BLACKSTONE'S GUIDE TO

The UK Internal Market Act 2020

BLACKSTONE'S GUIDE TO

The UK Internal Market Act 2020

Alan Bates
Brendan McGurk
George Peretz QC
Jack Williams

OXFORD
UNIVERSITY PRESS

OXFORD
UNIVERSITY PRESS

Great Clarendon Street, Oxford, OX2 6DP,
United Kingdom

Oxford University Press is a department of the University of Oxford.
It furthers the University's objective of excellence in research, scholarship,
and education by publishing worldwide. Oxford is a registered trade mark of
Oxford University Press in the UK and in certain other countries

First Edition published in 2021

Impression: 1

Published in the United States of America by Oxford University Press
198 Madison Avenue, New York, NY 10016, United States of America

British Library Cataloguing in Publication Data

Data available

Library of Congress Control Number: 2021946714

ISBN 978–0–19–285620–3

DOI: 10.1093/oso/9780192856203.001.0001

Printed and bound by
CPI Group (UK) Ltd, Croydon, CR0 4YY

Contents—Summary

Contents—Detailed

Table of Cases

United Kingdom

European Union

Table of Legislation

1
INTRODUCTION

A. THE CONCEPT OF A UK INTERNAL MARKET

The problem that lies at the heart of the United Kingdom Internal Market Act 2020 arises out of a tension that is inherent in any federal or confederal structure of government. Such **1.01**

Blackstone's Guide to the UK Internal Market Act 2020. Alan Bates, Brendan McGurk, George Peretz QC, and Jack Williams, Oxford University Press.

DOI: 10.1093/oso/9780192856203.003.0001

structures allow levels of regional or state government significant legislative autonomy, including powers to regulate commerce and trade. But it is also typically a characteristic of those structures that there is a strong policy objective of promoting commerce and trade across the whole federation: that policy objective usually has both economic motivations (promoting economic growth through increased trade) and political ones (encouraging greater integration). That leads to an inevitable tension: the greater the legislative autonomy of sub-central units, the more likely it is that they will regulate trade and commerce differently, and therefore, by accident or by design, throw up barriers to trade and movement between them.

1.02 The history of many European states over the last millennium illustrates various ways in which that tension has played out, as does much of the constitutional history of federal states such as the United States, Canada, and Australia. In Europe, the European Union (EU) (and its predecessors) provides a detailed case-study in managing the tension between allowing its Member States legislative autonomy while seeking to reduce barriers to trade in the name of political and economic integration—an objective that became known in the EU as the creation and development of the 'internal market' or 'single market'.

1. England

1.03 In contrast to many other European nations, England has had a unified system of law, and a unified executive and legislature, since early medieval times. It has virtually no, and certainly no recent, history of local government with any significant rule-making powers: further, under the English model of parliamentary sovereignty, English local government has no constitutionally protected status at all, such powers as it has being entirely the creation of statute passed by, and revocable by, Parliament. The tension between local legislative autonomy and the protection of the internal market is therefore almost entirely absent from English history.

1.04 But the story of the United Kingdom—the union of the four nations of England, Wales, Scotland, and (from 1800–1922) Ireland and (since 1922) Northern Ireland—is a different and far more complex story.

2. Wales

1.05 The Union of England and Wales—achieved by conquest by Edward I in the thirteenth century and by law by Henry VIII in the sixteenth century—is essentially one of complete integration of Wales into English law. The Statute of Rhuddlan issued by Edward I in 1284 provided for a complete union of executive power.[1] The Laws in Wales Acts of 1535 and 1542 removed the remaining traces of a separate Welsh legal system and separate Welsh laws, and though Wales preserved a separate court system until 1830 (the Courts of Great Sessions) those courts administered English common law and statutes made by the Westminster Parliament. Indeed, the Wales and Berwick Act 1746 created a statutory definition of 'England' as including Wales. In the nineteenth century, Parliament began to pass some

[1] 'The Divine Providence, which is unerring in its own government, among the gifts of its dispensation, wherewith it hath vouchsafed to distinguish us and our realm of England, hath now of its favour, wholly and entirely transferred under our proper dominion, the land of Wales, with its inhabitants, heretofore subject unto us, in feudal right, all obstacles whatsoever ceasing; and hath annexed and united the same unto the crown of the aforesaid realm, as a member of the same body.'

important legislation that applied only to Wales,[2] but the possibility of significant divergence between England and Wales in relation to any matters relating to the regulation of commerce and trade did not arise until Welsh devolution in 1998.

3. Scotland

The Union of England and Scotland is a more complex story. In the early medieval period, Scotland was established as a separate kingdom. Although Edward I succeeded in conquering Scotland in the late thirteenth century, that conquest proved short-lived and an independent kingdom was re-established by Robert I after the battle of Bannockburn in 1314. Scotland developed its own legal system, characterized (in distinction to English common law) by a greater willingness to accept Roman law. The fact that both kingdoms became Protestant in the middle of the sixteenth century began to bring them together, but it was a dynastic accident (the failure of any of Henry VIII's children to have children of their own) that led to the union of the crowns in 1603, when the English crown devolved to James VI of Scotland as the great-grandson of Henry VIII's sister, Margaret Tudor (who had married James IV of Scotland). That union of monarchs, in the person of James I and VI, did not however unite the kingdoms: and much of the constitutional drama of the seventeenth century found its origin in the continuing differences between them and in particular in the attempts of Charles I, Oliver Cromwell, and Charles II to impose the English religious settlement on Scotland (the Protestantism of each kingdom having taken very different forms). A brief annexation of Scotland under the Commonwealth was reversed on the restoration of Charles II in 1660. Although both kingdoms united in 1688 in accepting the ejection of James II and VII by a Dutch army and the accession of William III and II and Mary II, the kingdoms remained separate. 1.06

It was only in 1707, in the reign of Anne, that the Acts of Union passed by both the Scottish and English Parliaments united the kingdoms. The Acts of Union created a new Kingdom of Great Britain, with a single Parliament. 1.07

As the Lord President (Hamilton) said in *re Imperial Tobacco Ltd*:[3] '[i]t is generally accepted that free access to the English domestic and colonial markets formed, from the Scottish perspective, an important reason for entering into the Union. The background to the Union included the failure of the attempt by the Darien Co to establish a Scottish colony in the Americas, resentment of the Navigation Acts, increases in duties upon Scottish exports to England, and the threat in the Alien Act 1705 to prohibit such exports entirely.' 1.08

Accordingly, various provisions in the Treaty of Union dealt with what would now be called the creation of an internal market. Article IV provided for what might now be termed free movement: '[t]hat all the Subjects of the United Kingdom of Great Britain shall from and after the Union have full freedom and Intercourse of Trade and Navigation to and from any port or place within the said United Kingdom and the Dominions and Plantations thereunto belonging And that there be a Communication of all other Rights Privileges and Advantages which do or may belong to the Subjects of either Kingdom except where it is otherwise expressly agreed in these Articles'. 1.09

[2] See the Sunday Closing Act 1881, the Welsh Intermediate Education Act 1889, and the Welsh Church Act 1914.

[3] [2012] CSIH 9, [2012] SLT 749, at paragraph 157.

1.10 Most relevantly to the subject matter of this book, Article VI provided for common regulation of trade and common external tariffs: '[t]hat all parts of the United Kingdom for ever from and after the Union shall have the same Allowances Encouragements and Drawbacks and be under the same prohibitions restrictions and regulations of Trade and liable to the same Customs and Duties on Import and Export [a]nd that the Allowances Encouragements and Drawbacks prohibitions restrictions and regulations of Trade and the Customs and Duties on Import and Export settled in England when the Union commences shall from and after the Union take place throughout the whole United Kingdom.'

1.11 Further, Article XVIII provided that Scots law regulating trade and customs duties should be replaced by English law.

1.12 However, and importantly, Article XVIII also provided that generally Scots law would remain in force in Scotland, though amendable by the Parliament of Great Britain. Other provisions protected the autonomy of the Scottish legal system and courts.

1.13 That context has led the courts to give a restricted reading to what is meant by 'regulations of Trade' in Article VI: thus, in *Citizens Insurance Co of Canada v Parsons*,[4] the Privy Council (looking at the same phrase in the context of the British North America Act 1867) noted that 'Parliament has at various times since the Union passed laws affecting and regulating specific trades in one part of the United Kingdom only, without its being supposed that it thereby infringed the Articles of Union. Thus the Acts for regulating the sale of intoxicating liquors notoriously vary in the two kingdoms. So with regard to Acts relating to bankruptcy, and various other matters.'

1.14 As the Lord President said in *re Imperial Tobacco*,[5] Article VI 'is not . . . a general guarantee of freedom of trade in the widest sense, and it does not prohibit restrictions on trade. It is concerned with a more specific matter, namely that trade should not be advantaged or disadvantaged, in the respects mentioned, according to whether it is carried on in Scotland or in England and Wales. It is to be noted that the scope of Article VI has not been understood as extending to all distinctions between Scotland and England which may affect trade: *Citizens Insurance Co of Canada v Parsons*; nor could it have been intended that Article VI should proscribe all such distinctions, given the intention, reflected in Article XVIII, to retain a separate Scottish legal system.'

1.15 It can therefore be seen that Article VI has not been read as precluding what are now generally seen as non-tariff barriers between England and Scotland: indeed, the Privy Council's example of different regulation for the sale of alcohol on each side of the Tweed as a matter that was not prohibited by the Treaty of Union is particularly striking given that such regulations were very much affected by (though not necessarily prohibited by) EU internal market law,[6] and figured prominently in debates during the passage of the Act.

1.16 In the period between 1707 and 1998, the Westminster Parliament—as the Parliament of the United Kingdom—was the sole legislator for Scotland. That did not prevent legislation in many areas—including legislation that could be said to give rise to barriers to trade—differing across the Border: and Scotland retained its own distinctive legal system, and was, over the nineteenth and twentieth centuries, increasingly administered by a separate Government Department (the Scottish Office). But the fact that there was a common legislature and common executive meant that the fundamental tension between having different

[4] (1881–82) LR 7 App Cas 96.

[5] [2012] CSIH 9, [2012] SLT 749, at paragraph 157.

[6] See e.g. Case 120/78 *Cassis de Dijon* [1979] ECR 649 and *Scotch Whisky Association v Lord Advocate* [2017] UKSC 76.

rules in different parts of a State and ensuring that there were no barriers to trade within that State was a matter that was easily dealt with politically: and the courts' restrictive interpretation of Article VI meant that there was no real constitutional constraint on the ability of the common legislature and executive to decide what degree of difference in regulation was appropriate or acceptable.[7]

4. Northern Ireland

The complicated and in many respects tragic history of relations between England and Ireland is well beyond the scope of this work. From the early medieval period, Kings of England asserted overlordship of Ireland, and up until 1800 Ireland was a separate kingdom under the English (and later British) crown. In 1800, the Parliaments of Ireland and of Great Britain passed Acts of Union, creating a common UK Parliament. Ireland retained its own legal system, but (unlike Scotland) its system was based on English common law. 1.17

Article 6 of the Acts of Union provided that: '[t]he subjects of Great Britain and Ireland shall be on the same footing in respect of trade and navigation, and in all treaties with foreign powers the subjects of Ireland shall have the same privileges as British subjects.[8] From January 1, 1801, all prohibitions and bounties on the export of articles the produce or manufacture of either country to the other shall cease.' It went on to provide that exports and imports between Great Britain and Ireland should be duty-free, subject to exceptions that the united Parliament might impose. 1.18

In *Allister v Secretary of State for Northern Ireland* the High Court of Northern Ireland noted that the provisions of the Ireland/Northern Ireland Protocol resulted in: the requirement in Northern Ireland to comply with EU standards; bureaucracy and associated costs of complying with customs documentation and checks as between Great Britain and Northern Ireland; payment of tariffs for exports from Great Britain to Northern Ireland that are 'at risk'; and unfettered access enjoyed by Northern Ireland business to the EU. It held that those outcomes conflicted with the 'equal footing' requirement in Article 6.[9] However, it went on to hold that Article 6 was, to that extent, impliedly repealed by section 7A of the European Union (Withdrawal) Act 2018, rejecting arguments that the 1800 Act of Union was a 'constitutional statute' which could not be repealed without an express statement to that effect.[10] 1.19

[7] The debate—familiar to constitutional lawyers—as to the extent to which the legislative competence of the UK Parliament is, in any event, constrained by the Treaty of Union is beyond the scope of this work (although in *Philip v Scottish Ministers* [2021] CSOH 32, a case concerning the provisions of the Acts of Union that gave constitutional protection in Scotland to freedom of worship and to the independence of the Church of Scotland, it appears to have been common ground that it was: see paragraphs 64–65—though see also, in relation to the Act of Union with Ireland, paragraph 1.19 below). But whatever the answer, it should be noted that, as discussed at paragraph 1.45 below, paragraph 1 of Schedule 4 to the Scotland Act 1998 has the effect that the Scottish Parliament has no power to legislate in a way that contravenes Article VI.

[8] In *re Molyneaux* [1986] 1 WLR 331, Taylor J rejected a claim that the 1985 Anglo-Irish Agreement breached that part of Article 6, on the basis that the Republic of Ireland was not a 'foreign power' and that in any event the Agreement did not remove any privileges of Northern Ireland citizens vis-à-vis citizens living in Great Britain.

[9] [2021] NIQB 64, at paragraph 62.

[10] At paragraphs 63–114, where the Court pointed out that, as discussed below, various statutes since 1800 had modified the constitutional status of Ireland (and provided for the independence of the Republic of Ireland) notwithstanding the reference in the 1800 Act of Union to the Union being 'for ever'. The Court noted that the Prime Minister had, in Parliament, given an assurance that Article 6 had not been impliedly repealed, but did not consider that that assurance affected its analysis (see paragraphs 115–117).

1.20 During the nineteenth century, dissatisfaction in Ireland with the union settlement led to pressure for home rule: after various attempts by Liberal governments led by Gladstone and then Asquith to get legislation for home rule through Parliament, that objective was finally secured in 1914, despite vigorous opposition to home rule among the Protestant minority in Ireland, concentrated in the north. However, on the outbreak of the First World War later that year, implementation of the legislation was suspended. By the end of the war, and largely as a result of the 1916 Easter Rising, the political situation was transformed, as it became clear that the Catholic majority in Ireland now favoured independence. In an attempt to resolve the position, Parliament passed the Government of Ireland Act 1920, which established two devolved Parliaments in Ireland, one for the 'six counties' in the north of Ireland and one for the rest of the island, and set out the powers each had. The Northern Ireland Parliament began its work in 1921: but after a period of effective civil war in Ireland, the UK government signed a treaty with the leaders of the Southern Parliament (which had constituted itself as Dáil Éireann) which established the Irish Free State in Ireland. Under that treaty, implemented in the United Kingdom by the Irish Free State Constitution Act 1922, the Northern Ireland Parliament was given the right to opt out of the Irish Free State and retain Northern Ireland's status as part of the United Kingdom under the 1920 Act, which option it immediately exercised.

1.21 Between 1920 and 1972, Northern Ireland was governed by its own Parliament and Executive under the 1920 Act. Section 4 of that Act gave its legislature full power 'to make laws for the peace, order, and good government of . . . Northern Ireland' subject to a list of 'reserved matters', which included '[t]rade with any place out of [Northern Ireland], except so far as trade may be affected by the exercise of the powers of taxation given to the [Parliament], or by regulations made for the sole purpose of preventing contagious disease, or by steps taken by means of inquiries or agencies out of [Northern Ireland] for the improvement of the trade of that part or for the protection of traders of that part from fraud; the granting of bounties on the export of goods; quarantine; navigation, including merchant shipping (except as respects inland waters, the regulation of harbours, and local health regulations)'.

1.22 The extent of that reservation was considered by the House of Lords in *Gallagher v Lynn*,[11] which concerned legislation that prohibited farmers outside Northern Ireland, including from the Irish Free State, from obtaining licences to sell milk. Lord Atkin, delivering the only substantial speech, held that that legislation did not fall within the reservation, on the basis that 'the true nature and character of the Act, its pith and substance, is that it is an Act to protect the health of the inhabitants of Northern Ireland; and in those circumstances, though it may incidentally affect trade with County Donegal,[12] it is not passed "in respect of" trade, and is therefore not subject to attack on that ground'.

1.23 During that period, therefore, there was little legislative restraint on the ability of the Parliament of Northern Ireland to legislate in ways that created considerable barriers to trade, as long as the 'pith and substance' of the legislation was not about trade.

1.24 In 1972, as a result of growing tensions and violence in Northern Ireland, the Government of Ireland Act 1920 and the devolved institutions created by it were suspended. Devolution

[11] [1937] AC 863.

[12] The plaintiff in the case was a farmer from that county.

was restored only in 1998, after the Good Friday Agreement; however, that devolution was under entirely new legislation, as discussed below.

5. Summary

The issue identified at the start of this chapter—the tension in a federal or confederal system between legislative autonomy for the component parts and the desire to reduce barriers to trade between them—was largely absent from the United Kingdom for most of its history. No part of England has had significant legislative autonomy since the establishment of the kingdom in the ninth century, and it has had a common law since Norman times. As far as Wales was concerned there was, after 1542 and up until the 1998 devolution settlement, no or little legislative difference between it and England and no legislative autonomy. In the case of Scotland, though significant legal differences remained after union with England in 1707, the fact that it shared a common executive and legislature with the rest of the United Kingdom meant that the balance between maintaining difference in areas that affected trade and reducing trade barriers was one for those common institutions to decide. And although Northern Ireland, from 1921 until 1972, did have a very high degree of legislative autonomy and its Parliament was able to legislate in ways that created barriers to trade within the United Kingdom, its Parliament was permitted to strike that balance for itself without any substantial constitutional restraint. 1.25

As a result, although the UK internal market dates back centuries, there was no need for any legislation resembling the United Kingdom Internal Market Act 2020 to maintain it: the centralized nature of the UK state as it developed meant that, with the exception of Northern Ireland in the 1921–1972 period, the problems that that Act seeks to deal with could not in practice arise. 1.26

B. THE UNITED KINGDOM'S MEMBERSHIP OF THE EU AND ITS WITHDRAWAL

1. The United Kingdom's Membership of the EU and Its Predecessors

In the 1950s, the United Kingdom decided not to take part in the European Coal and Steel Community or in the European Economic Community. However, from the early 1960s, successive governments sought to join the Communities. After two failed attempts under the Macmillan and first Wilson governments, entry was finally negotiated by the Heath government and the United Kingdom acceded to the Communities on 1 January 1973. 1.27

The Labour government that took office in 1974 had promised a referendum on membership of the European Communities. That referendum took place in 1975, with a large majority voting to remain. 1.28

Under the Thatcher governments in the 1980s, the United Kingdom enthusiastically supported the creation of the 'single market': a programme of EEC legislation that built on the principles of free movement of goods and services in the Treaty of Rome to create a market with greatly reduced barriers to trade between Member States. Depending on the sector, that legislation typically harmonized regulation across Member States, or provided for mutual recognition of standards subject to common minimum standards. 1.29

1.30 There were, however, various ways in which the United Kingdom began to diverge from other Member States. From the outset in 1978 it refused to take part in the European Monetary System, joining only in 1990 shortly before the ousting of Mrs Thatcher as Prime Minister, and then crashing out in humiliating circumstances in 1992. In the 1990s, the Major government negotiated a series of 'opt-outs' from the Treaty of Maastricht, in particular from taking part in the Euro, the 'social chapter' of labour rights, and from the 'Schengen' common visa area. Although the 1997–2010 Labour government opted back into the social chapter, it refrained from taking any steps to join the Euro or Schengen.

2. The United Kingdom's Withdrawal from the EU

1.31 During the 1990s and 2000s, the Conservative Party became increasingly hostile to the EU (as it became after the 2009 Treaty of Lisbon). Its hostility was to a large extent constrained during its period of coalition government with the pro-EU Liberal Democrats in 2010–2015. But in 2013 David Cameron promised that if the Conservative Party were elected to government in 2015, it would call a second referendum on membership of the EU. When the Conservatives obtained a majority in the 2015 general election, Mr Cameron was obliged to make that promise good, in the form of the EU Referendum Act 2015, which provided for there to be a referendum on the question of whether the United Kingdom should remain in, or leave, the EU.

1.32 After a negotiation with the EU in which he obtained a series of further 'opt-outs', Mr Cameron set the date of the referendum in June 2016, and campaigned for a 'remain' vote. However, a number of his leading colleagues campaigned for 'leave'. The result of the referendum was a narrow win for 'leave'. Significantly for the future, however, voters in both Scotland and Northern Ireland voted by wide margins for 'remain'. Mr Cameron immediately resigned as Prime Minister, to be succeeded by Theresa May, who (although she had supported 'remain') made it clear that she would seek to implement the referendum result.

1.33 After the Supreme Court decided that the Prime Minister had no power under existing legislation or pursuant to any sufficient prerogative power to commence the process for withdrawal of a Member State under Article 50 of the Treaty on European Union,[13] Parliament passed the EU (Notification of Withdrawal) Act 2017, which gave her that power. Notification of the United Kingdom's intention to withdraw was given on 29 March 2017: that started a two-year period at the end of which (unless extended) the United Kingdom would cease to be a Member State. Mrs May then called a general election, in which she lost the Conservatives' overall majority: she continued as Prime Minister under a 'confidence and supply' arrangement with the Democratic Unionist Party, the largest unionist party in Northern Ireland. With their support, Mrs May succeeded in getting legislation enacted (the EU (Withdrawal) Act 2018) which dealt with the domestic legal consequences of withdrawal.

1.34 In parallel, Mrs May's government sought to negotiate a withdrawal agreement with the EU. This proved to be rather more difficult, largely due to the impossibility of reconciling her initial policy objectives of (a) avoiding the creation of a hard border with checks and infrastructure between Northern Ireland and Ireland; (b) avoiding the creation of such a barrier between Northern Ireland and Great Britain; and (c) freedom for the United Kingdom to

[13] *R(Miller) v Secretary of State for Exiting the EU* [2017] UKSC 5 ('*Miller I*').

adopt different regulatory standards and leaving the Customs Union. As was pointed out, it was possible to achieve only two of those three objectives. In the end, and after much political turmoil and several cabinet resignations, Mrs May negotiated a withdrawal agreement that achieved objectives (a) and (b) at the price of giving up (c): her negotiated withdrawal agreement in 2018 committed the whole United Kingdom to remain, in essence, part of the EU customs zone and regulatory zone for goods for an indefinite period (the 'backstop').

The House of Commons, however, repeatedly rejected that agreement, despite various attempts to obtain helpful 'clarifications' and two extensions to the Article 50 period. Unable to deliver on her 'flagship' policy, Mrs May resigned in July 2019. **1.35**

Her successor, Boris Johnson, had been one of the leaders of the 'leave' campaign, and had been one of the cabinet ministers who had resigned in protest at Mrs May's approach to negotiations with the EU. He promised to renegotiate the backstop, and to leave the EU without a withdrawal agreement (a result—a 'no-deal Brexit'—that would have led to enormous legal uncertainty and economic disruption) if no acceptable deal could be achieved. **1.36**

Since the House of Commons as a whole opposed the idea of a no-deal Brexit, but also lacked a majority for any alternative government, Mr Johnson's approach led to a constitutional crisis, during which Parliament passed legislation opposed by the government of the day (an extraordinary event in UK constitutional history) requiring it to seek a third extension to the Article 50 period, and was then prorogued, only for the prorogation to be found to be unlawful by the Supreme Court.[14] **1.37**

In October 2019, Mr Johnson succeeded in negotiating a revised withdrawal agreement with the EU (the 'Withdrawal Agreement')). On examination, however, it was clear that Mr Johnson had achieved that result by giving up objective (b) in the list above: the Withdrawal Agreement contained a revised Ireland/Northern Ireland Protocol which, though carefully drafted to avoid that result being too obvious to a casual reader,[15] essentially created a regulatory and customs border between Northern Ireland and Great Britain, and left Northern Ireland subject to EU regulation in the area of goods as well as (for all practical purposes) in the EU customs territory. On the other hand, the Withdrawal Agreement and accompanying political declaration left the rest of the United Kingdom free to set its own tariffs and regulation without reference to the EU—a key objective of the Johnson government (in contrast to that of Mrs May). **1.38**

After the Johnson government lost a motion for swift passage of the necessary legislation to implement the revised agreement through the House of Commons, Parliament passed legislation authorizing a general election in December 2019, in which Mr Johnson obtained a substantial Conservative majority. The new Parliament swiftly passed the EU (Withdrawal Agreement) Act 2020 implementing the revised agreement (and Ireland/Northern Ireland Protocol) into UK law, and the United Kingdom left the EU formally on 31 January 2020, though it remained for almost all practical purposes part of the EU until 31 December 2020, when the transition period provided for under the Withdrawal Agreement expired. Just before that, the United Kingdom and EU concluded a Trade and Cooperation Agreement providing for zero tariffs on all goods coming from the other party.[16] That Agreement confirmed that **1.39**

---

[14] *R(Miller) v Prime Minister* [2019] UKSC 41 ('*Miller II*').

[15] See S. Weatherill: 'The Protocol on Ireland/Northern Ireland: What it says is not what it does', 17 March 2020, http://eulawanalysis.blogspot.com/2020/03/the-protocol-on-ireland-northern.html.

[16] However, complex 'rules of origin' provisions meant that many goods exported from one to the other would not be regarded as coming from the other party and hence would be subject to tariffs.

the United Kingdom would be free to diverge from EU regulation, though at the risk of the imposition of tariffs under 'level playing field' provisions if it diverged too far.

3. The Consequences of Withdrawal for the UK Internal Market

1.40 The United Kingdom's withdrawal from the EU had three major consequences for the UK internal market.

1.41 First, at a political level, the fact that the United Kingdom had taken such a major constitutional and political step even though very substantial majorities of the people of Scotland and Northern Ireland had voted against it strengthened the hand of those who argued for Scottish independence or Irish re-unification: they could plausibly argue that voices from Scotland or Northern Ireland were simply ignored by the UK government. Particularly in Scotland, that led to calls for a second independence referendum and generally increased tension between the governments in London and Edinburgh. That tense political background meant that, in cases where actions of one government or another raised internal market issues, it was less plausible to rely on such difficulties being resolved through political negotiation and compromise.

1.42 Second, as discussed in detail below, the Ireland/Northern Ireland Protocol creates a very substantial barrier between Great Britain and Northern Ireland: despite the fact that the Protocol *says* that Northern Ireland has 'an integral place in the United Kingdom's internal market',[17] what it actually *does* is to remove it from the UK internal market in very substantial respects.[18]

1.43 Third, the United Kingdom's withdrawal from the EU had a major impact on the operation of the 'devolution settlement'—the general name for the creation[19] in 1998, and subsequent development, of powerful devolved legislatures and administrations in Scotland, Wales, and Northern Ireland. The essential problem was that the devolution settlement had been devised and developed against what was assumed at the time to be the permanent background of EU law. And at the heart of EU law is a complex and subtle network of Treaty provisions, case-law, and specific regulation that governs the 'internal market': that is to say, balances the need to allow for important legislative choices about regulation to be made at Member State (or sub-Member State) level against the objective of reducing barriers to trade, and in many cases provides for harmonization of rules, prescribes minimum standards, and/or requires recognition of goods or services coming from elsewhere in the EU as meeting national (or sub-national) standards. Essentially, because EU law—binding both the United Kingdom and devolved parliaments and governments—provided a strict framework for the exercise of rule-making powers so as not to obstruct the *EU's* internal market, it was at the time of the devolution settlements not thought necessary to address the question of whether the rule-making powers of the devolved parliaments should be constrained by concerns as to the *United Kingdom's* internal market. The United Kingdom's exit from the EU—and the radical form in which that was eventually achieved—removed that framework. The Act represents the Johnson government's attempt to replace it.

---

[17] Article 5(2) of the Protocol.

[18] See also the analysis in *Allister v Secretary of State for Northern Ireland* [2021] NIQB 64, at paragraphs 51–62.

[19] Re-creation, in the case of Northern Ireland.

C. THE DEVOLUTION SETTLEMENT

The 1974–1979 Labour government attempted to create devolved legislatures in Scotland and Wales; however, in referendums held in 1979, Scottish voters failed to approve devolution there by a sufficient majority, and Welsh voters overwhelmingly rejected devolution. 1.44

The Labour government elected in 1997 was committed to creating devolved parliaments in Scotland and in Wales, subject to a favourable referendum in each country. Such referendums were swiftly organized and resulted, in the case of Scotland, in a substantial majority for devolved institutions (a Parliament and an Executive) with substantial executive and legislative and limited tax-raising powers, and in the case of Wales a narrow majority for an Assembly with executive powers and limited legislative powers. 1.45

Over the period since 1998, the powers of the Scottish Parliament have steadily grown, and those of the Welsh Assembly (now the Senedd[20]) have been increased almost beyond recognition. The following discussion concentrates on Scotland, with brief sections on Wales and Northern Ireland that bring out any relevant differences. 1.46

1. Scotland

The Scotland Act 1998 created a Scottish Parliament and an Executive (the Scottish Ministers)—known since 2012 as the Scottish Government.[21] From the outset, the powers of the Scottish Parliament were on the 'reserved powers' model: section 29 of that Act provided that legislation of the Scottish Parliament was out of competence only if it (a) legislated for territories outside Scotland; (b) related to 'reserved matters' listed in Schedule 5 to the Act; (c) amended 'protected enactments' listed in Schedule 4; (d) was incompatible with EU law or the European Convention on Human Rights (ECHR); or (e) detracted from the constitutional position of the Lord Advocate. 1.47

The list of 'reserved matters' contains[22] a number of matters where regulation is capable of creating barriers to trade: for example, financial services and markets regulation;[23] data protection;[24] gambling regulation;[25] weights and measures;[26] much consumer protection and consumer credit regulation;[27] certain aspects of product safety;[28] road vehicle and freight operator licensing;[29] and aviation.[30] 1.48

---

[20] The Assembly became known as the Senedd as from May 2020, by virtue of the Senedd and Elections (Wales) Act 2020: to avoid confusion or repetition the term 'Senedd' is also here used in relation to periods before that date.

[21] See section 44(1) of the 1998 Act, as amended by the Scotland Act 2012.

[22] The Schedule 5 list has been significantly modified over the years, usually in the direction of decreasing the extent of reserved powers.

[23] Paragraphs A3 and A4 of Schedule 5.

[24] Paragraph B2 of Schedule 5.

[25] Paragraph B9 of Schedule 5.

[26] Paragraph C9 of Schedule 5.

[27] Paragraph C7 of Schedule 5 (NB that Scots consumer law, even within reserved areas, often differs significantly from English law, given the differences between Scots and English contract and tort/delict law).

[28] Paragraph C8 of Schedule 5.

[29] Paragraph E1 of Schedule 5.

[30] Paragraph E4 of Schedule 5.

1.49 However, from the outset the list of reserved powers in Schedule 5 has left the Scottish Parliament with extensive powers to regulate the production, sale, and supply of many goods and services.[31]

1.50 A further restriction on the powers of the Scottish Parliament is that, under paragraph 1(2)(a) of Schedule 4 to the 1998 Act, it has no power to amend Article VI of the Acts of Union. However, as will be clear from the discussion at paragraphs 1.13–1.15 above, Article VI is limited in its ability to prevent the Scottish Parliament regulating in ways that create substantial barriers to trade with the rest of the United Kingdom.

1.51 For those purposes, by far the most important restriction on the Scottish Parliament's rule-making powers was, during the United Kingdom's membership of the EU, EU law. By section 29(2)(d) of the Scotland Act, the Scottish Parliament simply had no competence to legislate in a way that was incompatible with EU law. That meant that, for example, the Scottish Parliament had no power to prevent goods or services being sold at all, or in a particular manner, if specific EU regulation or general Treaty provisions on free movement of goods or services precluded such regulation. To take a very prominent example, Scottish legislation in 2012 imposing minimum alcohol pricing—a matter that was not reserved under Schedule 5—was within competence only because the Scottish government was able to discharge the burden on it of showing 'objective justification' and proportionality, and hence that there was no infringement of Article 34 of the Treaty on the Functioning of the European Union (TFEU) (which prohibits quantitative restrictions on imports and measures having an equivalent effect).[32]

1.52 Since, in practice, almost any legislation or decision that affected the UK internal market also engaged EU rules that protected the EU single market, there was no need, at the time of the Scotland Act 1998 or subsequently, to impose any further constraint on the Scottish Parliament or government in order to protect the UK internal market.

1.53 A further critical element of the devolution settlement was the Sewel convention. The Scotland Act 1998 expressly reserved the competence of the UK Parliament to legislate for Scotland, even in non-reserved matters.[33] However, the UK government accepted that it would not normally be right for the UK Parliament to do so, without the consent of the Scottish Parliament. That acceptance was recorded in a Memorandum of Understanding between the United Kingdom and devolved governments.[34] Where it was thought right for the UK Parliament to legislate for the whole United Kingdom on a non-reserved matter, it was agreed that the respective governments would seek legislative consent from their legislatures: that process was also adopted where the UK Parliament sought to modify the competence of the devolved administrations or legislatures. As of December 2020, across the devolved legislatures, legislative consent had been given on 350 occasions, with only 13 refusals.[35]

---

[31] As well as extensive powers to grant subsidies, another area where EU law (in the form of State aid rules) operated as the main constraint on its ability to subsidize in ways that adversely affected trade and competition within the EU (and thus UK) internal market: see chapter 9 below.

[32] *Scotch Whisky Association v Lord Advocate* [2017] UKSC 76. The pursuers also claimed that the legislation infringed Regulation (EU) 1308/2013, the Single CMO Regulation, a claim that was also dismissed by the Supreme Court.

[33] Section 28(7).

[34] December 2001, Cm 5420. A revised version was published in October 2013.

[35] See Institute for Government: 'Explainer: Sewel Convention', updated 8 December 2020, https://www.instituteforgovernment.org.uk/explainers/sewel-convention

The Sewel convention was embodied in legislation by section 28(8) of the Scotland Act 1998,[36] which stated that 'it is recognised that the Parliament of the United Kingdom will not normally legislate with regard to devolved matters without the consent of the Scottish Parliament'. 1.54

However, in *Miller I*, the Supreme Court held that the Sewel convention, even with the benefit of that statutory recognition, was not a legal rule justiciable by the courts, commenting that: 'the Sewel convention has an important role in facilitating harmonious relationships between the UK Parliament and the devolved legislatures. But the policing of its scope and the manner of its operation does not lie within the constitutional remit of the judiciary, which is to protect the rule of law.'[37] 1.55

The effect of *Miller I* was that the UK Parliament remained free as a matter of law enforceable by the courts (a) to legislate in relation to devolved matters without the consent of the devolved legislatures; or (b) to restrict the powers of the devolved legislatures without their consent. That was notwithstanding section 63A of the Scotland Act 1998,[38] which declared that 'the Scottish Parliament and the Scottish Government are a permanent part of the United Kingdom's constitutional arrangements' and that they were not to be abolished save on the basis of a decision of the people of Scotland in a referendum. 1.56

2. Wales

As noted above, devolution in Wales was originally very much less extensive than devolution in Scotland. In 1998, the National Assembly for Wales was given powers to legislate only by way of secondary legislation and in defined areas, and there was no separate Welsh government (executive as well as legislative powers being conferred on the Assembly). It is unnecessary in this work to trace the development of devolution in Wales over the period since 1998. It is sufficient to say that it now closely resembles the Scottish model, with a Welsh government[39] and a Senedd with general legislative competence subject to reservations[40] (though the list of reserved matters is rather more extensive than in the Scottish model[41]). As in Scotland, by the time of the United Kingdom's withdrawal from the EU the Senedd had considerable competence to legislate in ways that were capable of creating barriers to trade.[42] 1.57

But, as in Scotland, that legislative competence was constrained by EU law: until the end of the transition period, section 108A(2)(e) of the Government of Wales Act (and its 1.58

[36] Inserted by section 2 of the Scotland Act 2016.

[37] Paragraph 151.

[38] Inserted by section 1 of the Scotland Act 2016.

[39] Section 45(1) of the Government of Wales Act 2006.

[40] Sections 107(1) and 108A of the Government of Wales Act.

[41] Reserved matters are set out in Schedule 7A to the Government of Wales Act. Examples of areas within the competence of the Scottish Parliament but not the Senedd include private law (contract, tort, property, etc.: paragraph 3) and criminal law (paragraph 4)—that reflects the fact that Scotland, unlike Wales, retained its own very distinct system of civil and criminal law after union with England. Note, however, that there is now statutory recognition of the concept of 'Welsh law': section A2 of the Government of Wales Act 2006.

[42] There being no equivalent to the Act of Union in the case of Wales (see paragraph 1.5 above), there is no equivalent in Wales to the provisions in the Scotland Act that limit competence in relation to provisions of the Act of Union, somewhat theoretical though those restrictions are.

predecessor provisions) provided that any legislation of the Senedd that infringed EU law were outside its competence.

1.59 As in Scotland: the UK Parliament's competence to make laws for Wales even in devolved matters is reserved;[43] the Sewel convention now takes statutory form;[44] and the Welsh government and Senedd are declared to be a permanent part of the United Kingdom's constitutional arrangements and not to be abolished save on the basis of a decision of the people of Wales in a referendum.[45]

3. Northern Ireland

1.60 As briefly described in section A above, the history of devolution in Northern Ireland stretches back for a century. But that devolution was suspended in 1972 as a result of what became known as the 'Troubles': Northern Ireland was then governed by a Secretary of State under legislation passed in the UK Parliament—although in most cases Northern Ireland legislation was made by the Secretary of State in the form of statutory instruments.

1.61 'Direct rule' was always regarded as a temporary expedient: most[46] unionist MPs wanted a resumption of devolution, as did the largest nationalist party, the SDLP (at least pending Irish re-unification, and subject to guarantees of power-sharing and equal treatment of the nationalist minority). Direct rule had obvious disadvantages: the UK Parliament had little time to debate legislation that applied to only a small percentage of the UK population;[47] and since none of the main parties in Great Britain put up candidates in Northern Ireland, no Northern Ireland MP was ever in a position to serve in government. However, it proved impossible for many years during the Troubles to negotiate a form of devolution that was acceptable to the bulk of both communities: the first attempt to set up a power-sharing executive and assembly collapsed in 1974 after protests on the unionist side.

1.62 Devolution only became possible as the result of lengthy and difficult negotiations involving not just the 'constitutional' parties but also the main armed organizations and parties sympathetic to them on each side. The 'Good Friday Agreement' (GFA) reached in 1998 established a process under which the armed organizations laid down their arms and substantial reforms were made to the governance of Northern Ireland, including the creation of a Northern Ireland Assembly and Executive.

1.63 A detailed account of the GFA is outside the scope of this work, as is an account of the operation of the Northern Ireland institutions (a complex regime involving an executive drawn from across the Assembly and with mechanisms to protect the position of both communities, and which on several occasions has been suspended, in two cases for periods of several years[48]).

1.64 Under the Northern Ireland Act 1998, the Assembly has general legislative competence, subject to exceptions and reservations.[49] Excepted matters, listed in Schedule 2[50] are generally

[43] Section 107(5) of the Government of Wales Act 2006.

[44] Section 107(6) of the Government of Wales Act 2006.

[45] Section A1 of the Government of Wales Act 2006.

[46] Enoch Powell MP, who served as an Ulster Unionist MP from 1974 to 1987 after many years as a Conservative MP and Minister, being an exception who favoured complete integration of Northern Ireland into the United Kingdom: he was a firm opponent of devolution in all parts of the United Kingdom.

[47] A problem that also applied to Scottish legislation.

[48] October 2002 to May 2007, and January 2017 to January 2020.

[49] Sections 5 and 6 of the Northern Ireland Act 1998.

[50] Which may be amended by the Secretary of State after a request by the Assembly.

outside the legislative competence of the Assembly.[51] Legislation by the Assembly in relation to reserved matters, listed in Schedule 3, requires the consent of the Secretary of State.[52] A number of UK Acts are entrenched and may not be amended by the Assembly.[53] As in the other devolution statutes, the Northern Ireland Act 1998 expressly maintains the powers of the UK Parliament to legislate for Northern Ireland in devolved matters.[54] However, there is no provision recording the Sewel convention (which is, nonetheless, accepted to apply).

One provision has no parallel in the other devolution statutes: section 1—which reflects the terms of the GFA—provides that, while 'Northern Ireland in its entirety remains part of the United Kingdom and shall not cease to be so without the consent of a majority of the people of Northern Ireland voting in a poll held for the purposes of this section', if the people of Northern Ireland choose in such a poll to 'cease to be part of the United Kingdom and form part of a united Ireland, the Secretary of State shall lay before Parliament such proposals to give effect to that wish as may be agreed between Her Majesty's Government in the United Kingdom and the Government of Ireland'.[55] **1.65**

In broad terms, the list of excepted matters in Schedule 2 (matters entirely outside competence) concerns areas such as the constitution, international relations, defence and United Kingdom-wide taxation. Areas such as financial services and aviation (which are outside the competence of the Scottish Parliament and the Senedd) are 'reserved' under Schedule 3, and can be the subject of Northern Ireland Assembly legislation with the Secretary of State's consent. But the Assembly has a very substantial ability to legislate in ways that could raise barriers to commerce and trade without needing the Secretary of State's consent. **1.66**

Until the end of the EU withdrawal transition period, and in parallel with the other devolved legislatures, the main constraint on the ability of the Assembly to pass legislation in ways that could adversely affect the operation of the UK internal market was its lack of competence in relation to legislation in contravention of EU law: section 6(2)(d) of the Northern Ireland Act 1998. **1.67**

However, unlike Scotland and Wales, Northern Ireland remains—under the Ireland/Northern Ireland Protocol—subject to EU law in a large number of areas (see chapter 8): section 6(2)(d) now places any legislation that is incompatible with that Protocol outside competence. **1.68**

4. England

The effect of the devolution settlement is that the UK Parliament—when it respects the Sewel convention—now, in many areas of national life, legislates only for England. That has **1.69**

---

[51] Unless ancillary to other provisions dealing with matters that are not excepted and where the Secretary of State consents: sections 6(2)(b) and 8(a) of the Northern Ireland Act 1998.

[52] Section 8(b) of the Northern Ireland Act 1998.

[53] Section 7 of the Northern Ireland Act 1998.

[54] Section 6(6) of the Northern Ireland Act 1998. During the suspension periods, the UK Parliament passed various legislation for Northern Ireland in relation to devolved matters: most controversially, the Northern Ireland (Executive Formation etc) Act 2019 contained provisions that led to the extension of legal abortion and same-sex marriage to Northern Ireland.

[55] In *Allister v Secretary of State for Northern Ireland* [2021] NIQB 64, at paragraph 136, it was held that the Ireland/Northern Ireland Protocol was consistent with section 1, which did not regulate any other constitutional change apart from the right to determine whether to remain part of the United Kingdom or to become part of a united Ireland.

given rise to two issues: the issue that legislation for England is passed by a legislature that contains many MPs from other parts of the United Kingdom unaffected by that legislation (often known as the 'West Lothian Question'[56]); and the question of whether there should be devolution within England.

1.70 The West Lothian Question remains, though measures were taken in 2015 as a matter of House of Commons procedure ('English Votes for English Laws'[57]) to ensure that at various stages only English MPs could vote on legislation that affected only England. Those procedural measures were, however, reversed in 2021.[58]

1.71 As for English devolution, that has been limited to non-existent. Many parts of England now have elected mayors (and, in the case of London, an elected assembly), but they lack any significant law-making powers and their executive powers are essentially those of local government (transport, police, planning). In areas where rule-making could disrupt the UK internal market, it is the UK government and UK Parliament that acts for England.

1.72 In consequence the United Kingdom under the devolution settlement differs from 'genuine' federal systems in two profound ways: first, the central legislature and executive are also the legislature and executive for (by far) the largest component of the state; and, second, the central legislature has constitutional power, restrained only by a non-justiciable convention, to alter and reduce the powers of the sub-central components of the State at will. That constitutional position forms the background to the political controversies surrounding first Brexit and then the United Kingdom Internal Market Act.

D. THE IMPACT OF EU WITHDRAWAL ON THE DEVOLUTION SETTLEMENT

1. The Powers of the Devolved Legislatures in Relation to Brexit

1.73 Relations with the EU were not a matter within the competence of any of the devolved legislatures.[59] However, as discussed above, the competence of all the devolved legislatures was limited to measures that complied with EU law.

1.74 In *Miller I* the Supreme Court considered the implications of that position for the role of the devolved legislatures in the Brexit process. It stated that: 'in imposing the EU constraints and empowering the devolved institutions to observe and implement EU law, the devolution legislation did not go further and require the United Kingdom to remain a member of the European Union'.[60] It further noted that 'the removal of the EU constraints on withdrawal from the EU Treaties will alter the competence of the devolved institutions unless new legislative constraints are introduced. In the absence of such new restraints, withdrawal

---

[56] Because the MP who persistently raised it as an objection to devolution during debates in the 1970s, Tam Dalyell, was MP for West Lothian. The point was not however new, and formed a major argument against Irish Home Rule in the late nineteenth century.

[57] See https://www.parliament.uk/about/how/laws/bills/public/english-votes-for-english-laws/.

[58] By a vote of the House of Commons, amending its standing orders: see Hansard HC, 13 July 2021, cols 306–26.

[59] Relations with the EU were a reserved matter (Scotland), an excepted matter (Northern Ireland), and initially not a matter on which competence was conferred on the Assembly and then a reserved competence (Wales).

[60] *Miller I*, paragraph 129.

from the EU will enhance the devolved competence.'[61] However, since, as noted above, the Supreme Court ruled that the Sewel convention was not justiciable, the fact that the Sewel convention (at least 'normally') required the devolved legislatures' consent to legislation that had the effect of augmenting their powers was not a legal obstacle to the United Kingdom's withdrawal if the UK Parliament chose to proceed with such legislation in any event.

Miller I therefore established that the UK Parliament could decide to authorize withdrawal from the EU, and could pass legislation necessary to give effect to that withdrawal, without the consent of the devolved legislatures. Indeed, the Scottish Parliament refused legislative consent to the EU (Withdrawal) Act 2018, all three devolved legislatures refused legislative consent to the EU (Withdrawal Agreement) Act 2020, and the Scottish Parliament and Senedd refused legislative consent to the United Kingdom Internal Market Act 2020. But those Acts became law in any event. **1.75**

The Supreme Court also rejected the claim that section 1 of the Northern Ireland Act 1998 (see paragraph 1.64 above) required the consent of the people of Northern Ireland before the United Kingdom could withdraw from the EU.[62] **1.76**

2. The EU (Withdrawal) Act 2018

The EU (Withdrawal) Act 2018 dealt with the far-reaching legal consequences of the United Kingdom's withdrawal. In essence, it provided for the continued effect in the United Kingdom of directly effective EU law, as it stood at the moment of withdrawal, after the United Kingdom's withdrawal from the EU.[63] That body of 'retained EU law' could be modified by Ministers (including devolved Ministers within their respective areas of competence): Ministers' powers to do that, under section 8 of the 2018 Act, were wide but not unlimited: fundamental changes to retained EU law required primary legislation.[64] **1.77**

Section 12 of the 2018 Act modified the devolution statutes: it replaced the provisions to the effect that legislation that infringed EU law was outside the competence of the devolved legislatures with a provision that their legislation 'cannot modify, or confer power by subordinate legislation to modify, retained EU law so far as the modification is of a description specified in regulations made by a Minister of the Crown'.[65] In each case, the devolved legislature could refuse consent, but if consent was not given within 40 days the Minister could proceed without it. However, such regulations could only be made within two years of exit day,[66] and any constraints imposed by them ceased to apply to any legislation passed more than five years after exit day. Moreover, while the section 12 modifications remained in force, Ministers are required to publish quarterly reviews of whether it was appropriate to retain **1.78**

[61] *Miller I*, paragraph 129.

[62] *Miller I*, paragraph 135.

[63] After the agreement, in the Withdrawal Agreement, of a transition period after the United Kingdom's exit from the EU during which EU would continue to apply in full, the 2018 Act was amended by the EU (Withdrawal Agreement Act) 2020 to apply from the end of the transition period ('IP completion day').

[64] The Welsh Assembly passed legislation designed to achieve the same effect in relation to EU law in Wales within its area of competence: the Law Derived from the EU (Wales) Act 2018: given the passage of the UK legislation that Act was however repealed a few months later (under powers given to Welsh Ministers to repeal it).

[65] Section 30A of the Scotland Act 1998; section 109A(1) of the Government of Wales Act 2006; section 6A of the Northern Ireland Act 1998.

[66] On this occasion, the term 'exit day' (i.e. 31 January 2020, the date on which the United Kingdom withdrew from the EU) was left unchanged by the EU (Withdrawal Agreement) Act 2020.

them (or any provisions made under them).[67] In short, therefore, section 12 left the devolved legislatures free to repeal or amend retained EU law after IP completion day[68] unless UK Ministers made 'freezing' regulations.

1.79 As noted above, in accordance with the usual operation of the Sewel convention, the Welsh Assembly gave legislative consent to the 2018 Act. The Scottish Parliament refused it, on the basis of objections to section 12.[69] However, as discussed above, that refusal did not prevent the 2018 Act from becoming law.

1.80 Under the powers given to them by section 8 of the 2018 Act, Ministers have (with effect from IP completion day) repealed the elements of EU law that formed the basis of protection of the EU internal market. For example, the provisions in the TFEU on free movement of goods (Articles 34–36 TFEU) were repealed by the Prohibition on Quantitative Restrictions (EU Exit) Regulations 2020[70] and the provisions on free movement of services (Articles 56 and 57 TFEU) by the Freedom of Establishment and Free Movement of Services (EU Exit) Regulations 2019.[71]

3. Common Frameworks

1.81 The result of those developments was that, as from IP completion day, the United Kingdom's withdrawal from the EU would remove the EU law constraint on the exercise of devolved legislative power. Further, that constraint would not be replaced: the cessation of fundamental elements of EU single market law pursuant to the 2018 Act meant that those fundamental elements would no longer form any part of UK law; and those elements of EU law that were maintained in UK law (retained EU law) could be freely amended by devolved legislatures as they chose within their areas of competence, subject only to the time-limited possibility of a freezing regulation under section 12.

1.82 The upshot was that the main constraint on the ability of devolved legislatures (or the UK Parliament acting for England) to legislate in ways that created substantial barriers to the UK internal market was going to disappear, with little to replace it.

1.83 In October 2017, the UK government (at that time under Mrs May) and the devolved governments issued a Joint Communiqué[72] announcing that they had agreed principles for 'common frameworks'. The Communiqué stated that the administrations 'agree to work together to establish common approaches in some areas that are currently governed by EU law, but that are otherwise within areas of competence of the devolved administrations or legislatures. A framework will set out a common UK, or GB, approach and how it will be operated and governed. This may consist of common goals, minimum or maximum standards, harmonisation, limits on action, or mutual recognition, depending on the policy area and the objectives being pursued. Frameworks may be implemented by legislation, by executive action, by memorandums of understanding, or by other means depending on the context in which the framework is intended to operate.'

1.84 The Communiqué then set out a number of principles. Common frameworks would be established where, among other things, they were needed: to 'enable the functioning of the

[67] Section 12(10) of the 2018 Act.

[68] See n. 58 above.

[69] The Northern Ireland Assembly and Executive were suspended at the relevant time.

[70] SI 2020/1625.

[71] SI 2019/1401.

[72] Joint Ministerial Committee (EU Negotiations) Communiqué, 16 October 2017, https://assets.publishing.service.gov.uk/government/uploads/system/uploads/attachment_data/file/652285/Joint_Ministerial_Committee_communique.pdf.

UK internal market, while acknowledging policy divergence'; to 'ensure compliance with international obligations'; or to 'ensure the UK can negotiate, enter into and implement new trade agreements and international treaties'. The frameworks would 'respect the devolution settlements and the democratic accountability of the devolved legislatures' and so would: 'be based on established conventions and practices, including that the competence of the devolved institutions will not normally be adjusted without their consent; maintain, as a minimum, equivalent flexibility for tailoring policies to the specific needs of each territory as is afforded by current EU rules; [and] lead to a significant increase in decision-making powers for the devolved administrations'.[73]

In April 2019 the Cabinet Office identified 154 areas of policy where EU law intersected with devolved competences, including include environmental regulation, agriculture, food standards, animal welfare, public procurement and aspects of justice, transport, and energy. The Cabinet Office took the view that only 40 of those required a common framework, the others being areas where informal cooperation was sufficient: and of those 40, 22 did not require a binding legal framework because sufficient cooperation could be achieved by concordats or memoranda of understanding, or by the operation of retained EU law. In the remaining 18 areas (the bulk of which involved agriculture, food standards, or the environment) 'legislative common frameworks arrangements might be needed, in whole or in part'.[74] **1.85**

According to the Institute for Government, as of October 2020 'there has been substantial intergovernmental working on common frameworks, mainly at civil service level. In 2018, over 30 "deep dive" workshops were held, each bringing together civil servants from different administrations to discuss common frameworks for a specific policy area, and on cross-cutting themes such as the UK internal market. In 2019, these continued alongside two joint UK government/devolved administration Project Board meetings and stakeholder engagement events.' The Covid-19 crisis, however, slowed down that work.[75] **1.86**

E. LEGISLATIVE HISTORY AND DEVOLUTION CONCERNS

1. The White Paper

It was against that background that, in July 2020, the Johnson government published a White Paper setting out its proposals for what became the United Kingdom Internal Market Bill.[76] **1.87**

In his foreword, the then Secretary of State for Business, Energy and Industrial Strategy (BEIS) explained the proposals as follows: **1.88**

[73] In relation to Northern Ireland (the position of which after Brexit was very unclear at that stage) the Communiqué stated that 'Frameworks will ensure recognition of the economic and social linkages between Northern Ireland and Ireland and that Northern Ireland will be the only part of the UK that shares a land frontier with the EU. They will also adhere to the [GFA].'

[74] Cabinet Office, 'Revised Frameworks Analysis: Breakdown of areas of EU law that intersect with devolved competence in Scotland, Wales and Northern Ireland', April 2019, https://assets.publishing.service.gov.uk/government/uploads/system/uploads/attachment_data/file/792738/20190404-FrameworksAnalysis.pdf.

[75] Institute for Government: 'Explainer: Devolution: common frameworks and Brexit', updated October 2020, https://www.instituteforgovernment.org.uk/explainers/devolution-common-frameworks-brexit.

[76] White Paper: 'UK Internal Market', CP 278, July 2020 (hereafter 'the White Paper').

[F]rom 1 January 2021, hundreds of powers previously exercised at EU level will flow directly to the UK government and the devolved administrations in Edinburgh, Cardiff, and Belfast. Devolved administrations will have unprecedented regulatory freedom within new UK frameworks, allowing them to benefit from opportunities to innovate. To allow each home nation to take full advantage of these new opportunities, and ensure businesses can continue to trade freely across the UK as they do now, we are consulting on legislating for a UK Internal Market.

Northern Ireland sells more to the rest of the UK than to all EU member states combined. Scotland sells more to the rest of the UK than to the rest of the world put together. And in some parts of Wales, a quarter of workers commute in from England on a daily basis.

Under the plans in this white paper, the UK will continue to operate as a coherent Internal Market. A Market Access Commitment will guarantee UK companies can trade unhindered in every part of the United Kingdom—ensuring the continued prosperity and wellbeing of people and businesses across all 4 nations. At the same time, we will maintain our high standards for consumers and workers.

This will give business certainty. If a baker sells bread in both Glasgow and Carlisle, they will not need to create different packaging because they are selling between Scotland and England. Likewise, engineering firms in Scotland using parts made in Wales will know that the parts are compliant with regulations across other home nations.

By enshrining the principle of mutual recognition into law, our proposals will ensure regulations from one part of the UK are recognised across the country. The principle of non-discrimination will support companies trading in the UK, regardless of where in the UK they are based.

These principles will not undermine devolution, they will simply prevent any part of the UK from blocking products or services from another part while protecting devolved powers to innovate, such as introducing plastic bag minimum pricing or introducing smoking bans.

1.89 The White Paper sought to place its proposals in the context of the history of the UK internal market:

Centuries before we joined the European Union, the UK's Internal Market received its own articulation through the Acts of Union, guaranteeing basic economic freedoms to all British citizens. Since 1973, these age-old rules were replaced by European law. Decades later, the British people voted to leave the European Union. As EU laws cease to apply, we once again gain the opportunity to articulate our centuries-old rules of the Internal Market, drawing on the laws that constitute an integral part of our shared British history.[77]

1.90 The White Paper identified significant risks to the economy if its proposals were not implemented:

As the EU regulatory powers fall away, there is a danger of regulatory barriers emerging. These would bring risks not just to the wider UK economy, but also to England, Scotland, Wales and Northern Ireland individually. Any reduction in Scottish and Welsh GDP is likely to be 4 and more than 5 times larger respectively, in comparison to the overall UK GDP loss, given their high degree of integration with the rest of the UK.

[77] White Paper, paragraph 1. See section A above for a more detailed account of the history there alluded to.

Without an up-to-date, coherent market structure, economic barriers could block or inhibit trade in goods across the UK, and services could be significantly and detrimentally impacted. Complexities in key sectors such as construction could arise, were differences in regulations to emerge over time. If England and Scotland diverged on their approach to building regulations or processes for obtaining construction permits, it would become significantly more difficult for construction firms to design and plan projects effectively across the UK. Moreover, different approaches to the regulation of construction professionals, such as differing qualifications for plumbers and technicians, could limit access to skilled construction workers, and make it harder for Scottish construction companies to bid for contracts in England.[78]

The White Paper claimed that the common frameworks process could not be expected to avoid those problems: 1.91

Common Frameworks aim to protect the UK Internal Market by providing high levels of regulatory coherence in specific policy areas through close collaboration with devolved administrations to manage regulation. They do this by enabling officials to work together to set and maintain high regulatory standards. However, Frameworks on their own cannot guarantee the integrity of the entire Internal Market. As they tend to be sector-specific, they do not address the totality of economic regulation or the cumulative effects of divergence, ie the consequences of regulatory difference in one sector that affects other sectors. Finally, they do not fully address the question of how best to substitute the wider EU ecosystem of institutions and treaty rights had on the UK Internal Market.

The UK Internal Market legislation discussed in this white paper complements Frameworks by providing a baseline level of regulatory coherence across a wider range of sectors. This means that the areas without a Common Framework will still benefit from a low-level regulatory coherence underpinning. Crucially, market coherence will be provided for issues that fall around or between individual sector-focused frameworks.[79]

The White Paper finally identified another reason for its proposals: that it would make it easier for the UK government to reach trade agreements with third countries (agreements on regulatory matters being a critical aspect of modern free trade agreements): 1.92

Ensuring the UK remains a coherent and integrated economy will be key to fostering all the opportunities in trade. A system that delivers across the whole of the UK will help develop and implement ambitious trade deals that can bring UK-wide benefits to businesses and citizens. It will also help make the whole UK more attractive to foreign investment and build confidence in our present and future trade partners. Helping business thrive will support UK exports, and enable companies to become more competitive, boosting the UK's trading reputation around the world. A well-functioning Internal Market system, tailored to the interests of businesses across the UK, will therefore play a vital role in supporting our long-term global trade ambitions, ensuring the UK as a whole is capable of competing on the international stage.[80]

The White Paper then went on to set out proposals for a mutual recognition principle and a non-discrimination principle, inviting views on whether the latter should include indirect as well as direct discrimination and on what areas should be covered by which principle. It sketched out proposals for an independent body with monitoring functions and to make subsidy control a reserved (or, in Northern Ireland, excepted) matter.[81] 1.93

[78] White Paper, paragraphs 16 and 17.

[79] White Paper, paragraphs 21 and 22. See also paragraphs 93–94.

[80] White Paper, paragraph 45. See also paragraphs 123–125.

[81] See chapter 9 below.

2. Reaction to the White Paper

1.94 The Scottish government expressed its strong opposition to the White Paper proposals.[82] It stated that they were 'fundamentally inconsistent with devolution' because 'the approach in the paper centralises control in the UK Government and UK Parliament, cutting across devolved powers by imposing new domestic constraints on the exercise of these functions; the approach sees devolved decision-making as an obstacle or problem that needs to be bypassed through UK-wide legislation, rather than taking an approach which prioritises agreement by means of negotiation and consensus between different decision-making centres across the UK.' It also claimed that the proposals were 'unnecessary' because negotiations on common frameworks were 'already providing considered and agreed approaches in areas of policy and regulation relevant to UK internal trade'. Moreover, the Scottish government argued that the proposals would lead to a lowering of standards because 'Scotland will be compelled to accept standards, set by the UK Government and Parliament for England (most probably using the English Votes for English Laws mechanism[83] which will exclude MPs from Scotland), regardless of the views and decisions of the Scottish Government and Parliament, and regardless of whether they are appropriate for circumstances in Scotland'.

1.95 The Welsh government also criticized the UK government's failure to consult before issuing the White Paper, stating that 'we support having rules across the UK to regulate the internal market, but these rules must be agreed between the four Governments in the UK, each of which has their own responsibility for economic development'.[84]

a) *The Bill*

1.96 On 9 September 2020, BEIS published the proposed Bill[85] and a response to the consultation exercise.[86] The response reaffirmed the decision to introduce the market access principles and stated that the principle of non-discrimination would include indirect discrimination. The task of monitoring the internal market and the operation of the legislation would be conferred on an Office for the Internal Market within the Competition and Markets Authority (CMA).

1.97 That response was, however, overwhelmed, in terms of press and political attention, by clauses in the Bill that had not been foreshadowed in the White Paper and whose existence had been trailed only the day before publication: those clauses (42, 43, and 45, in Part 5 of the Bill) provided for UK Ministers to have power to disapply, modify, or interpret provisions of the Ireland/Northern Ireland Protocol, including in particular Article 10 relating to subsidies. As the Secretary of State for Northern Ireland had admitted when trailing those proposals,[87] the use of any such power would have involved a breach of international law (in fact,

---

[82] Scottish Government, 'UK internal market: initial assessment of UK Government proposals', 12 August 2020, https://www.gov.scot/publications/uk-internal-market/.

[83] See paragraph 1.69 above.

[84] See Politics Home, 'Ministers promise "power surge" to devolved nations after Brexit amid bitter row with Scotland and Wales', 16 July 2020, https://www.politicshome.com/news/article/ministers-promise-power-surge-to-devolved-nations-after-brexit-amid-bitter-row-with-scotland-and-wales,

[85] Copies of the Bill as introduced and all subsequent versions of the Bill as it went through Parliament are available at https://bills.parliament.uk/bills/2775/publications.

[86] https://assets.publishing.service.gov.uk/government/uploads/system/uploads/attachment_data/file/929306/ukim-consultation-government-response.pdf.

[87] 'I would say to my hon. Friend that yes, this [proposal] does break international law in a very specific and limited way. We are taking the power to disapply the EU law concept of direct effect, required by article

of the Withdrawal Agreement negotiated by the Johnson government less than 12 months previously). The intention that such powers would be used to breach the provisions of the Withdrawal Agreement was made clear on the face of the Bill: clause 45(1)(a) stated in terms that 'regulations under section 42(1) or 43(1) are not to be regarded as unlawful on the grounds of any incompatibility or inconsistency with relevant international or domestic law' and clause 45(1)(b) expressly modified section 7A of the EU (Withdrawal) Act 2018—which gave direct effect to the Withdrawal Agreement as required by Article 4 of that Agreement—to the extent that it was inconsistent with such regulations.[88]

One issue that was immediately raised was whether, in making that proposal, Ministers **1.98**
were in breach of the Ministerial Code: as Jeremy Wright MP (former Attorney General in the Cameron and May governments) asked the Prime Minister during the Second Reading debate on 14 September: 'When I was the Attorney General in the previous Government, I was happy to confirm that the ministerial code obliged Ministers to comply with international as well as domestic law. This Bill will give Ministers overt authority to break international law. Has the position on the ministerial code changed?'[89] The Prime Minister, in answering, referred to a briefing paper issued on behalf of the then Law Officers.[90] That paper contained the pronouncement that '[i]t is an established principle of international law that a state is obliged to discharge its treaty obligations in good faith. This is, and will remain, the key principle in informing the UK's approach to international relations. However, in the difficult and highly exceptional circumstances in which we find ourselves, it is important to remember the fundamental principle of Parliamentary sovereignty.' However, as many legal commentators pointed out,[91] that pronouncement contained nothing which dealt with the point that what was being proposed was a breach of international law: a point to which the principle of parliamentary sovereignty as a matter of domestic law was simply irrelevant.

The Second Reading debate concentrated on that issue, and was notable for concerns **1.99**
expressed by a number of Conservative MPs.[92] Nonetheless, the proposals in Part 5 were, in the Commons (during an accelerated committee and report process), amended only to strengthen them: provisions were added to prevent the courts from annulling regulations made under clause 42 or 43 on the ground of incompatibility with the Human Rights Act 1998.[93]

A number of other minor changes were made, but the Bill as introduced to the House of **1.100**
Lords on 30 September was in substantially the same form as introduced to the Commons.

4 [of the Withdrawal Agreement], in certain very tightly defined circumstances.' Hansard HC, 8 September 2020, col. 509.

[88] For a critique of clause 45 of the Bill, see https://eurelationslaw.com/blog/clause-45-of-internal-market-bill-a-striking-attempt-to-exclude-judicial-review.

[89] Hansard HC, 14 September 2020, col. 44.

[90] https://assets.publishing.service.gov.uk/government/uploads/system/uploads/attachment_data/file/916702/UKIM_Legal_Statement.pdf.

[91] See e.g. M. Elliott, 'Legal Kryptonite? Parliamentary Sovereignty, International Law and the Internal Market Bill', Public Law for Everyone, 10 October 2020, https://publiclawforeveryone.com/2020/10/10/legal-kryptonite-parliamentary-sovereignty-international-law-and-the-internal-market-bill/.

[92] See e.g. Sir Robert Neill MP: 'Part 5 of the Bill, as it stands, gives me real concern as to its leading the United Kingdom into a breach of our international obligations and the law that stems from them. That is, as many others have observed, not something that any country should do, save in the most extreme and pressing circumstances.' Hansard (HC) 14 September 2020, col. 62.

[93] Clause 47(1)(a) and (3) in the Bill as introduced to the House of Lords.

1.101 Passage through the House Lords proved far more difficult. First, after voting to agree to Second Reading only after also passing a motion regretting that the enactment of Part 5 would undermine the rule of law and damage the United Kingdom's international reputation, the House of Lords simply removed Part 5 (including the much-criticized Clauses 42–45) of the Bill in totality, by 433 votes to 165, with the supporters of the amendment including many prominent Conservative politicians.[94]

1.102 With somewhat less attention, however, the House of Lords also made various important amendments to other parts of the Bill.[95] The most important of those were, first, in amendments supported by the Welsh government, that clauses were added to Part 1 and Part 2 that made the market access principles inapplicable to any statutory provision or requirement that gave effect to a decision agreed to through the common frameworks process, and removed UK Ministers' powers to regulate in regard to a matter under discussion in the common frameworks process. Second, UK Ministers were required to consult the devolved administrations before exercising their regulation-making powers under Parts 1 and 2, and duties to review the making of such regulations were added. Third, a list of broad public interest derogations from the market access principles were added. Fourth, the Secretary of State was required to seek the consent of the devolved administrations to appointments to the Office of the Internal Market, and to separate it from the CMA.

1.103 Although the government succeeded in reinstating parts of Part 5 of the Bill when it returned to the Commons, the government finally abandoned the proposals to give it power to make regulations that breached the Withdrawal Agreement. The final position in relation to the other Lords' amendments is discussed in the following chapters of this work.

3. The Devolved Governments and the Bill

1.104 Both the Senedd and the Scottish Parliament refused legislative consent to the Bill: the Senedd simply rejected the legislative consent motion, and the Scottish Parliament passed a motion refusing consent on the basis that it 'reduces and constrains the competence of the Scottish Parliament and breaches international law'.[96]

1.105 The central concerns set out by the devolved administrations were those set out at paragraph 1.93 above. The effect of the market access principles in Part 1 (and the equivalent provisions in Parts 2 and 3) was, it was said, to make it impossible for the devolved governments to legislate to impose stricter requirements than those applicable in England: if they tried, English producers or suppliers could simply invoke those principles. Although the Act also in theory applied to the UK government, legislating for England, that was, it was

[94] See e.g. Lord Howard of Lympne, former leader of the Conservative Party: 'Ministers, both in your Lordships' House and elsewhere, have sought to make the case that circumstances make it expedient to break international law. But is that not what lawbreakers always say? Is that not the excuse of lawbreakers everywhere? What sort of a precedent are the Government setting when they admit that position? How can we reproach other countries—Russia, China, Iran—if their behaviour becomes reprehensible, when we ourselves have such scant regard for the treaties we sign up to and we set such a lamentable example?' Hansard HL, 9 November 2020, col. 860; Lord Clarke of Nottingham, former Conservative Chancellor of the Exchequer: 'I again would have expected some explanation of what dire circumstances the Government were contemplating to justify such an amazing break from our traditions, as a liberal democracy and one of the world's principal upholders of the rules-based international order.' Hansard HL, 9 November 2020, col. 882.

[95] https://publications.parliament.uk/pa/bills/cbill/58-01/0224/200224.pdf.

[96] Copies of the relevant correspondence from the Clerks to the Senedd and to the Scottish Parliament to the Clerks of Parliament are at https://bills.parliament.uk/bills/2775/publications.

said, a somewhat theoretical constraint: England was, on every measure of economic weight, far larger than any of the other nations of the United Kingdom, and so any concerns that Scottish and Welsh producers or suppliers might not be affected by such regulation would be unlikely to act as a real policy constraint; and, moreover, the UK government could, in the event of any difficulties caused to its regulatory policy by the Act, either use its powers to modify the Act or use its control of the sovereign UK Parliament simply to amend the Act.

A further set of concerns related to the limited possible exclusions and justifications, on public policy grounds, applying to the mutual recognition and non-discrimination principles. **1.106**

Finally, as discussed in chapter 9 below, the devolved administrations objected to the provisions on subsidy control and financial assistance. **1.107**

After Royal Assent, the Counsel General for Wales applied for permission to apply for judicial review, seeking declarations that (a) the provisions of the Act did not have the effect of impliedly limiting the legislative competence of the Senedd to enact legislation which is inconsistent with the mutual recognition principle contained in section 2 of the Act; and (b) the power conferred on the Secretary of State to make regulations amending provisions of that Act could not be exercised in a way which would substantively limit the legislative competence of the Senedd. That application was, however, dismissed and permission refused by the Divisional Court on the basis that it was premature, and that the issues raised should be considered as and when the Senedd, or the Secretary of State, exercised the powers at issue.[97] **1.108**

F. STRUCTURE OF THE ACT

Part 1 of the Act deals with the 'market access principles' (mutual recognition and non-discrimination) in relation to goods. Each principle is defined, and the types of restrictions to which they potentially apply set out along with certain exclusions: section 10 provides for general exclusions from both the principles. Part 1 is discussed in chapters 2 and 3. **1.109**

Part 2 of the Act contains provision that limit the application of regulatory requirements in relation to services, covering both requirements as to authorization to supply services and requirements that must be complied with in order to supply services. Part 2 is discussed in chapters 4 and 5. **1.110**

Part 3 deals with mutual recognition of qualifications, and creates a general rule (with exceptions) that a person authorized to carry out an activity in one part of the United Kingdom must be treated as authorized to carry out that activity in other parts of the United Kingdom. Part 3 is discussed in chapter 6. **1.111**

Part 4 deals with the Office of the Internal Market, established within the CMA in order to monitor and report on the functioning of the internal market, both generally and, on the request of one of the national governments, on particular issues. It also confers powers of investigation on the CMA. Part 4 is discussed in chapter 7. **1.112**

Part 5 makes various provisions in relation to the Ireland/Northern Ireland Protocol. Part 5 is discussed in chapter 8. **1.113**

Part 6 confers a general power on the UK government to give financial assistance throughout the United Kingdom for a wide range of purposes. Part 6 is discussed in chapter 9. **1.114**

[97] *R(Counsel General for Wales) v Secretary of State for Business, Energy and Industrial Strategy* [2021] EWHC 950 (Admin). Permission was given for the judgment to be cited in court.

1.115 Part 7 makes subsidy control a reserved (or excepted) matter. Part 7 is also discussed in chapter 9.

1.116 Part 8 makes various general provisions, and adds the Act to the list of Acts in each of the devolution statutes that may not be amended by the relevant legislature. Part 8 is discussed below.

G. EXTENT AND COMMENCEMENT OF THE ACT

1.117 The Act extends to England and Wales, Scotland, and Northern Ireland: section 59(1).

1.118 The Act comes into force on such days as the Secretary of State may appoint by regulations: section 59. As of 20 September 2021, all parts of the Act had been brought into force.[98]

H. MODIFICATION OF THE ACT

1.119 Section 54 of the Act adds the Act to the lists of 'protected enactments' ('entrenched enactments' in Northern Ireland) in each of the devolution statutes.[99] In each case, the effect is remove amendment of the Act from the competence of the relevant legislature.

[98] United Kingdom Internal Market Act 2020 (Commencement No. 1) Regulations 2020 (SI 2020/1621), United Kingdom Internal Market Act 2020 (Commencement No. 2) Regulations 2021 (SI 2021/706), and United Kingdom Internal Market Act 2020 (Commencement No. 3) Regulations 2021 (SI 2021/1062).

[99] Schedule 4 to the Scotland Act 1998; Schedule 7B to the Government of Wales Act 2006; section 7(1) of the Northern Ireland Act 1998.

2
THE MUTUAL RECOGNITION PRINCIPLE FOR GOODS

A. INTRODUCTION

This chapter examines the first of the two 'market access principles' established in section 1 of the Act, namely the mutual recognition principle for goods (hereafter referred to in this chapter as 'the mutual recognition principle' or 'the principle'). The relevant provisions in the **2.01**

Blackstone's Guide to the UK Internal Market Act 2020. Alan Bates, Brendan McGurk, George Peretz QC, and Jack Williams, Oxford University Press. © Alan Bates, Brendan McGurk, George Peretz QC, and Jack Williams 2021.
DOI: 10.1093/oso/9780192856203.003.0002

Act for the mutual recognition principle are found in Part I at sections 2–4 and 14–16,[1] with modifications for the purposes of Northern Ireland found in section 11.[2] Exclusions from the mutual recognition principle are found in section 10 and Schedule 1 to the Act.

2.02 This chapter answers five overarching questions. What is the mutual recognition principle? What are the conditions for its applicability? What 'relevant requirements' are covered by the principle? When is the principle excluded? What effect does it have in practice?

B. THE MUTUAL RECOGNITION PRINCIPLE FOR GOODS

2.03 Section 2(1) of the Act provides that:

> The mutual recognition principle for goods is the principle that goods which—
> (a) have been produced in, or imported into, one part of the United Kingdom ('the originating part'), and
> (b) can be sold there without contravening any relevant requirements that would apply to their sale, should be able to be sold in any other part of the United Kingdom, free from any relevant requirements that would otherwise apply to the sale.

2.04 This mutual recognition principle means that any good that meets regulatory requirements (so-called 'relevant requirements') relating to sale in one part of the United Kingdom (England, Northern Ireland, Scotland, and Wales[3]) in which it is produced or imported into, can be sold in any other part of the United Kingdom without having to adhere to any additional or different relevant requirement in that other, destination part.

2.05 For example:

a. a bag of flour made in England that met the relevant requirements in England (e.g. on the composition of the flour) can be sold in Wales without having to meet any other relevant requirements that apply in Wales;[4]

b. a jam producer in Wales does not need to worry about meeting any Scottish relevant requirements for jam when selling in Scotland, as long as the jam produced conforms to the Welsh requirements;[5] and

c. chlorinated chicken lawfully imported into and sold within England from the United States as part of a (hypothetical) trade deal would be allowed to be sold in Wales, despite any ban on the product introduced by the Senedd Cymru (the Welsh Parliament).

2.06 The function of the mutual recognition principle is thus to preserve an internal market for goods within the United Kingdom, which provides unfettered access for qualifying goods. The principle ensures that goods need only comply with one set of rules when they are sold

---

[1] Each of these provisions commenced at 11 p.m. on 31 December 2020 (defined as 'IP completion day' in Schedule 1 to the Interpretation Act 1978 by reference to section 39 of the European Union (Withdrawal Agreement) Act 2020): see Regulation 2 of the United Kingdom Internal Market Act 2020 (Commencement No. 1) Regulations 2020.

[2] Section 11 ('Modifications in connection with the Northern Ireland Protocol') is addressed in chapter 8.

[3] See section 58, which defines 'part of the United Kingdom' accordingly.

[4] Explanatory Notes to the United Kingdom Internal Market Act 2020, paragraph 11 (hereafter, 'Explanatory Notes').

[5] Department for Business, Energy and Industrial Strategy, Policy Paper, Mutual recognition of goods: general principles and relevant requirements (17 November 2020) (hereafter, 'Mutual Recognition Policy Paper').

in the United Kingdom, thus preventing businesses from having to comply with multiple requirements for sales of their goods or otherwise having their market restricted. This reduces complexity and costs. If a particular good meets the required standards of one part of the United Kingdom, then it is essentially deemed to be fit for sale across all parts of the United Kingdom.

In cases where there are no relevant requirements that would apply to the sale of a good in the part of the United Kingdom in which it was produced or imported into (i.e. the 'originating part'), the mutual recognition principle still permits the good to be sold in other parts of the United Kingdom without complying with the relevant requirements that apply in those other parts (s. 2(1)(b)). 2.07

The mutual recognition principle also does not prevent local producers being bound by local regulation. The UK government (in respect of England) and the devolved administrations retain, within their respective areas of legislative competence, the capacity to enforce their own requirements on goods produced in that part of the United Kingdom or imported into that part of the United Kingdom. For example, a Welsh producer and an English producer of flour may make identical goods (flour) which are in compliance with the English requirements, but not the Welsh requirements. The Welsh producer would still be bound by any Welsh relevant requirements concerning the composition of flour in respect of sales in Wales. The English producer, however, could market its flour across the whole of the United Kingdom, including in Wales, by virtue of the fact that its goods were produced in England (where they were in compliance with the rules), thus triggering the mutual recognition principle. 2.08

The effect of this may be to disincentivize devolved administrations (or the UK government in respect of England) from raising standards in their respective areas, as these higher standards would apply only to their own producers or importers, which could then be undercut by goods imported from another part of the United Kingdom due to the mutual recognition principle. This may also encourage a 'race to the bottom', whereby devolved administrations, for example, are incentivized to lower standards in response to relaxation of regulations elsewhere. On account of the size of England, the economic reality may be that whatever standard is set in England will be followed in the other parts of the United Kingdom to prevent traders in those nations being at a competitive disadvantage.[6] 2.09

Section 14 provides that: 2.10

> Nothing in this Part [1] prevents goods produced in or imported into a part of the United Kingdom from being sold in another part of the United Kingdom if (apart from this Part) the sale complies with any requirements applicable in that other part of the United Kingdom (or there are no such requirements).

This means, for example, that where goods do not meet the criteria for the mutual recognition principle to apply, or where traders do not wish to make use of the principle for their goods, these goods can continue to be sold in a part of the United Kingdom by complying with the requirements relating to sale that apply there.[7] 2.11

---

[6] According to the Office for National Statistics, in 2019 the economy of England generated around 87 per cent of total economic activity; the remainder was split between the other parts of the United Kingdom, with Scotland contributing 8 per cent, Wales generating 3 per cent, and Northern Ireland being responsible for 2 per cent of overall output measured by gross value added.

[7] Explanatory Notes (n. 4), paragraph 166.

C. THE APPLICABILITY OF THE MUTUAL RECOGNITION PRINCIPLE

2.12 There are two overarching requirements for the mutual recognition principle to apply to particular goods. First, those goods must have been produced in or imported into one part of the United Kingdom, the 'originating part' (s. 2(1)(a)). Second, those goods must also be capable of being sold in the originating part without contravening[8] any relevant requirements that would apply to their sale (s. 2(1)(b)).[9] Only then can the good be sold in any other part of the United Kingdom (the destination part), free from any relevant requirements that would otherwise apply to the sale (s. 2(1)).

2.13 There are thus a number of specific conditions for the applicability of the mutual recognition principle. It only applies to 'goods', which have either been 'produced in' or 'imported into' the so-called 'originating part' of the United Kingdom. It then only applies to 'the sale' of those goods in the destination part of the United Kingdom. More broadly, the principle generally only applies to relevant requirements which post-date the commencement of the Act, that is, it does not generally have retrospective effect (s. 4). Each of these conditions for the applicability of the principle are examined in turn.

1. The Definition of 'goods'

2.14 The term 'goods' is defined in section 16(2) of the Act as 'any tangible movable, or corporeal moveable, thing (including any packaging or label), but not water or gas that is not offered for sale in a limited volume or set quantity'.

2.15 This definition encompasses agricultural goods, including live animals, germinal products, and animal by-products.[10]

2.16 The reference to water or gas 'that is not offered for sale in a limited volume or set quantity' means that bottled water or canisters of gas are covered by the concept of 'goods', whereas water or gas that is piped into buildings as a utility are not covered.[11]

2. The Definition of 'produced in'

2.17 The mutual recognition principle applies to goods from an 'originating part' of the United Kingdom (s. 2(1)(a)). A good can originate from that part in one of two ways, namely having either been 'produced in' that part of the United Kingdom or having been 'imported into' that part.

2.18 The concept of 'production' is defined in section 16(3)–(7) and (11) of the Act. Goods are to be regarded as 'produced in' the originating part of the United Kingdom if either they are wholly produced there, or 'if the most recent significant production step which is a regulated

---

[8] Section 16(13) of the Act defines 'contravening' as including the failure to comply.

[9] Paragraph 6 of Schedule 1 to the Act states that an authorization under Chapter 2 of Title 7 of Regulation (EC) No 1907/2006 of the European Parliament and of the Council of 18 December 2006 as it forms part of retained EU law ('the UK REACH Regulation') 'is to be disregarded (for the purposes of the mutual recognition principle for goods) whether goods can be sold as mentioned in section 2(1)(b)'.

[10] Explanatory Notes (n. 4), paragraph 173.

[11] ibid.

step has occurred there' (s. 16(3)). For both situations, section 16(11) states that a reference to 'production' (however expressed e.g. 'produced in') includes 'cultivation, harvesting and similar activities (in relation to plants or fungi)' (s. 16(11)(a)) and 'rearing, keeping, handling, killing and similar activities in relation to livestock or other animals' (s. 16(11)(b)). This reflects the fact that the definition of 'goods' in section 14 includes agricultural products.

If the good is not wholly produced in the originating part of the United Kingdom, then the most recent production step has to have occurred there and be both (i) a 'regulated step' and (ii) a 'significant' step (s. 16(3)). 2.19

In respect of the 'regulated step' requirement in section 16(3), section 16(4) states that a production step is 'regulated' for the purposes of section 16(3) in one of two distinct circumstances. First, it is a regulated production step if it is the subject of any statutory requirement in that part of the United Kingdom in which it is produced (s. 16(4)(a)). A 'statutory requirement' is an obligation, condition, or prohibition (however described) imposed by legislation (including legislation imposing mandatory terms into contracts for the sale of goods) (see ss 16(14) and 3(8)).[12] Second, alternatively section 16(4)(b) states that it is also a regulated production step if: 2.20

it is a step that could materially affect a person's ability to sell the goods without contravening—
(i) any relevant requirement for the purposes of the mutual recognition principle for goods, or
(ii) any statutory requirement that is excluded from being a relevant requirement by section 4(1) [regarding the exclusion of certain requirements existing before the commencement of the Act], that would be applicable to a sale of the goods in that part of the United Kingdom (being a sale of a kind for which the goods are being produced).

For example, the manufacture of a crane in Scotland would constitute a regulated step. If, however, another company in England purchased the crane and changed its colour before sale, the crane would still count as being produced in Scotland, as changing the colour is not a regulated step.[13] 2.21

For the definition of 'relevant requirements' see section D below. 2.22

In respect of the second, cumulative requirement in section 16(3) that the (most recent and regulated) production step be 'significant', section 16(5) states that a production step is significant 'if it is significant in terms of the character of the goods being produced and the purposes for which they are sold or used', subject to section 16(6) and (7). For example, the baking of a loaf of bread would constitute a significant step.[14] 2.23

Section 16(6) confirms that a production step falling within any of the following descriptions is not significant (whether or not it is regulated): 2.24

a. activities carried out specifically to ensure goods do not deteriorate before being sold (such as maintaining them at or below a particular temperature). For example, preserving activities, such as cooling or freezing, high temperature treatment, drying, sealing,

[12] Pursuant to section 58, 'legislation' includes primary legislation, subordinate legislation, and retained direct EU legislation, whereby (i) 'primary legislation' includes Acts of the UK Parliament, Acts of the Scottish Parliament, Acts or Measures of the Senedd Cymru (the Welsh Parliament), and Northern Ireland legislation; and (ii) 'subordinate legislation' means an instrument made under primary legislation or retained direct EU legislation.

[13] Department for Business, Energy and Industrial Strategy, Policy Paper, Mutual recognition of goods: location of production (17 November 2020) (hereafter, 'Location of Production Policy Paper').

[14] ibid.

adding preservatives, and similar measures would not count as 'significant' unless significant to the character of the goods (e.g. pickling);[15]

b. activities carried out solely for purposes relevant to their presentation for sale (such as cleaning or pressing fabrics or sorting different coloured items for packaging together);

c. activities involving a communication of any kind with a regulatory or trade body (such as registering the goods or notifying the goods or anything connected with them or their production); and

d. activities carried out for the purpose of testing or assessing any characteristic of the goods (such as batch testing a pharmaceutical product). For example, taking samples from goods or similar quality assurance activities would not count as 'significant'.[16]

2.25 Section 16(7) states that a product step 'involving the packaging, labelling or marking of goods is not significant (whether or not it is regulated) unless the step is fundamental to the character of the goods and the purposes for which they are to be sold or used'. For example, jam made in Scotland but where the jar is labelled in England would be Scottish, but collectable trading cards where the card stock is made in Scotland but the information on the cards is applied in England would be English because the information is fundamental to those goods.[17]

3. The Definition of 'imported into'

2.26 The second way in which a good originates from one part of the United Kingdom (such that s. 2(1)(a) applies) is if it has been 'imported into' that part.[18]

2.27 The concept of 'importation' is defined in section 16(8)–(10) of the Act. Goods are 'imported into' a part of the United Kingdom 'only if they are imported into that part from outside the United Kingdom' (<IBT>s. 16(8)</IBT>). For this purpose, the Isle of Man is treated as outside the United Kingdom (ibid). Section 16(9) states that goods are to be treated as imported:

a. for goods brought by sea, when the ship carrying them enters the limits of the port at which they are discharged (s. 16(9)(a)). For these purposes, 'port' means a port appointed by the Commissioners for Her Majesty's Revenue and Customs (see ss 1 and 19 of the Customs and Excise Management Act 1979) and 'ship' includes any boat or other vessel whatsoever and, in some circumstances, hovercraft (see ss 1 and 2 of the Customs and Excise Management Act 1979);

b. for goods brought by air, when they are unloaded; and

---

[15] ibid.

[16] ibid.

[17] ibid.

[18] The application of the mutual recognition principle to imported goods was justified by the Parliamentary Under-Secretary of State, Department for Business, Energy and Industrial Strategy (Lord Callanan) on the basis that '[r]emoving imported goods from the mutual recognition principle would mean that those goods, simply because of where they were sourced, could not benefit from the same regulatory treatment as goods produced in the United Kingdom. Even when produced to identical specification and quality as domestic products, this discriminatory impact would put imported goods at a conspicuously unfair disadvantage. Under such a discriminatory approach, we would be likely to be in clear breach of our World Trade Organization commitments to treat imports from other countries no less favourably than similar products produced domestically': Hansard HL, 28 October 2020, col. 249.

c. for goods brought by land, when they enter the United Kingdom.

Section 16(10) provides that where a good is either produced in or imported into one part of the United Kingdom ('the original part of the United Kingdom'), and is then exported outside of the United Kingdom before subsequently being re-imported back into the United Kingdom, the good should still be regarded as having been produced in or imported into the original part of the United Kingdom. For example, biscuits which are made in Northern Ireland and transported to Wales via the Republic of Ireland are considered to be produced in Northern Ireland and not imported into Wales.[19] Therefore, they will benefit from mutual recognition if they comply with the requirements of Northern Ireland. They do not need to comply with the requirements in Wales to be sold there (or in other parts of the United Kingdom). 2.28

4. The Definition of 'sold' and 'sale'

Section 2(1)(b) states that the mutual recognition principle applies only to goods which can be 'sold' in the originating part of the United Kingdom without contravening any relevant requirements that would apply to their 'sale', Where section 2(1)(a) and (b) apply, the goods should be able to be 'sold' in the destination part of the United Kingdom, free from any relevant requirements that would otherwise apply to the 'sale' (s. 2(1)). 2.29

Section 15 defines references to the sale of goods (however expressed in Part 1 of the Act: s. 15(1)) for these purposes. The terms are defined broadly. The sale of goods includes some earlier actions with a view to sale: agreement to sell, offering or exposing for sale, or having in possession or holding for sale (s. 15(4)). Part 1 of the Act also applies 'in relation to a supply of goods other than a sale as it applies in relation to a sale' (s. 15(5)). For that purpose, 'supply of goods' means the transfer of possession or property in goods (whether or not under or by virtue of a contract) (s. 15(6)) and includes, for example, supply by way of barter or exchange (s. 15(6)(a)); the leasing or hiring out of goods, hire purchase, or bailment of goods (s. 15(6)(b)); or a gift (or anything else done free of charge) (s. 15(6)(c)). Earlier actions with a view to these types of supply would also be covered for example, an agreement to hire.[20] Activities which are not related to sale and in particular those which happen after sale are generally not captured. So for example, requirements as to how a product may or may not be used or those related to disposal at the end of a product's life would not normally be in scope.[21] 2.30

Relevant requirements for the purposes of the mutual recognition principle will thus include any requirements relating to the activities listed in section 15. This is subject to section 2(2), which provides: 2.31

> Where goods are to be sold in a particular way in the other part of the United Kingdom, the condition in subsection (1)(b) [namely that the goods 'can be sold there without contravening any relevant requirement that would apply to their sale'] has effect as if the reference to 'their sale' were a reference to their sale in that particular way.

The reference in section 2(2) to the 'other part' of the United Kingdom refers to the destination part, as opposed to the originating part. This sub-section means that the effect of the 2.32

[19] Location of Production Policy Paper (n. 13).
[20] Explanatory Notes (n. 4), paragraph 170.
[21] Mutual Recognition Policy Paper (n. 5).

mutual recognition principle is limited by reference to the particular type of sale that is taking place in the nation where the good is being sold. Section 2(2) provides an example: 'if goods are to be sold by auction, the condition is met if (and only if) they can be sold by auction in the originating part without contravening any applicable relevant requirements there'.

2.33 Moreover, there are exclusions to the concept of 'sale'. References to the sale of goods do not include sales which are not made in the course of a business (s. 15(2)(a)), or those which are made in the course of a business but only for the purpose of performing a function of a public nature (s. 15(2)(b)). The latter does not, however, exclude sales which are made by a public body or authority for commercial purposes and are also not made for the purpose of performing a function of a public nature (other than a function relating to the carrying on of commercial activities) (s. 15(3)).

2.34 For example:

a. the supply of medication by the NHS to a patient through a prescription would not be covered as it is a sale made by a public authority fulfilling a public function;[22] and
b. if a public body were to set up a gift shop selling merchandise, this would be captured as a 'sale' for the purposes of Part 1 as it would be commercial activity not directly related to its public functions.[23]

5. The Exclusion of Requirements Existing Prior to Commencement

2.35 Pursuant to section 4, the mutual recognition principle generally only applies to relevant requirements (see section D below) which post-date the commencement of the Act, that is, it does not generally have retrospective effect. Therefore, where different regulatory requirements existed in different parts of the United Kingdom prior to the commencement of the Act, those requirements are generally permitted and remain unaffected by the mutual recognition principle.

2.36 Section 4(1) provides that a 'statutory requirement'[24] in a part of the United Kingdom (the so-called 'relevant part' for these purposes) which applies in relation to a particular sale of goods in that part of the United Kingdom and would otherwise fall within section 3 of the Act as a relevant requirement 'is not a relevant requirement (so far as relating to that sale) for the purposes of the mutual recognition principle' where the two conditions in section 4(2) are both met.

2.37 The conditions in section 4(2) are that:

a. the same statutory requirement would have applied in relation to the sale if it had taken place on the relevant day (s. 4(2)(a)). For these purposes (and for the purposes of s. 4(5)),

---

[22] Explanatory Notes (n. 4), paragraphs 16 and 168.

[23] Explanatory Notes (n. 4), paragraph 168.

[24] A 'statutory requirement' is an obligation, condition, or prohibition (however described) imposed by legislation (including legislation imposing mandatory terms into contracts for the sale of goods) (see ss 16(14) and 3(8)). Pursuant to section 58, 'legislation' includes primary legislation, subordinate legislation, and retained direct EU legislation, whereby (i) 'primary legislation' includes Acts of the UK Parliament, Acts of the Scottish Parliament, Acts or Measures of the Senedd Cymru (the Welsh Parliament), and Northern Ireland legislation; and (ii) 'subordinate legislation' means an instrument made under primary legislation or retained direct EU legislation.

a statutory requirement is to be regarded 'the same' as another statutory requirement, or having the same effect, if any differences between them are not substantive (s. 4(6)); and

b. there was no corresponding requirement in force in each of the other three parts of the United Kingdom on the relevant day (s. 4(2)(b)). For these purposes, 'corresponding requirement', in relation to the statutory requirement in 'the relevant part' of the United Kingdom means a statutory requirement in another part of the United Kingdom that would have had the same effect in relation to the sale (if it had taken place there on the relevant day) (s. 4(5)).

These conditions must both apply on 'the relevant day' (s. 4(2)). This is defined as 'the day before the day on which this section comes into force' (s. 4(3)). As section 4 came into force at 11 p.m. on 31 December 2020 (see Regulation 2 of the United Kingdom Internal Market Act 2020 (Commencement No. 1) Regulations 2020 in conjunction with Schedule 1 to the Interpretation Act 1978 by reference to section 39 of the European Union (Withdrawal Agreement) Act 2020), the 'relevant day' is therefore 30 December 2020. Therefore, any existing regulatory differences across the United Kingdom on 30 December 2020 are time-barred in the sense that these are not retrospectively subject to the mutual recognition principle and can still be lawfully maintained and applied. For example, the pre-existing (as of 30 December 2020) Scottish rules on raw cow's drinking milk are unaffected by the introduction of the mutual recognition principle in the Act.[25] 2.38

Section 4(4) provides that the 're-enactment (without substantive change)' of a statutory requirement does not affect its continuity for the purposes of section 4(2)(a). In essence, this means that if a time-barred relevant requirement is re-enacted without substantive change, then the mutual recognition principle still does not apply despite it being enacted after the relevant day. The rationale for this is that consumers and businesses have already adapted to these differences, whereas the aim of the Act is to ensure that businesses will continue to enjoy internal trade without any new barriers. 2.39

By contrast, the implication is that substantive changes to any pre-existing (and thus time-barred) relevant requirements will then be brought into the scope of the mutual recognition principle. For example, where existing legislation receives technical or minor amendments that do not alter the substance of the legislation, that would continue to be out of scope, whereas re-enactments that would change the effect or outcome of the legislation would then come within the scope of the mutual recognition principle. 2.40

D. RELEVANT REQUIREMENTS

For goods to benefit from the mutual recognition principle, those goods must be capable of being sold in the originating part without contravening[26] any 'relevant requirements' that would apply to their sale (s. 2(1)(b)). Where that condition is met in addition to the requirement that the goods have been produced in or imported into one part of the United Kingdom (the 'originating part') (s. 2(1)(a)), then the goods can be sold in any other part of 2.41

[25] Mutual Recognition Policy Paper (n. 5). In Scotland it is an offence to place raw milk or cream on the market for direct consumption in Scotland—this includes distribution. The ban includes sheep, goats, buffalo, and any other species farmed for its milk.

[26] Section 16(13) of the Act defines 'contravening' as including the failure to comply.

the United Kingdom (the destination part) free from any 'relevant requirements' that would otherwise apply to the sale (s. 2(1)). In those circumstances, any 'relevant requirements' in the destination part of the United Kingdom 'do not apply in relation to the sale' (s. 2(3)).

2.42 Section 3(2) defines 'relevant requirements' for these purposes as follows:

> A statutory requirement in the part of the United Kingdom concerned which—
> (a) prohibits the sale of the goods or, in the case of an obligation or condition, results in their sale being prohibited if it is not complied with, and
> (b) is within the scope of the mutual recognition principle, is a relevant requirement in relation to the sale unless excluded from being a relevant requirement by any provision of this Part.

1. The Definition of 'statutory requirement'

2.43 A 'statutory requirement' for the purposes of section 3(2) is an obligation, condition, or prohibition (however described) imposed by legislation (including legislation imposing mandatory terms into contracts for the sale of goods) (see ss 16(14) and 3(8)). Pursuant to section 58, 'legislation' includes primary legislation, subordinate legislation, and retained direct EU legislation, whereby (i) 'primary legislation' includes Acts of the UK Parliament, Acts of the Scottish Parliament, Acts or Measures of the Senedd Cymru (the Welsh Parliament), and Northern Ireland legislation; and (ii) 'subordinate legislation' means an instrument made under primary legislation or retained direct EU legislation.

2.44 Therefore, non-legislative, administrative practices and actions of private parties (including industry-wide standards, for example) are not covered by the concept of relevant requirements and thus fall outside the scope of the mutual recognition principle. This is distinct from the position under EU law, which covers administrative[27] and non-binding measures.[28]

2. The Relevant Requirements 'within the scope' of the Mutual Recognition Principle

2.45 Pursuant to section 3(3), a statutory requirement is 'within the scope of' the mutual recognition principle for the purposes of section 3(2)(b) if it 'relates to' any one or more of the following:

a. characteristics of the goods themselves (such as their nature, composition, age, quality, or performance);
b. any matter connected with the presentation of the goods (such as the name or description applied to them or their packaging, labelling, lot-marking, or date-stamping);
c. any matter connected with the production of the goods or anything from which they are made or is involved in their production, including the place at which, or the circumstances in which, production or any step in production took place;
d. any matter relating to the identification or tracing of an animal (such as marking, tagging or micro-chipping, or the keeping of particular records);

[27] For example, Case C-21/84 *Commission v France* ECLI:EU:C:1985:184 and Case C-192/01 *Commission v Denmark* ECLI:EU:C:2003:492.

[28] For example, Case 249/81 *Commission v Ireland* ECLI:EU:C:1982:402.

e. the inspection, assessment, registration, certification, approval, or authorization of the goods or any other similar dealing with them;
f. documentation or information that must be produced or recorded, kept, accompany the goods, or be submitted to an authority; and
g. anything not falling within paragraphs (a) to (f) which must (or must not) be done to, or in relation to, the goods before they are allowed to be sold.

Section 3(7) also provides that a statutory requirement which requires the person selling or acquiring the goods to keep or submit, after the sale takes place, any documentation or information required to be produced or recorded beforehand is to be treated as a relevant requirement relating to the sale. **2.46**

Relevant requirements for the mutual recognition principle therefore relate to anything which must be done to or in relation to the good before it can be lawfully sold, and are broadly those requirements that relate to the good itself, for example relating to its characteristics, presentation, production, or the documentation that must be supplied alongside it. For example: **2.47**

a. a requirement that jam can only have a particular amount of sugar is something that relates to the composition of the jam (that is a characteristic of the good itself pursuant to s. 3(3)(a));[29]
b. a ban on single-use plastics would be caught by mutual recognition. Devolved administrations could introduce a ban on the sale of a particular good, but the ban would only cover local products produced in that part of the United Kingdom (or those imported into that territory from outside the United Kingdom). Devolved administrations could not enforce that ban against sellers of goods produced in, or imported into, other parts of the United Kingdom;[30] and
c. a requirement that the sugar content of the jam be printed on the front label in large bright type would also be covered by mutual recognition (that is the presentation of the good pursuant to s. 3(3)(b)).[31]

Other types of requirements not related to lawful sale, such as conditions on the carriage of goods or policies concerning the use of products (such as a smoking ban or building regulations), are not covered by the concept of 'relevant requirements' and are thus not covered by the mutual recognition principle (though may be covered by the non-discrimination principle).[32] **2.48**

---

[29] Mutual Recognition Policy Paper (n. 5).

[30] Department for Business, Energy and Industrial Strategy, Policy Paper, Goods market access: approach to restrictions and bans (17 November 2020) (hereafter, the 'Restrictions and Bans Policy Paper').

[31] Mutual Recognition Policy Paper (n. 5).

[32] See Hansard HL, 23 November 2020, col. 72: 'A number of noble Lords ... raised yet again the sale of coal across the English-Welsh border, and my noble friend Lord Randall introduced the new issue of peat. The same thing applies in both cases: there is a clear distinction between sale and use. Under mutual recognition, the use of coal or, indeed, peat ... could be banned, regardless of its origin in the UK. Requirements related to the use of goods are not within the scope of the mutual recognition principle. If the requirement instead relates specifically to the sale of coal or peat, the interaction with mutual recognition is slightly more complex and depends on whether the requirement in question counts as a relevant requirement for the purposes of mutual recognition. Broadly speaking, mutual recognition captures requirements that are intrinsic to the good itself, such as requirements for the composition of the good, whereas non-discrimination captures, among other things, requirements for the circumstances or manner in which a good can be sold.'

2.49 The list of relevant requirements in section 3 is not open to amendment, other than amendment to the Act itself (i.e. by primary legislation).

3. Manner of Sale Requirements

2.50 Subject to an important caveat addressed below, 'manner of sale requirements' are not within the scope of the mutual recognition principle (s. 3(4)).[33] A 'manner of sale requirement' is defined by section 3(5) as a statutory requirement (as to which see above) 'that governs any aspect of the circumstances or manner in which the goods are sold (such as where, when, by whom, to whom, or the price or other terms on which they may be sold)'. Manner of sale requirements thus cover the circumstances or manner in which goods are sold. For example:

a. pricing requirements, such as minimum unit alcohol pricing and plastic bag charges, are therefore not in the scope of the mutual recognition principle;[34] and
b. a requirement that a certain good can only be sold to persons above the age of 18 would not be in scope of mutual recognition (provided it is not artificially designed to ban the sale of the good).[35]

2.51 As noted above, the exclusion of manner of sale requirements from the concept of relevant requirements is subject to a caveat. A statutory requirement that is worded as a manner of sale requirement but 'appears to be designed artificially to avoid the operation of the mutual recognition principle in relation to what would otherwise be a requirement within the scope of that principle' is, however, to be regarded as a relevant requirement despite section 3(4) (s. 3(6)). Thus, where a manner of sale requirement involves an unusually restrictive condition such that it would be impossible to comply with the condition and have a practical chance of selling the goods, the effect of section 3(6) is that that requirement would nevertheless be a 'relevant requirement' subject to the mutual recognition principle. For example:

a. if jam was not explicitly banned but instead made subject to 'manner of sale' requirements which would in effect be a ban, these requirements could still be disapplied through the mutual recognition principle;[36] and
b. if legislation is introduced that says a good can only be sold to persons aged 150 years or older, this is a manner of sale requirement; however, while it does not expressly ban the sale of the good, it would in practice result in a total ban on sale and it is therefore within the scope of the mutual recognition principle.[37]

---

[33] They are, however, within the scope of the non-discrimination principle addressed in chapter 3.

[34] Explanatory Notes (n. 4), paragraph 102.

[35] Mutual Recognition Policy Paper (n. 5). See, also, Hansard HC, 29 September 2020, col. 189: '[W]e are taking the opportunity to put it beyond any possible doubt that alcohol minimum unit pricing-type regulation and any other sales requirements are not in the scope of the mutual recognition principle, unless they amount in practice to a total ban on a good being sold.'

[36] ibid.

[37] Restrictions and Bans Policy Paper (n. 30).

E. EXCLUSIONS FROM THE MUTUAL RECOGNITION PRINCIPLE

There are circumstances and requirements that are excluded from the application of the mutual recognition principle. An exclusion is a policy area, area of regulation, or type of relevant requirement that is not subject to the principle, meaning that divergences between regulatory requirements in each part of the United Kingdom are permissible. Exclusions from the mutual recognition principle are found in section 10 and Schedule 1 to the Act. 2.52

1. Out of Scope

This chapter has already discussed various situations which are out of scope of the mutual recognition principle. These are not exclusions as such, as they mean the situation never falls within the scope of the mutual recognition principle in the first place. They are nonetheless helpful to have in mind at this juncture. Examples include the following. Sales that are not made in the course of business and sales which, despite being made in the course of business, are made only for the purpose of performing a public function are not covered by the principle. Relevant requirements which pre-existed the commencement of the Act are not within the scope of the principle where there was no corresponding requirement in force in each of the other three parts of the United Kingdom. Certain manner of sale requirements and non-legislative requirements (i.e. those of private parties) are also not within scope of the concept of 'relevant requirements', and so are not covered by the mutual recognition principle. 2.53

In addition to these out-of-scope circumstances, the following sub-sections address relevant parts of section 10 and Schedule 1 to the Act which provide 'further'[38] exclusions from the application of the mutual recognition principle. 2.54

2. Pest and Disease Control

Pursuant to paragraph 1 of Schedule 1, the mutual recognition principle does not apply to and does not affect the operation of legislation (often referred to as sanitary and phytosanitary (SPS) legislation) to prevent or reduce the movement of a 'pest or disease' insofar as certain conditions are met. The phrase 'pest or disease' includes any organism or agent that is liable to cause a disease or other harm to the health of humans, animals, or plants (paragraph 1(8) of Schedule 1). This exclusion will allow the nations of the United Kingdom to preserve and protect the health of their animals, citizens, and plants, in line with existing international and national practice. 2.55

There are five conditions for the application of this exclusion. 2.56

The first condition is that the aim of the legislation is to prevent or reduce the movement of a pest or disease into the part of the United Kingdom in which the legislation applies ('the restricting part') from another part of the United Kingdom ('the affected part') (paragraph 1(2) of Schedule 1).[39] 2.57

---

[38] The heading of section 10 is: 'Further exclusions from market access principles'.

[39] Paragraph 3 of Schedule 1 provides that where a decision is taken to exercise powers conferred by legislation in a particular way for the purpose referred to in paragraph 1(2) of Schedule, the reference to 'legislation' in that sub-paragraph is to be read as a reference to the use of the legislation in that way.

2.58 The second condition is that it is reasonable to believe that the pest or disease (i) is present in the affected part, and (ii) is not present, or is significantly less prevalent, in the restricting part (paragraph 1(3) of Schedule 1).

2.59 The third condition is that the potential movement of that pest or disease into the restricting part from the affected part poses (or would in the absence of the legislation pose) a serious threat to the health of humans, animals, or plants in the restricting part (paragraph 1(4) of Schedule 1).

2.60 The fourth condition is that the 'responsible administration'[40] has provided to the 'other administrations'[41] an assessment of the available evidence in relation to (i) the threat to the health of humans, animals, or plants in the restricting part, and (ii) the likely effectiveness of the legislation in addressing that threat (paragraph 1(5) of Schedule 1).

2.61 The fifth condition is that the legislation can reasonably be justified as necessary in order to address the threat to the health of humans, animals, or plants in the restricting part (paragraph 1(6) of Schedule 1). In determining whether the fifth condition is met, paragraph 1(7) of Schedule 1 provides that the following consideration is to be taken into account: 'whether the legislation, taken together with any similar legislation applying in the restricting part, imposes measures of similar severity arising from the potential movement of the pest or disease into, or within, the restricting part (wherever those threats originate)'.

3. Unsafe Food or Feed

2.62 Pursuant to paragraph 2 of Schedule 1, the mutual recognition principle does not apply to and does not affect the operation of legislation to prevent or reduce the movement of 'unsafe food or feed' insofar as certain conditions are met. This will give each nation of the United Kingdom the ability to prevent goods moving into their markets in the case of an emergency, for example. The definitions of 'food', 'feed', and 'unsafe' are generally given the same meanings as those used in Regulation (EC) No 178/2002 of the European Parliament and of the Council of 28 January 2002 laying down the general principles and requirements of food law (etc), as it forms part of retained EU law (the 'UK General Food Law Regulation') (paragraph 2(7) of Schedule 1).[42] Accordingly:

a. 'food' means any substance or product, whether processed, partially processed, or unprocessed, intended to be, or reasonably expected to be ingested by humans (<IBT>Article 2 of the UK General Food Law Regulation</IBT>). It includes drink, chewing gum, and any substance, including water, intentionally incorporated into the food during its manufacture, preparation, or treatment (ibid). It includes water after the point of compliance (ibid).[43] It does not include: feed, live animals unless they are prepared for placing on the market for human consumption, plants prior to harvesting, medicinal products,[44]

[40] The term 'responsible administration' is defined in paragraph 4(1)–(5) of Schedule 1. Essentially, it refers to the Secretary of State, Scottish Ministers, Welsh Ministers, or a Northern Ireland department acting within their respective legislative competences.

[41] The term 'the other administrations' is defined in paragraph 4(6) of Schedule 1. It means each of the Secretary of State, Scottish Ministers, the Welsh Ministers, and a Northern Ireland department other than the 'responsible administration'.

[42] The UK General Food Law Regulation forms part of retained EU law in accordance with section 3 of the European Union (Withdrawal) Act 2018. It was amended by the General Food Law (Amendment etc.) (EU Exit) Regulations 2019/641.

[43] See Article 6 of Directive 98/83/EC.

[44] See Directives 65/65/EEC and 92/73/EEC.

cosmetics,[45] tobacco and tobacco products,[46] narcotic or psychotropic substances,[47] residues and contaminants, or medical devices;[48]

b. 'feed' means any substance or product, including additives, whether processed, partially processed or unprocessed, intended to be used for oral feeding to animals (Article 3 of the UK General Food Law Regulation);

c. 'unsafe' in relation to food means if it is considered to be 'injurious to health'[49] or 'unfit for human consumption'[50] (Article 14(2) of the UK General Food Law Regulation).[51] In determining whether any food is unsafe, regard shall be had to the normal conditions of use of the food by the consumer and at each stage of production, processing, and distribution, and to the information provided to the consumer, including information on the label, or other information generally available to the consumer concerning the avoidance of specific adverse health effects from a particular food or category of foods (Article 14(3) of the UK General Food Law Regulation). Where any food which is unsafe is part of a batch, lot, or consignment of food of the same class or description, it shall be presumed that all the food in that batch, lot, or consignment is also unsafe, unless following a detailed assessment there is no evidence that the rest of the batch, lot, or consignment is unsafe (Article 14(6) of the UK General Food Law Regulation); and

d. 'unsafe' in relation to feed means 'unsafe for its intended use' (paragraph 2(7) of Schedule 1) which means if it is considered to have an adverse effect on human or animal health, or considered to make the food derived from food-producing animals unsafe for human consumption (Article 15(2) of the General Food Law Regulation). Unlike in connection with the definition of 'unsafe' in respect of food in paragraph 2(7)(a) to Schedule 1, which refers to Article 14 of the General Food Law Regulation in its entirety, the definition of 'unsafe' in respect of feed refers only to Article 15(2) of the General Food Law Regulation specifically. It is unclear whether this is an intentional difference in treatment, such that the provisions in Article 15(3) and (4) of the General Food Law Regulation on batches (etc.) and compliance with certain legislation leading to deemed safeness are inapplicable for feed, unlike the corresponding provisions in respect of unsafeness in relation to food (as discussed above).

---

[45] See Directive 76/768/EEC.

[46] See Directive 89/622/EEC.

[47] See the United Nations Single Convention on Narcotic Drugs 1961, and the United Nations Convention on Psychotropic Substances 1971.

[48] See Regulation (EU) 2017/745.

[49] Article 14(4) of the General Food Law Regulation provides that, in determining whether any food is injurious to health, regard shall be had (i) not only to the probable immediate and/or short-term and/or long-term effects of that food on the health of a person consuming it, but also on subsequent generations; (ii) to the probable cumulative toxic effects; and (iii) to the particular health sensitivities of a specific category of consumers where the food is intended for that category of consumers.

[50] Article 14(5) of the General Food Law Regulation provides that, in determining whether any food is unfit for human consumption, regard shall be had to whether the food is unacceptable for human consumption according to its intended use, for reasons of contamination, whether by extraneous matter or otherwise, or through putrefaction, deterioration, or decay.

[51] Food that complies with specific legislation in force in the relevant constituent territory of Great Britain governing food safety shall nonetheless be deemed to be safe insofar as the aspects covered by the specific provisions are concerned: Article 14(7) of the UK General Food Law Regulation.

2.63 There are five conditions for the application of the exclusion in paragraph 2 of Schedule 1 to the Act.

2.64 The first condition is that the aim of the legislation is to prevent or reduce the movement of unsafe food or feed into the part of the United Kingdom in which the legislation applies ('the restricting part') from another part of the United Kingdom ('the affected part') (paragraph 2(2) of Schedule 1).

2.65 The second condition is that it is reasonable to believe that the food or feed affected by the legislation is, is likely to be, or is at particular risk of being unsafe in a particular respect (paragraph 2(3) of Schedule 1).

2.66 The third condition is that the potential movement of food or feed that is unsafe in that respect into the restricting part from the affected part poses (or would in the absence of the legislation pose) a serious threat to the health of humans or animals in the restricting part (paragraph 2(4) of Schedule 1)

2.67 The fourth condition is that the 'responsible administration'[52] has provided to the 'other administrations'[53] an assessment of the available evidence in relation to the health of humans or animals in the restricting part and the likely effectiveness of the legislation in addressing that threat (paragraph 2(5) of Schedule 1).

2.68 The fifth condition is that the legislation can reasonably be justified as necessary in order to address the threat to the health of humans or animals in the restricting part (paragraph 2(6) of Schedule 1).

4. Chemicals

2.69 Pursuant to paragraph 7 of Schedule 1, the mutual recognition principle does not apply to and does not affect the operation of either Article 67 of Regulation (EC) No 1907/2006 of the European Parliament and of the Council of 18 December 2006 as it forms part of retained EU law ('the UK REACH Regulation'[54]), or a restriction imposed in accordance with Article 129 of the UK REACH Regulation. This provides an exclusion from mutual recognition for chemicals in relation to authorizations and restrictions under the UK REACH Regulation. As the mutual recognition principle does not apply, this enables the relevant regulatory authorities to take account of local environmental and workplace factors when considering the authorization of the use of particularly hazardous chemicals in their territories, and which chemicals should be restricted or banned because they pose an unacceptable human health or environmental risk.

2.70 The UK REACH Regulation is retained EU law in accordance with section 3 of the European Union (Withdrawal) Act 2018. The UK REACH Regulation was amended by the REACH etc. (Amendment etc.) (EU Exit) Regulations 2019/758.

2.71 Article 67 of the UK REACH Regulation provides that:

1. A substance on its own, in a mixture or in an article, for which Annex XVII contains a restriction shall not be manufactured, placed on the market or used unless it complies with

[52] The term 'responsible administration' is defined in paragraph 4(1)–(5) of Schedule 1. Essentially, it refers to the Secretary of State, Scottish Ministers, Welsh Ministers, or a Northern Ireland department acting within their respective legislative competences.

[53] The term 'the other administrations' is defined in paragraph 4(6) of Schedule 1. It means each of the Secretary of State, Scottish Ministers, the Welsh Ministers, and a Northern Ireland department other than the 'responsible administration'.

[54] As defined by paragraph 8 of Schedule 1.

> the conditions of that restriction. This shall not apply to the manufacture, placing on the market or use of a substance in scientific research and development. Annex XVII shall specify if the restriction shall not apply to product and process orientated research and development, as well as the maximum quantity exempted.
>
> 2. Paragraph 1 shall not apply to the use of substances in cosmetic products, as defined by Regulation 1223/2009, with regard to restrictions addressing the risks to human health within the scope of that Regulation.

The term 'substance' in Article 67 of the UK REACH Regulation means 'a chemical ele- 2.72
ment and its compounds in the natural state or obtained by any manufacturing process, including any additive necessary to preserve its stability and any impurity deriving from the process used, but excluding any solvent which may be separated without affecting the stability of the substance or changing its composition' (<IBT>Article 3 of the UK REACH Regulation</IBT>). A 'mixture' refers to a mixture or solution composed of two or more substances (ibid) and 'article' means 'an object which during production is given a special shape, surface or design which determines its function to a greater degree than does its chemical composition' (ibid).

'Regulation 1223/2009' in Article 67(2) of the UK REACH Regulation refers to Regulation 2.73
(EC) No 1223/2009 of the European Parliament and of the Council of 30 November 2009 on cosmetic products (recast) as it forms part of retained EU law in accordance with section 3 of the European Union (Withdrawal) Act 2018 (the 'UK Cosmetic Products Regulation'). The UK Cosmetic Products Regulation was amended by the Product Safety and Metrology etc. (Amendment etc.) (EU Exit) Regulations 2019/696. Article 2(1)(a) of the UK Cosmetic Products Regulation, as amended, defines 'cosmetic products' as:

> any substance or mixture intended to be placed in contact with the external parts of the human body (epidermis, hair system, nails, lips and external genital organs) or with the teeth and the mucous membranes of the oral cavity with a view exclusively or mainly to cleaning them, perfuming them, changing their appearance, protecting them, keeping them in good condition or correcting body odours and related expressions are to be construed accordingly.

Article 129 of the UK REACH Regulation provides that: 2.74

a. an appropriate authority (namely, the Secretary of State in relation to England, the Scottish Ministers in relation to Scotland, and the Welsh Ministers in relation to Wales[55]) may impose an appropriate provisional 'restriction' in respect of a substance if that authority (i) has justifiable grounds for believing that urgent action is essential to protect human health or the environment in respect of the substance, on its own, in a mixture or in an article, even if satisfying the requirements of this Regulation, and (ii) has competence to impose the provisional restriction (Article 129(1));
b. the Secretary of State has competence to impose a provisional restriction if, or to the extent that, the exercise of that function to impose that restriction relates to England, or relates to Scotland or Wales and is not within the respective devolved competences pursuant to section 54 of the Scotland Act 1998 and the section 58A of the Government of Wales Act 2006 respectively (Article 129(5)); and

[55] Article 3 of the UK REACH Regulation.

c. the Scottish and Welsh Ministers have competence to impose a provisional restriction if, or to the extent that, the exercise of that function to impose that restriction is within their respective devolved competences pursuant to section 54 of the Scotland Act 1998 and the section 58A of the Government of Wales Act 2006 respectively (Article 129(5)).

2.75 The term 'restriction' in Article 129 of the UK REACH Regulation means 'a restriction on the placing on the market or use of a substance' (Article 129(4)).

2.76 According to the Department for Business, Energy and Industrial Strategy,[56] authorizations for dangerous chemicals reflect the circumstances of individual chemical plants and specific manufacturing conditions and local environmental circumstances. They are granted to individual applicants for specific uses, including for sale down their supply chain. The exclusion in paragraph 7 of Schedule 1 to the Act will, according to the Exclusions Policy Paper, ensure that manufacturers outside of this supply chain will have to obtain their own authorization on the basis of their own specific circumstances and local environmental or workplace conditions.

2.77 For restrictions, the Exclusions Policy Paper states that the levels and effects of exposure to chemicals are not uniform, which means the need to take action to remove unacceptable risks may be particularly urgent, or only exist, in some areas. For example, the Exclusions Policy Papers states that there are lower river flows in England, and therefore a toxic chemical could build up more quickly and have a worse environmental impact than it would have in Scotland. The exclusion will ensure that restrictions can be focused on the areas where they are needed. It will also ensure that an administration can take urgent action to ban a particular chemical within its territory, and prevent the chemical entering its market from elsewhere.

5. Fertilizers and Pesticides

2.78 Pursuant to paragraphs 9 and 10 of Schedule 1, the mutual recognition principle does not apply to and does not affect the operation of certain prohibitions, conditions, and regulations in respect of fertilizers and pesticides.

2.79 Paragraph 9(a) of Schedule 1 provides that the principle does not apply to and does not affect the operation of prohibitions or conditions imposed in accordance with Article 15(1) of Regulation (EC) No 2003/2003 of the European Parliament and of the Council of 13 October 2003 relating to fertilisers, as it forms part of retained EU law (the 'UK Fertilisers Regulation').[57] Article 15(1) of the UK Fertilisers Regulation, as amended, provides that:

> Where the appropriate authority has justifiable grounds for believing that a specific UK fertiliser, although satisfying the requirements of this Regulation, constitutes a risk to safety or health of humans, animals or plants or a risk to the environment, nothing in this Regulation prevents the appropriate authority from using any power the appropriate authority has to temporarily prohibit the placing on the market of that fertiliser in its territory or make it subject to special conditions.

2.80 The 'appropriate authority' for the purposes of Article 15(1) means: (i) in relation to a decision in respect of ammonium nitrate fertilizers of high nitrogen content where the decision

[56] Department for Business, Energy and Industrial Strategy, Policy Paper, Goods market access: exclusions (17 November 2020) (hereafter, 'Exclusions Policy Paper').

[57] The UK Fertilisers Regulation forms part of retained EU law in accordance with section 3 of the European Union (Withdrawal) Act 2018. It was amended by the Fertilisers and Ammonium Nitrate Material (Amendment) (EU Exit) Regulations 2019/601.

is outside devolved competence, the Secretary of State, and (ii) in relation to a decision in respect of other fertilizers, the Secretary of State in relation to England, the Welsh Ministers in relation to Wales, the Scottish Ministers in relation to Scotland, and the Department of Agriculture, Environment and Rural Affairs in relation to Northern Ireland (Article 2 of the UK Fertilisers Regulation).

Paragraph 9(b) provides that the principle does not apply to and does not affect the operation of regulations made under section 74A(1) of the Agriculture Act 1970, to the extent that such regulations can reasonably be justified as a response to a risk to the health or safety of humans, animals, or plants, or the environment. Regulations under section 74A(1) of the Agriculture Act 1970 are made with a view to controlling in the public interest the composition or content of fertilizers and of material intended for the feeding of animals, and may make provision for: 2.81

a. prohibiting or restricting, by reference to its composition or content, the importation into and exportation from the United Kingdom, the sale or possession with a view to sale, or the use, of any prescribed material; and
b. regulating the marking, labelling, and packaging of prescribed material and the marks to be applied to any container or vehicle in which any prescribed material is enclosed or conveyed.

The exclusions in paragraph 9 of Schedule 1 therefore allow devolved administrations (and the UK government in relation to England) to ban the sale of, or place further restrictions on, unsafe fertilizers where these present a risk to the safety or health of humans, animals, or plants, or the environment. For example, if devolved administrations considered that, because of either the geography or farming approach in their region, a fertilizer needed further safeguarding measures and protections, this exclusion from mutual recognition would allow them to act quickly and effectively.[58] 2.82

Paragraph 10 of Schedule 1 provides that the mutual recognition principle does not apply to and does not affect the operation of three Regulations concerning pesticides, namely Regulation (EC) No. 1107/2009 of the European Parliament and of the Council of 21 October 2009 concerning the placing of plant protection products on the market (etc), as it forms part of retained EU law;[59] the Plant Protection Products Regulations 2011 (SI 2011/2131); and the Plant Protection Products Regulations (Northern Ireland) 2011 (SR (N.I.) 2011/295). 2.83

This exclusion ensures that each part of the United Kingdom remains responsible for deciding which pesticide products can be authorized for sale and use in its respective territory. This will retain the ability of each devolved administration to take account of local environmental conditions, such as wildlife, soil types, water environment, climatic conditions, or cultivation methods, when considering which pesticides should be authorized for sale and use in its respective territory. For example, different decisions could be taken on the risks posed to upland crops and forestry in Scotland, where there are generally cooler temperatures and higher rainfall, than in the generally warmer southern parts of England.[60] 2.84

[58] Exclusions Policy Paper (n. 56).

[59] This forms part of retained EU law in accordance with section 3 of the European Union (Withdrawal) Act 2018.

[60] Exclusions Policy Paper (n. 56).

6. Taxation

2.85 Pursuant to paragraph 11 of Schedule 1, the mutual recognition principle does not apply to and does not affect the operation of any legislation so far as it imposes, or relates to the imposition of, any tax, rate, duty, or similar charge. Section 58 defines 'legislation' as including primary legislation, subordinate legislation, and retained direct EU legislation, whereby (i) 'primary legislation' includes Acts of the UK Parliament, Acts of the Scottish Parliament, Acts or Measures of the Senedd Cymru (the Welsh Parliament), and Northern Ireland legislation; and (ii) 'subordinate legislation' means an instrument made under primary legislation or retained direct EU legislation.

7. Future Regulations

2.86 Pursuant to section 10(2), the Secretary of State is provided with a power to amend Schedule 1 by regulations to alter or add to the exclusions addressed above. This provides flexibility for the internal market system to respond to changes in market conditions.[61]

2.87 Section 10(3) provides an example for which the power may be exercised, namely to give effect to an agreement that forms part of a common framework agreement[62] and provides that certain cases, matters, requirements, or provision should be excluded from the application of the market access principles.

2.88 In making regulations pursuant to section 10, the Secretary of State must have regard to the importance of facilitating the access to the market within Great Britain of 'qualifying Northern Ireland goods' as defined in section 47 (as to which see chapter 8). The making of regulations under section 10 is subject to the affirmative resolution procedure (s. 10(8)).[63]

2.89 There is a requirement on the Secretary of State to seek the consent of the devolved administrations before exercising the power in section 10(2) (s. 10(9)). If consent is not given by any of the devolved administrations within a month, the Secretary of State may still exercise the power (s. 10(10). Before doing so, however, the Secretary of State must publish an explanation for proceeding in the absence of consent (s. 10(11)).

---

[61] For example, the Parliamentary Under-Secretary of State, Department for Business, Energy and Industrial Strategy (Lord Callanan) stated that the flexibility to add new exceptions would 'be needed if implementation shows the need for a review, or if further areas are identified that need exclusion due to a shifting economic landscape. This would be the case, for example, if the application of the market access principles to a new technology would pose a threat to public security or the environment': Hansard HL, 28 October 2020, col. 272.

[62] A common framework agreement is a consensus between a Minister of the Crown and one or more devolved administrations as to how devolved or transferred matters previously governed by EU law are to be regulated after IP completion day (s. 10(4)). See chapter 1, section D.3 above for the pre-Act history of common frameworks: in June 2021 the UK government explained in its 'Response to the House of Lords Common Frameworks Scrutiny Committee report: "Common Frameworks: building a cooperative Union" ' (https://committees.parliament.uk/publications/6175/documents/68906/default/) how it saw that process working in future. IP completion day is defined as 11 p.m. on 31 December 2020: see Schedule 1 to the Interpretation Act 1978 by reference to section 39 of the European Union (Withdrawal Agreement) Act 2020). When determining whether a matter is a devolved or transferred matter for the purposes of section 10(4), section 30A of the Scotland Act 1998, section 109A of the Government of Wales Act 2006, and section 6A of the Northern Ireland Act 1998 are to be ignored (s 10(6)). Those sections each relate to restrictions on legislative competence relating to retained EU law as defined by the European Union (Withdrawal) Act 2018. See, further, the Joint Ministerial Committee (EU Negotiations) communiqué (16 October 2017).

[63] The affirmative procedure is a type of parliamentary procedure that applies to statutory instruments ('SIs'). Its name describes the form of scrutiny that the SI receives from Parliament. An SI laid under the affirmative procedure must be actively approved by both Houses of Parliament.

F. THE EFFECT OF THE MUTUAL RECOGNITION PRINCIPLE

Section 1(3) states that the mutual recognition principle has 'no direct effect except as provided by this Part' of the Act. What, then, is the consequence of the mutual recognition principle's application? Where a situation is within the principle's scope and not excluded, section 2(1) provides that the goods from the originating part of the United Kingdom can be sold in any other part of the United Kingdom (the destination part) free from any 'relevant requirements' that would otherwise apply to the sale (s. 2(1)) and that any 'relevant requirements' in the destination part of the United Kingdom 'do not apply in relation to the sale' (s. 2(3)). For example, if Scotland introduced a new law that all fizzy drinks had to be coloured orange, that law would be inapplicable to goods produced in England, Northern Ireland, and Wales, but would continue to apply to fizzy drinks produced in Scotland. Any Scottish agency or public body with power to enforce this law would be unable to enforce it against those non-Scottish goods. 2.90

There are two ways in which a dispute may arise in court to enforce the market access principles. 2.91

First, a business or individual may claim that a relevant requirement should be disapplied or given no effect pursuant to the Act and seek a relevant declaration from the court that that is the case and perhaps other relief to prevent or un-do an attempt to enforce such an impermissible application of the relevant requirement. This will be by way of judicial review. 2.92

Second, a regulator may try to enforce a relevant requirement against a business or individual or prosecute them for non-compliance, and that business or individual may use the market access principles as a shield by submitting that such enforcement should not have been brought or such penalty is of no application or effect on account of the market access principles. 2.93

3

THE NON-DISCRIMINATION PRINCIPLE FOR GOODS

Blackstone's Guide to the UK Internal Market Act 2020. Alan Bates, Brendan McGurk, George Peretz QC, and Jack Williams, Oxford University Press.
DOI: 10.1093/oso/9780192856203.003.0003

A. INTRODUCTION

This chapter examines the second of the two market access principles established in section 1 of the Act, namely the non-discrimination principle for goods (hereafter referred to in this chapter as 'the non-discrimination principle' or 'the principle'). The relevant provisions in the Act for the non-discrimination principle are found in Part I at sections 5–9 and 14–16,[1] with modifications for the purposes of Northern Ireland found in section 11.[2] Exclusions from the non-discrimination principle are found in section 10 and Schedule 1 to the Act. 3.01

This chapter answers six overarching questions. What is the non-discrimination principle? What are the conditions for its applicability? What 'relevant requirements' are covered by the principle? What are the differences between direct and indirect discrimination? When is the non-discrimination principle excluded? What effect does it have in practice? 3.02

B. THE NON-DISCRIMINATION PRINCIPLE FOR GOODS

Section 5(1) of the Act provides that: 3.03

> The non-discrimination principle for goods is the principle that the sale of goods in one part of the United Kingdom should not be affected by relevant requirements that directly or indirectly discriminate against goods that have a relevant connection with another part of the United Kingdom.

For these purposes, section 5(2) provides that the part of the United Kingdom where sale should not be affected is referred to as the 'destination part' (s. 5(2)(a)); the goods that have a relevant connection with another part of the United Kingdom are referred to as the 'incoming goods' (s. (5)(2)(b)); and that other part is referred to as the 'originating part' (s. 5(2)(c)). 3.04

The non-discrimination principle means that discrimination based on differential treatment between local goods in the destination part of the United Kingdom (England, Northern Ireland, Scotland, and Wales[3]) and incoming goods from the originating part of the United Kingdom is prohibited. The non-discrimination principle covers both direct discrimination (see section E below) and indirect discrimination (see section F below). 3.05

For example: 3.06

a. a bag of flour made in England can be sold in Wales without having to meet a Welsh requirement that incoming flour from England must be chilled whereas local (Welsh) flour does not;

b. a jam producer in Wales does not need to worry about meeting any Scottish relevant requirements for jam when selling in Scotland that only apply to jam from England, Wales, and Northern Ireland, but do not apply to Scottish jams; and

[1] Each of these provisions commenced at 11 p.m. on 31 December 2020 (defined as 'IP completion day' in Schedule 1 to the Interpretation Act 1978 by reference to section 39 of the European Union (Withdrawal Agreement) Act 2020): see Regulation 2 of the United Kingdom Internal Market Act 2020 (Commencement No. 1) Regulations 2020.

[2] Section 11 ('Modifications in connection with the Northern Ireland Protocol') is addressed in chapter 8.

[3] See section 58, which defines 'part of the United Kingdom' accordingly.

c. chlorinated chicken lawfully imported into England from the United States of America as part of a (hypothetical) trade deal that then travels to Wales would be allowed to be sold in Wales without certification, despite any requirement by the Senedd Cymru (the Welsh Parliament) that non-Welsh chicken that comes from England has to be certified prior to sale whereas Welsh chicken does not.

3.07 The function of the non-discrimination principle is thus to preserve an internal market within the United Kingdom by ensuring, subject to conditions and exceptions, that one nation within the United Kingdom cannot regulate in a way that affords less favourable treatment to goods originating in or coming from another part of the United Kingdom compared to regulations concerning its own, local goods. This ensures equal access and treatment to producers based in and goods circulating within the United Kingdom by reducing (discriminatory) trading barriers.

3.08 Section 14 provides that:

> Nothing in this Part [1] prevents goods produced in or imported into a part of the United Kingdom from being sold in another part of the United Kingdom if (apart from this Part) the sale complies with any requirements applicable in that other part of the United Kingdom (or there are no such requirements).

3.09 This means, for example, that where goods do not meet the criteria for non-discrimination principle to apply, or where traders do not wish to make use of the principle for their goods, these goods can continue to be sold in a part of the United Kingdom by complying with the requirements relating to sale that apply there.[4]

C. THE APPLICABILITY OF THE NON-DISCRIMINATION PRINCIPLE

3.10 There are a number of specific conditions for the applicability of the non-discrimination principle. It applies only to 'goods', which have a 'relevant connection' with the so-called 'originating part' of the United Kingdom, having been 'produced in', produced by a business 'based in', or having 'come from, or passing through' that part. It then only applies to 'the sale' of those goods in the destination part of the United Kingdom. More broadly, the principle generally only applies to relevant requirements which post-date the commencement of the Act, that is, it does not generally have retrospective effect (s. 9). Each of these conditions for the applicability of the principle are examined in turn.

1. The Definition of 'goods'

3.11 The term 'goods' is defined in section 16(2) of the Act as 'any tangible movable, or corporeal moveable, thing (including any packaging or label), but not water or gas that is not offered for sale in a limited volume or set quantity'.

3.12 This definition encompasses agricultural goods, including live animals, germinal products, and animal by-products.[5]

[4] Explanatory Notes to the United Kingdom Internal Market Act 2020, paragraph 166 (hereafter, 'Explanatory Notes').

[5] Explanatory Notes (n. 4), paragraph 173.

The reference to water or gas 'that is not offered for sale in a limited volume or set quantity' means that bottled water or canisters of gas are covered by the concept of 'goods', whereas water or gas that is piped into buildings as a utility are not covered.[6] 3.13

2. The Definition of 'relevant connection'

The non-discrimination principle applies to the sale of goods in the destination part of the United Kingdom that are affected by relevant requirements that discriminate against goods that 'have a relevant connection' with another part of the United Kingdom (s. 5(1)), namely the 'originating part' (s. 5(2)(c)). Goods that have a relevant connection with the originating part of the United Kingdom are referred to as the 'incoming goods' (s. 5(2)(b)). 3.14

Pursuant to section 5(4), goods have 'a relevant connection' with a part of the United Kingdom (and so are 'incoming goods') if they or any of their components[7] fall with at least one of three scenarios. These are the matters on the basis of which discrimination is not permitted. 3.15

a) *Produced in that part*

The first scenario is that the incoming goods or any of their components are produced in that part, that is, the originating part (s. 5(4)(a)). 3.16

The concept of 'production' is defined in section 16(3)–(7) and (11) of the Act. Goods are to be regarded as 'produced in' the originating part of the United Kingdom if either they are wholly produced there, or 'if the most recent significant production step which is a regulated step has occurred there' (s. 16(3)). For both situations, section 16(11) states that a reference to 'production' (however expressed, e.g. 'produced in') includes 'cultivation, harvesting and similar activities (in relation to plants or fungi)' (s. 16(11)(a)) and 'rearing, keeping, handling, killing and similar activities in relation to livestock or other animals' (s. 16(11)(b)). This reflects the fact that the definition of 'goods' in section 14 includes agricultural products. 3.17

If the good is not wholly produced in the originating part of the United Kingdom, then the most recent production step has to have occurred there and be both (i) a 'regulated step' and (ii) a 'significant' step (s. 16(3)). 3.18

In respect of the 'regulated step' requirement in section 16(3), section 16(4) states that a production step is 'regulated' for the purposes of section 16(3) in one of two distinct circumstances. First, it is a regulated production step if it is the subject of any statutory requirement in that part of the United Kingdom in which it is produced (s. 16(4)(a)). A 'statutory requirement' is an obligation, condition, or prohibition (however described) imposed by legislation (including legislation imposing mandatory terms into contracts for the sale of goods) (see ss 16(14) and 3(8)).[8] Second, alternatively, section 16(4)(b) states that it is also a regulated production step if: 3.19

> it is a step that could materially affect a person's ability to sell the goods without contravening—

[6] ibid.

[7] The term 'components' includes parts, ingredients, and constituent materials (s. 5(5)(a)).

[8] Pursuant to section 58, 'legislation' includes primary legislation, subordinate legislation, and retained direct EU legislation, whereby (i) 'primary legislation' includes Acts of the UK Parliament, Acts of the Scottish Parliament, Acts or Measures of the Senedd Cymru (the Welsh Parliament), and Northern Ireland legislation; and (ii) 'subordinate legislation' means an instrument made under primary legislation or retained direct EU legislation.

(i) any relevant requirement for the purposes of the mutual recognition principle for goods, or
(ii) any statutory requirement that is excluded from being a relevant requirement by section 4(1) [regarding the exclusion of certain requirements existing before the commencement of the Act], that would be applicable to a sale of the goods in that part of the United Kingdom (being a sale of a kind for which the goods are being produced).

3.20 For example, the manufacture of a crane in Scotland would constitute a regulated step. If, however, another company in England purchased the crane and changed its colour before sale, the crane would still count as being produced in Scotland, as changing the colour is not a regulated step.[9]

3.21 In respect of the second, cumulative requirement in section 16(3) that the (most recent and regulated) production step be 'significant', section 16(5) states that a production step is significant 'if it is significant in terms of the character of the goods being produced and the purposes for which they are sold or used', subject to section 16(6) and (7). For example, the baking of a loaf of bread would constitute a significant step.[10]

3.22 Section 16(6) confirms that a production step falling within any of the following descriptions is not significant (whether or not it is regulated):

a. activities carried out specifically to ensure goods do not deteriorate before being sold (such as maintaining them at or below a particular temperature). For example, preserving activities, such as cooling or freezing, high temperature treatment, drying, sealing, adding preservatives and similar measures would not count as 'significant' unless significant to the character of the goods (e.g. pickling);[11]
b. activities carried out solely for purposes relevant to their presentation for sale (such as cleaning or pressing fabrics or sorting different coloured items for packaging together);
c. activities involving a communication of any kind with a regulatory or trade body (such as registering the goods or notifying the goods or anything connected with them or their production); and
d. activities carried out for the purpose of testing or assessing any characteristic of the goods (such as batch testing a pharmaceutical product). For example, taking samples from goods or similar quality assurance activities would not count as 'significant'.[12]

3.23 Section 16(7) states that a product step 'involving the packaging, labelling or marking of goods is not significant (whether or not it is regulated) unless the step is fundamental to the character of the goods and the purposes for which they are to be sold or used'. For example, jam made in Scotland but where the jar is labelled in England would be Scottish, but collectable trading cards where the card stock is made in Scotland but the information on the cards is applied in England would be English because the information is fundamental to those goods.[13]

---

[9] Department for Business, Energy and Industrial Strategy, Policy Paper, Mutual recognition of goods: location of production (17 November 2020) (hereafter, 'Location of Production Policy Paper').

[10] ibid.

[11] ibid.

[12] ibid.

[13] ibid.

b) *Produced by a business based in that part*

The second scenario is where the goods or any of their components are produced by a business based in that part, that is, the originating part (s. 5(4)(b)). For these purposes, a business is 'based' either where its registered office is; if it does not have a registered office, where its head office is; or, if it has neither a registered office nor a head office, where its principal place of business is (s. 5(5)(b)). 3.24

c) *Come from or pass through that part*

The third scenario is where the goods or any of their components come from, or pass through, that part (i.e. the originating part) before reaching the destination part (s. 5(4)(c)). 3.25

3. The Definition of 'sale'

Section 5(1) states that the non-discrimination principle applies only to goods that are 'sold' in one part of the United Kingdom, namely the 'destination part' where the sale should not be affected (s. 5(2)(a)). 3.26

Section 15 defines references to the sale of goods (however expressed in Part 1 of the Act: s. 15(1)) for these purposes. The terms are defined broadly. The sale of goods includes some earlier actions with a view to sale: agreement to sell, offering or exposing for sale, or having in possession or holding for sale (s. 15(4)). Part 1 of the Act also applies 'in relation to a supply of goods other than a sale as it applies in relation to a sale' (s. 15(5)). For that purpose, 'supply of goods' means the transfer of possession or property in goods (whether or not under or by virtue of a contract) (s. 15(6)) and includes, for example, supply by way of barter or exchange (s. 15(6)(a)); the leasing or hiring out of goods, hire purchase, or bailment of goods (s. 15(6)(b)); or a gift (or anything else done free of charge) (s. 15(6)(c)). Earlier actions with a view to these types of supply would also be covered, for example an agreement to hire.[14] Activities which are not related to sale and in particular those which happen after sale are generally not captured. So, for example, requirements as to how a product may or may not be used or those related to disposal at the end of a product's life would not normally be in scope.[15] 3.27

There are, however, exclusions to the concept of 'sale'. References to the sale of goods do not include sales which are not made in the course of a business (s. 15(2)(a)), or those which are made in the course of a business but only for the purpose of performing a function of a public nature (s. 15(2)(b)). The latter does not, however, exclude sales which are made by a public body or authority for commercial purposes and are also not made for the purpose of performing a function of a public nature (other than a function relating to the carrying on of commercial activities) (s. 15(3)). 3.28

For example: 3.29

a. the supply of medication by the NHS to a patient through a prescription would not be covered as it is a sale made by a public authority fulfilling a public function;[16] and

[14] Explanatory Notes (n. 4), paragraph 170.

[15] Department for Business, Energy and Industrial Strategy, Policy Paper, Mutual recognition of goods: general principles and relevant requirements (17 November 2020).

[16] Explanatory Notes (n. 4), paragraphs 16 and 168.

b. if a public body were to set up a gift shop selling merchandise, this would be captured as a 'sale' for the purposes of Part 1 as it would be commercial activity not directly related to its public functions.[17]

4. The Exclusion of Requirements Existing Prior to Commencement

3.30 Pursuant to section 9, the non-discrimination principle generally only applies to relevant requirements (see section D below) which post-date the commencement of the Act, that is, it does not generally have retrospective effect. Therefore, where different regulatory requirements existed in different parts of the United Kingdom prior to the commencement of the Act, those requirements are generally permitted and remain unaffected by the non-discrimination principle.

3.31 Section 9(1) provides that a 'statutory provision'[18] is not a relevant requirement for the purposes of the non-discrimination principle if the same provision was in force in the part of the United Kingdom concerned on the day before the day on which this section comes into force.

3.32 The 'relevant day' is defined as 'the day before the day on which this section comes into force' (s. 4(3)). As section 9 came into force at 11 p.m. on 31 December 2020 (see Regulation 2 of the United Kingdom Internal Market Act 2020 (Commencement No. 1) Regulations 2020 in conjunction with Schedule 1 to the Interpretation Act 1978 by reference to section 39 of the European Union (Withdrawal Agreement) Act 2020), the 'relevant day' is therefore 30 December 2020. Therefore, any existing regulatory differences across the United Kingdom on 30 December 2020 are time-barred in the sense that these are not retrospectively subject to the non-discrimination principle and can still be lawfully maintained and applied.

3.33 Section 9(3) states that the 'same provision' for the purposes of section 9(1) is to be regarded as in force on 30 December 2020 only if any differences are 'not substantive'.

3.34 Section 9(2) provides that the 're-enactment (without substantive change)' of a statutory provision does not affect its continuity for the purposes of section 9(1). In essence, this means that if a time-barred relevant requirement is re-enacted without substantive change, then the non-discrimination principle still does not apply despite it being enacted after the relevant day. The rationale for this is that consumers and businesses have already adapted to these differences, whereas the aim of the Act is to ensure that businesses will continue to enjoy internal trade without any new barriers.

3.35 By contrast, the implication is that substantive changes to any pre-existing (and thus time-barred) relevant requirements will then be brought into the scope of the non-discrimination principle. For example, where existing legislation receives technical or minor amendments that do not alter the substance of the legislation, that would continue to be out of scope, whereas re-enactments that would change the effect or outcome of the legislation would then come within the scope of the non-discrimination principle.

---

[17] Explanatory Notes (n. 4), paragraph 168.

[18] A 'statutory provision' means provision contained in legislation (see ss 9(4) and 6(10)). Pursuant to section 58, 'legislation' includes primary legislation, subordinate legislation, and retained direct EU legislation, whereby (i) 'primary legislation' includes Acts of the UK Parliament, Acts of the Scottish Parliament, Acts or Measures of the Senedd Cymru (the Welsh Parliament), and Northern Ireland legislation; and (ii) 'subordinate legislation' means an instrument made under primary legislation or retained direct EU legislation.

D. RELEVANT REQUIREMENTS

The non-discrimination principle in section 5(1) states that the sale of goods in the destination part of the United Kingdom should not be affected by 'relevant requirements' that directly or indirectly discriminate against goods that have a relevant connection with the originating part of the United Kingdom. If and to the extent that it directly or indirectly discriminates against the incoming goods, any 'relevant requirement' in the destination part of the United Kingdom 'is of no effect' (s. 5(3)). 3.36

Section 6(2) defines 'relevant requirements' for these purposes as follows: 3.37

A relevant requirement, for the purposes of the principle as it has effect in relation to a part of the United Kingdom, is a statutory provision that—
(a) applies in that part of the United Kingdom to, or in relation to, goods sold in that part, and
(b) is within the scope of the non-discrimination principle.

1. The Definition of 'statutory provision'

A 'statutory provision' for the purposes of section 6(2) is a provision contained in legislation (s. 6(10)). Pursuant to section 58, 'legislation' includes primary legislation, subordinate legislation, and retained direct EU legislation, whereby (i) 'primary legislation' includes Acts of the UK Parliament, Acts of the Scottish Parliament, Acts or Measures of the Senedd Cymru (the Welsh Parliament), and Northern Ireland legislation; and (ii) 'subordinate legislation' means an instrument made under primary legislation or retained direct EU legislation. 3.38

Therefore, non-legislative, administrative practices and actions of private parties (including industry-wide standards, for example) are not covered by the concept of relevant requirements and thus fall outside the scope of the non-discrimination principle. This is distinct from the position under EU law, which covers administrative[19] and non-binding measures.[20] 3.39

Moreover, contrasted with the position in respect of the mutual recognition principle for goods, the use of the term 'statutory provision' in section 6 as opposed to 'statutory requirement' in section 3 means that mandatory terms implied into contracts by statute are not relevant for the non-discrimination principle. 3.40

2. The Relevant Requirements 'within the scope' of the Non-Discrimination Principle

Pursuant to section 6(3), a statutory provision is 'within the scope of' the non-discrimination principle if it 'relates to' any one or more of the following: 3.41

a. the circumstances or manner in which goods are sold (such as where, when, by whom, to whom, or the price or other terms on which they may be sold);
b. the transportation, storage, handling, or display of goods;

[19] For example, Case C-21/84 *Commission v France* ECLI:EU:C:1985:184 and Case C-192/01 *Commission v Denmark* ECLI:EU:C:2003:492.

[20] For example, Case 249/81 *Commission v Ireland* ECLI:EU:C:1982:402.

c. the inspection, assessment, registration, certification, approval, or authorization of the goods or any similar dealing with them; and

d. the conduct or regulation of businesses that engage in the sale of certain goods or types of goods.

3.42 Relevant requirements for the non-discrimination principle therefore relate to regulations about the manner of sale of goods and the circumstances in which goods come to be sold. For example:

a. rules that regulate how or where goods are displayed on shop shelves cannot provide for better treatment of local goods;

b. a ban in Scotland on internet sales of products produced in Northern Ireland would be caught by the concept of 'relevant requirements'; and

c. a requirement that premises shall not accept customers under the age of 18 is subject to the non-discrimination principle.

3.43 Unlike with relevant requirements for the purposes of the mutual recognition principle for goods, the list of relevant questions in section 6 for the purposes of the non-discrimination principle is open to amendment by secondary legislation. Section 6(5) provides that the Secretary of State may by regulations amend the list in section 6(3) so as to 'add, vary or remove' relevant requirements for the purposes of the non-discrimination principle.[21] The making of regulations under section 6(5) is subject to the affirmative resolution procedure (s. 6(6)).[22] There is a requirement on the Secretary of State to seek the consent of the devolved administrations before exercising the power in section 6(5) (s. 6(7)). If consent is not given by any of the devolved administrations within a month, the Secretary of State may still exercise the power (s. 6(8)). Before doing so, however, the Secretary of State must publish an explanation for proceeding in the absence of consent (s. 6(9)).

3. Exclusions from 'relevant requirements'

3.44 Section 6(4) expressly states that a statutory provision is not a relevant requirement if either section 9 applies concerning the exclusion of certain existing provisions prior to the commencement of the Act (s. 6(4)(b)), or 'to the extent that it is a relevant requirement for the purposes of the mutual recognition principle for goods' (s. 6(4)(a)). Requirements which fall within mutual recognition are excluded from the application of the non-discrimination

[21] The Parliamentary Under-Secretary of State, Department for Business, Energy and Industrial Strategy (Lord Callanan) explained that 'the power to amend will enable [the government] to carry out practical and useful amendments that might be needed early in the operation of the regime. They will also enable [the government] to respond to business and consumer experience of the principles. For example, there are several types of regulatory requirements currently not covered by the market access principles, such as those on the recycling of goods. If it becomes clear that the exclusion of these categories is creating significant barriers to trade, say by allowing specific, discriminatory and unwarranted restrictions to be enforced that could add to business costs, the power in [section] 6 would provide a means of resolving this by adapting the scope of the non-discrimination principle. To reiterate: these powers are not intended for casual redrafting but simply to enable the provisions to work properly': Hansard HL, 28 October 2020 col. 271.

[22] The affirmative procedure is a type of parliamentary procedure that applies to statutory instruments ('SIs'). Its name describes the form of scrutiny that the SI receives from Parliament. An SI laid under the affirmative procedure must be actively approved by both Houses of Parliament.

principle by definition, because if mutual recognition applies the good already has market access free of relevant requirements which would otherwise apply and so cannot suffer discrimination.

E. DIRECT DISCRIMINATION

The non-discrimination principle prevents the sale of goods in the destination part of the United Kingdom from being affected by relevant requirements that 'directly or indirectly discriminate' against goods that have a relevant connection with the originating part of the United Kingdom (s. 5(1)). This section examines direct discrimination. 3.45

Section 7(1) provides: 3.46

> A relevant requirement directly discriminates against incoming goods if, for reason that the goods have the relevant connection with the originating part, the requirement applies to, or in relation to, the incoming goods in a way—
> (a) in which it does not or would not apply to local goods, and
> (b) that puts the incoming goods at a disadvantage compared to local goods.

The terms 'relevant requirement', 'goods', 'relevant connection', 'originating part', and 'incoming goods' have already been defined above. 3.47

Direct discrimination therefore applies where an incoming good (from one part of the United Kingdom) is put at a disadvantage compared to a local good (from another part of the United Kingdom) by virtue of a relevant requirement applying to it but not the local good, on account of the fact that it, the originating good, originates from another part of the United Kingdom. For example, a requirement that incoming produce from Scotland must be chilled, but local produce from England does not would be direct discrimination as it makes it more difficult or less attractive to buy or sell the produce.[23] 3.48

1. The Definition of 'local goods'

In order for the non-discrimination principle to apply on account of direct discrimination, section 7(1)(a) requires that the relevant requirement applies to, or in relation to, the incoming goods in a way in which it does not or would not apply to 'local goods', and section 7(1)(b) requires that that requirement puts the incoming goods at a disadvantage compared to 'local goods'. 3.49

Local goods are defined in section 7(3) as 'actual or hypothetical goods'[24] that (i) lack the relevant connection of the incoming goods with the originating part (s. 7(3)(a)), but (ii) 3.50

---

[23] Explanatory Notes (n. 4), paragraph 19.

[24] The fact that the local goods are defined in section 7(3) as including hypothetical, local goods explains the use of 'or would not' in section 7(1)(a). The Parliamentary Under-Secretary of State, Department for Business, Energy and Industrial Strategy (Lord Callanan) explained that 'The inclusion of "actual and hypothetical goods" within this [section] is necessary, as it means that the provisions work effectively in scenarios where there are no actual local goods against which impacts on incoming goods can be compared. To explain further, if a company has a product that is subject to a patent, it can therefore be made by only one company in the UK. If an authority were to regulate against that product because of where it is produced, there could not possibly be a local good to compare it to in order to determine relative disadvantage. Being able to compare it to a hypothetical good addresses this, and allows the rules against direct discrimination to operate properly and

otherwise are materially the same as, and share the material circumstances of, the incoming goods (s. 7(3)(b)).

3.51 Section 7(4) states that the local goods (referred to as 'the other goods') lack the relevant connection of the incoming goods with the originating part for section 7(3)(a) in the following circumstances (which differ depending on the way in which the incoming goods have a relevant connection to the originating part of the United Kingdom pursuant to section 5):

a. where the incoming goods have a relevant connection within section 5(4)(a) (i.e. where they were produced in the originating part), if the other goods (i.e. the local goods) or their components were produced in the destination part (s. 7(4)(a));
b. where the incoming goods have a relevant connection within section 5(4)(b) (i.e. where they were produced by a business based in the originating part), if the other goods (i.e. the local goods) or their components were produced by a business based in the destination part (s. 7(4)(b)); and
c. where the incoming goods have a relevant connection within section 5(4)(c) (i.e. where they came from, or pass through, the originating part before reaching the destination part), if the other goods (i.e. the local goods) or their components came from the destination part and did not pass through anywhere outside that part (s. 7(4)(c)).

3.52 The term 'components' includes parts, ingredients, and constituent materials (s. 5(5)(a)).

2. The Definition of 'disadvantage'

3.53 In order for the non-discrimination principle to apply on account of direct discrimination, section 7(1)(b) requires that the relevant requirement puts the incoming goods 'at a disadvantage' compared to local goods.

3.54 Section 7(2) states that goods are put at a disadvantage 'if it is made in any way more difficult, or less attractive, to sell or buy the goods or do anything in connection with their sale'.

F. INDIRECT DISCRIMINATION

3.55 The non-discrimination principle prevents the sale of goods in the destination part of the United Kingdom from being affected by relevant requirements that 'directly or indirectly discriminate' against goods that have a relevant connection with the originating part of the United Kingdom (s. 5(1)). This section examines indirect discrimination.

3.56 Section 8(1) provides that:

A relevant requirement indirectly discriminates against incoming goods if—
(a) it does not directly discriminate against the goods,
(b) it applies to, or in relation to, the incoming goods in a way that puts them at a disadvantage,

protect all businesses across the UK. The existing wording is also important to deal with situations where arguments could be posited that a local good is similar to, but not the same as, an incoming good, and therefore would not be a good comparator in determining whether discrimination exists. Being able to compare to a hypothetical good that is the same as the incoming good, save for location, enables that determination to take place ... This means that regulators can focus on determining whether discrimination might take effect, rather than identifying comparable goods': Hansard HL, 28 October 2020, col. 252.

(c) it has an adverse market effect, and
(d) it cannot reasonably be considered a necessary means of achieving a legitimate aim.

Indirect discrimination therefore applies where incoming goods from one part of the United Kingdom (the originating part) are not directly discriminated against in the destination part of the United Kingdom, but where regulation in the destination part nevertheless disadvantages those incoming goods and has an adverse market affect. Thus, requirements which appear neutral as they apply equally to both local and incoming goods, may nevertheless have the effect, in practice, of putting incoming goods from the other, originating part of the United Kingdom at a disadvantage. These requirements will thus be prohibited by the non-discrimination principle because they are indirectly discriminatory. For example, where a (hypothetical) English requirement imposed a rule that dairy goods can only travel 20 miles from the site of production, although dairy goods from other parts of the United Kingdom would not be expressly banned and although the requirement also applies to English goods, the effect in practice would be to exclude products from Wales, Scotland, and Northern Ireland.[25] 3.57

There are four conditions set out in section 8(1) for the applicability of indirect discrimination. Each is addressed in turn. 3.58

1. Direct Discrimination

The first condition, whether a relevant requirement directly discriminates against incoming goods—with the effect that it cannot also indirectly discriminate against such goods—is addressed in section E above. 3.59

2. The Definition of 'disadvantage'

The second condition is that the relevant requirement puts the incoming goods 'at a disadvantage' (s. 8(1)(b)). Section 8(2) states that goods are put at a disadvantage 'if it is made in any way more difficult, or less attractive, to sell or buy the goods or do anything in connection with their sale than if the requirement did not apply'. 3.60

3. The Definition of 'adverse market effects'

The third condition is that the relevant requirement has 'an adverse market effect' (s. 8(1)(c)). Section 8(3) states that a requirement has an adverse market effect for these purposes if it 'causes a significant adverse effect on competition in the market for such goods in the United Kingdom' because it: 3.61

a. puts at a disadvantage the incoming goods (and any 'comparable goods' that also have a relevant connection with the originating part and are also put at that disadvantage) (s. 8(3)(a)), but

[25] Department for Business, Energy and Industrial Strategy, Policy Paper, Non-discrimination of goods: general principles (17 November 2020) (hereafter, 'Non-discrimination Policy Paper').

b. does not put at that disadvantage (at all or to the same extent) some or all 'comparable goods' that have a relevant connection with the destination part and no other part of the United Kingdom (s. 8(3)(b)).

3.62 Whether these circumstances apply is to be determined 'with regard both to the content of the requirement and to the way in which it operates, or is administered, in practice (as a whole or in particular classes of case)' (s. 8(5)).

3.63 For the purposes of section 8(3)(a) and (b), 'comparable goods' is defined to mean 'like goods or interchangeable goods' (s. 8(4)), where 'like goods' means 'goods that are alike the incoming goods in all respects, or otherwise have characteristics closely resembling those of the incoming goods' (s. 8(4)(a)), and 'interchangeable goods' means 'goods that, from the point of view of a purchaser of the goods, could reasonably be said to be interchangeable with the incoming goods' (s. 8(4)(b)).

3.64 There are thus five cumulative exercises required to be undertaken in connection with section 8(3).

3.65 First, the relevant goods in question need to be identified. This requires an assessment of the nature and characteristics of the incoming goods in order to determine what 'comparable goods' exist, if any. It also requires an assessment of whether the incoming goods have a relevant connection with the originating part of the United Kingdom (s. 5) and whether comparable goods have a relevant connection with the destination part and no other part of the United Kingdom (ss 5 and 8).

3.66 Whether a good is 'comparable' (on account of either being a 'like good' or an 'interchangeable good') (s. 8(4)), involves similar enquiries to those in defining the relevant product markets for the purposes of market definition in competition law.[26] In that context, it is necessary to investigate the 'characteristics of the products in question by virtue of which they are particularly apt to satisfy an inelastic need and are only to a limited extent interchangeable with other products'.[27] In determining the range of products which are viewed as substitutes by consumers for these purposes, a key question asked in competition law is whether the consumers would switch to readily available substitutes or to suppliers located elsewhere in response to a hypothetical small (in the range of 5–10 per cent) but permanent relative price increase in the products and areas being considered. If substitution were enough to make the price increase unprofitable because of the resulting loss of sales, additional substitutes are included in the relevant product market. This is referred to as the SSNIP test. The following evidence may be available to assist: an assessment of the characteristics and uses of the good in question; evidence of substitution in the recent past; econometric and statistical evidence estimating own-price and cross-price elasticities for the demand of products based on the similarity of price movements over time, the causality between price series and the similarity of price levels and/or their convergence; consumer or business surveys; and consideration of barriers and costs associating with switching demand to potential substitutes.

3.67 Second, it must be determined whether the incoming good is 'put at a disadvantage' by the relevant requirement that does not apply (at all or to the same extent) to some or all comparable goods identified pursuant to the first exercise that have a relevant connection with the destination part of the United Kingdom only and not the originating part of the United Kingdom. Section 8(2) defines 'put at a disadvantage' broadly, namely if it is made

[26] See the European Commission's Notice on the Definition of the Relevant Market for the Purposes of [EU] Competition Law OJ [1997] C/372/5 (hereafter, the 'Market Definition Notice').

[27] Case 6/72 *Continental Can v Commission* EU:C:1973:22, paragraph 32.

'in any way more difficult, or less attractive, to sell or buy the goods or do anything in connection with their sale'. Whether there is 'disadvantage' is also to be determined not just on an objective basis (i.e. looking at the content of the requirement alone), but also looking at the way in which the relevant requirement operates, or is administered in practice, that is, an effects analysis (s. 8(5)).

Third, after identifying the incoming and comparable goods, the 'market for such goods in the United Kingdom' (s. 8(3)) must be defined. The term 'such goods' appears to be a reference to both the incoming goods and comparable goods together. This requires a market definition exercise that will be familiar to competition lawyers.[28] That exercise is not confined to demand-side factors, such as those referred to in section 8(4) when determining what the 'comparable goods' are for the purposes of the comparative disadvantage stage of the analysis. Whilst in most cases demand-side substitutability is the key factor for market definition purposes, it is also appropriate to consider supply-side substitutability and potential competition (e.g. whether producers could readily adapt their production and barriers to entry). **3.68**

Fourth, whether there are 'significant adverse effects on competition' within the defined market needs to be examined (s. 8(3)). Whether there are significant adverse effects is to be determined not just on an objective basis (i.e. looking at the content of the relevant requirement alone), but also looking at the way in which it operates, or is administered in practice, that is, an effects analysis (s. 8(5)). Significant adverse effects on competition may, for example, include: the imposition or increase of restrictive barriers of entry to trade; the prevention of new market entrants; the reduction in number of traders trading on the market; a reduction in choice for consumers; or increased and excessive prices for the relevant goods. **3.69**

Fifth, it must finally be assessed whether the significant adverse effect on competition in the market for such goods is 'caused' by the relevant requirement (s. 8(3)), as opposed to some other factor or condition. Again, competition law provides a helpful insight for this assessment. **3.70**

For example, in considering whether conduct by a dominant undertaking was capable of restricting competition and, in particular capable of producing alleged foreclosure effects, the European Commission is required to analyse all the circumstances, including the 'share of the market covered by the challenged practice', 'conditions and arrangements' for the conduct in question, and 'their duration'.[29] **3.71**

4. The Definition of 'legitimate aim'

The fourth condition is that the relevant requirement 'cannot reasonably be considered a necessary means of achieving a legitimate aim' (s. 8(1)(c)). Section 8(12) provides that whether this condition is met is to be determined with regard, in particular, to the effects of the requirement in all the circumstances, and the availability of alternative means of achieving the aim in question. **3.72**

For these purposes, the definition of 'legitimate aim' is restricted to one, or a combination of, only two aims, namely 'the protection of the life or health of humans, animals or plants' (s. 8(6)(a)) and 'the protection of public safety or security' (s. 8(6)(b)). An example of where a legitimate aim may be used is where a disease has been identified in cattle with evidence that processing meat from these animals to enter the human food chain, could pose a risk **3.73**

[28] See the Market Definition Notice (n. 26).

[29] See e.g. Case C-413/14 P *Intel v Commission* EU:C:2017:632, paragraphs 138–139.

to people's health.[30] In this circumstance the legitimate aim could be invoked to ban the transportation and processing of meat from the affected cattle to ensure the public's health is protected.

3.74 Section 8(7) states that the Secretary of State may by regulations amend section 8(6) so as to 'add, vary or remove an aim'. The making of regulations under section 8(7) is subject to the affirmative resolution procedure (s. 8(8)).[31] There is a requirement on the Secretary of State to seek the consent of the devolved administrations before exercising the power in section 8(7) (s. 8(9)). If consent is not given by any of the devolved administrations within a month, the Secretary of State may still exercise the power (s. 8(10)). Before doing so, however, the Secretary of State must publish an explanation for proceeding in the absence of consent (s. 8(11)).

G. EXCLUSIONS FROM THE NON-DISCRIMINATION PRINCIPLE

3.75 There are circumstances and requirements that are excluded from the application of the non-discrimination principle. An exclusion is a policy area, area of regulation, or type of relevant requirement that is not subject to the principle, meaning that divergences between regulatory requirements in each part of the United Kingdom are permissible. Exclusions from the non-discrimination principle are found in section 10 and Schedule 1 to the Act.

1. Out of Scope

3.76 This chapter has already discussed various situations which are out of scope of the non-discrimination principle. These are not exclusions as such, as they mean the situation never falls within the scope of the non-discrimination principle in the first place. They are nonetheless helpful to have in mind at this juncture. Examples include the following. Sales that are not made in the course of business and sales which, despite being made in the course of business, are made only for the purpose of performing a public function are not covered by the principle. Relevant requirements which pre-existed the commencement of the Act are not within the scope of the principle. Requirements already covered by the mutual recognition principle and non-legislative requirements (i.e. those of private parties) are also not within scope of the concept of 'relevant requirements', and so are not covered by the non-discrimination principle. Finally, there are in-built exceptions for indirect discrimination, where the relevant requirement can reasonably be considered a necessary means of achieving certain legitimate aims.

3.77 In addition to these out-of-scope circumstances, the following sub-sections address relevant parts of section 10 and Schedule 1 to the Act which provide 'further' exclusions from the application of the non-discrimination principle.

[30] Non-discrimination Policy Paper (n. 25).

[31] The affirmative procedure is a type of parliamentary procedure that applies to statutory instruments ('SIs'). Its name describes the form of scrutiny that the SI receives from Parliament. An SI laid under the affirmative procedure must be actively approved by both Houses of Parliament.

2. Pest and Disease Control

Pursuant to paragraph 1 of Schedule 1, the non-discrimination principle does not apply to and does not affect the operation of legislation (often referred to as sanitary and phytosanitary (SPS) legislation) to prevent or reduce the movement of a 'pest or disease' insofar as certain conditions are met. The phrase 'pest or disease' includes any organism or agent that is liable to cause a disease or other harm to the health of humans, animals, or plants (paragraph 1(8) of Schedule 1). This exclusion will allow the nations of the United Kingdom to preserve and protect the health of their animals, citizens, and plants, in line with existing international and national practice. 3.78

There are five conditions for the application of this exclusion. 3.79

The first condition is that the aim of the legislation is to prevent or reduce the movement of a pest or disease into the part of the United Kingdom in which the legislation applies ('the restricting part') from another part of the United Kingdom ('the affected part') (paragraph 1(2) of Schedule 1).[32] 3.80

The second condition is that it is reasonable to believe that the pest or disease (i) is present in the affected part, and (ii) is not present, or is significantly less prevalent, in the restricting part (paragraph 1(3) of Schedule 1). 3.81

The third condition is that the potential movement of that pest or disease into the restricting part from the affected part poses (or would in the absence of the legislation pose) a serious threat to the health of humans, animals, or plants in the restricting part (paragraph 1(4) of Schedule 1). 3.82

The fourth condition is that the 'responsible administration'[33] has provided to the 'other administrations'[34] an assessment of the available evidence in relation to (i) the threat to the health of humans, animals, or plants in the restricting part, and (ii) the likely effectiveness of the legislation in addressing that threat (paragraph 1(5) of Schedule 1). 3.83

The fifth condition is that the legislation can reasonably be justified as necessary in order to address the threat to the health of humans, animals, or plants in the restricting part (paragraph 1(6) of Schedule 1). In determining whether the fifth condition is met, paragraph 1(7) of Schedule 1 provides that the following consideration is to be taken into account: 'whether the legislation, taken together with any similar legislation applying in the restricting part, imposes measures of similar severity arising from the potential movement of the pest or disease into, or within, the restricting part (wherever those threats originate)'. 3.84

3. Public Health Emergency

Pursuant to paragraph 5 of Schedule 1, a relevant requirement is not to be taken to directly discriminate against incoming goods for the purposes of section 7 'to the extent that it can 3.85

[32] Paragraph 3 of Schedule 1 provides that where a decision is taken to exercise powers conferred by legislation in a particular way for the purpose referred to in paragraph 1(2) of Schedule 1, the reference to 'legislation' in that sub-paragraph are to be read a references to the use of the legislation in that way.

[33] The term 'responsible administration' is defined in paragraph 4(1)–(5) of Schedule 1. Essentially, it refers to the Secretary of State, Scottish Ministers, Welsh Ministers, or a Northern Ireland department acting within their respective legislative competences.

[34] The term 'the other administrations' is defined in paragraph 4(6) of Schedule 1. It means each of the Secretary of State, Scottish Ministers, the Welsh Ministers, and a Northern Ireland department other than the 'responsible administration'.

reasonably be justified as a response to a public health emergency'.[35] The term 'public health emergency' is defined as 'an event or a situation that is reasonably considered to pose an extraordinary threat to human health in the destination part' of the United Kingdom.

4. Taxation

3.86 Pursuant to paragraph 11 of Schedule 1, the non-discrimination principle does not apply to and does not affect the operation of any legislation so far as it imposes, or relates to the imposition of, any tax, rate, duty, or similar charge. Section 58 defines 'legislation' as including primary legislation, subordinate legislation, and retained direct EU legislation, whereby (i) 'primary legislation' includes Acts of the UK Parliament, Acts of the Scottish Parliament, Acts or Measures of the Senedd Cymru (the Welsh Parliament), and Northern Ireland legislation; and (ii) 'subordinate legislation' means an instrument made under primary legislation or retained direct EU legislation.

5. Provision Having Effect in More Than One Part of the United Kingdom

3.87 Pursuant to paragraph 12 of Schedule 1, a relevant requirement is not to be taken indirectly to discrimination against goods for the purposes of section 8 where four cumulative conditions apply:

a. the relevant requirement is a statutory provision contained in, or in subordinate legislation made under, an Act of Parliament (paragraph 12(1)(a) of Schedule 1). A 'statutory provision' means provision contained in legislation (s. 6(10));
b. the same, or substantially the same, statutory provision applies in the originating part of the United Kingdom (paragraph 12(1)(b) of Schedule 1). The originating part of the United Kingdom is where the incoming goods have a relevant connection (e.g. where they are produced) and is counterpoint to the 'destination part' (s. 5);
c. the statutory provision that applies in the originating part is also contained in, or in subordinate legislation made under, an Act of Parliament (paragraph 12(1)(c) of Schedule 1); and
d. no substantive change to the statutory provision has come into force (i) in the destination part but not the originating part, or (ii) in the originating part but not the destination part (paragraph 12(1)(d) of Schedule 1).

3.88 The effect of this exclusion is that a relevant requirement made by an Act of Parliament, or under an Act of Parliament, which has effect in more than one part of the United Kingdom is excluded from the principle of indirect discrimination where the place of origin (the originating part) and the place of destination are both covered by the relevant requirement. For example, a relevant requirement under an Act of Parliament that applies to both England and Wales will be excluded from indirect discrimination if the good originated in England and was destined to Wales, or vice versa.[36]

---

[35] 'Relevant requirement', 'incoming goods', and 'destination part' are each defined in sections 5 and 6 (paragraph 5(2) of Schedule 1).

[36] Explanatory Notes (n. 4), paragraph 30.

6. Future Regulations

Pursuant to section 10(2), the Secretary of State is provided with a power to amend Schedule 1 by regulations to alter or add to the exclusions addressed above. This provides flexibility for the internal market system to respond to changes in market conditions.[37] 3.89

Section 10(3) provides an example for which the power may be exercised, namely to give effect to an agreement that forms part of a common framework agreement[38] and provides that certain cases, matters, requirements, or provision should be excluded from the application of the market access principles. 3.90

In making regulations pursuant to section 10, the Secretary of State must have regard to the importance of facilitating the access to the market within Great Britain of 'qualifying Northern Ireland goods' as defined in section 47 (as to which see chapter 8). The making of regulations under section 10 is subject to the affirmative resolution procedure (s. 10(8)).[39] 3.91

There is a requirement on the Secretary of State to seek the consent of the devolved administrations before exercising the power in section 10(2) (s. 10(9)). If consent is not given by any of the devolved administrations within a month, the Secretary of State may still exercise the power (s. 10(10). Before doing so, however, the Secretary of State must publish an explanation for proceeding in the absence of consent (s. 10(11)). 3.92

H. THE EFFECT OF THE NON-DISCRIMINATION PRINCIPLE

Section 1(3) states that the non-discrimination principle has 'no direct effect except as provided by this Part' of the Act. What, then, is the consequence of the non-discrimination principle's application? Where a situation is within the principle's scope and not excluded, section 5(1) states that the sale of goods in the destination part of the United Kingdom 'should not be affected' by the discriminatory relevant requirement. Section 5(3) reinforces this, saying that any such relevant requirement 'is of no effect'[40] in the destination part 'if 3.93

[37] For example, the Parliamentary Under-Secretary of State, Department for Business, Energy and Industrial Strategy (Lord Callanan) stated that the flexibility to add new exception would 'be needed if implementation shows the need for a review, or if further areas are identified that need exclusion due to a shifting economic landscape. This would be the case, for example, if the application of the market access principles to a new technology would pose a threat to public security or the environment': Hansard HL, 28 October 2020, col. 272.

[38] A common framework agreement is a consensus between a Minister of the Crown and one or more devolved administrations as to how devolved or transferred matters previously governed by EU law are to be regulated after IP completion day (s. 10(4)). IP completion day is defined as 11 p.m. on 31 December 2020: see Schedule 1 to the Interpretation Act 1978 by reference to section 39 of the European Union (Withdrawal Agreement) Act 2020). When determining whether a matter is a devolved or transferred matter for the purposes of section 10(4), section 30A of the Scotland Act 1998, section 109A of the Government of Wales Act 2006 and section 6A of the Northern Ireland Act 1998 are to be ignored (s. 10(6)). Those sections each relate to restrictions on legislative competence relating to retained EU law as defined by the European Union (Withdrawal) Act 2018. See, further, the Joint Ministerial Committee (EU Negotiations) communiqué (16 October 2017).

[39] The affirmative procedure is a type of parliamentary procedure that applies to statutory instruments ('SIs'). Its name describes the form of scrutiny that the SI receives from Parliament. An SI laid under the affirmative procedure must be actively approved by both Houses of Parliament.

[40] See Hansard HL, 28 October 2020, cols 251–2: '[Section] 5(3) will operate so that any future requirements that fall within the scope of the non-discrimination principle will be of no effect to the extent that they are discriminatory. For the benefit of the lawyers, this does not mean that the requirement is to be treated as if

and to the extent that'[41] it directly or indirectly discriminates against the incoming goods. The 'destination part' is the part of the United Kingdom where the goods are sold (s. 5(2)(a)). For example, if Scotland introduced a new law that all fizzy drinks from England had to be displayed on the bottom shelf, that law would be inapplicable and any Scottish agency or public body with power to enforce this law would be unable to enforce it.

3.94 There are two ways in which a dispute may arise in court to enforce the market access principles.

3.95 First, a business or individual may claim that a relevant requirement should be disapplied or given no effect pursuant to the Act and seek a relevant declaration from the court that that is the case and perhaps other relief to prevent or un-do an attempt to enforce such an impermissible application of the relevant requirement. This will be by way of judicial review.

3.96 Second, a regulator may try to enforce a relevant requirement against a business or individual or prosecute them for non-compliance, and that business or individual may use the market access principles as a shield by submitting that such enforcement should not have been brought or such penalty is of no application or effect on account of the market access principles.

---

it never had any legal effect. Rather, it allows the continued operation of the requirement, except to the extent that it has discriminatory effects. This aims to ensure that businesses can continue in their trade and goods can continue to be sold, despite protectionist measures that might treat goods from one part of the UK more favourably than goods from another.'

[41] See Hansard HL, 18 November 2020, col. 1492: 'This wording was chosen by the Government because it targets discrimination, while leaving intact other elements of a regulation that may be perfectly useful or serviceable. For example, consider the case of one requirement covering two products. One of those products is not discriminated against, but the other faces indirect discrimination due to the particular market structure for that product. [Section 5(3)] ensures that the regulation of the product which is not facing discrimination continues. This would not be the case if the requirement were struck down in its entirety when any part of it is discriminatory.'

4
MUTUAL RECOGNITION OF AUTHORIZATIONS TO PROVIDE SERVICES

A. INTRODUCTION

This chapter examines the application and effect of section 19 of the Act, which provides for the mutual recognition of authorizations to provide services. Section 19(1) provides that 'an authorisation requirement in relation to the provision of services in one part of the United Kingdom does not apply to a person who is authorised to provide those services in another part of the United Kingdom'. The term 'authorisation requirement' means 'a legislative requirement that a service provider must have the permission of a regulator before carrying on a business of providing particular services' (s. 17(3)). 4.01

Blackstone's Guide to the UK Internal Market Act 2020. Alan Bates, Brendan McGurk, George Peretz QC, and Jack Williams, Oxford University Press.
DOI: 10.1093/oso/9780192856203.003.0004

4.02 In this chapter, the term 'mutual recognition rule' is used to refer to the rule laid down in section 19(1). The term 'mutual recognition *principle*' is not used herein in relation to section 19(1), since the 'market access principles' in section 1(2) are in relation to trade in goods, not services. The word 'rule' anyway seems more appropriate in relation to section 19(1) since that section lays down a specific rule rather than a broader 'principle'.

4.03 Section 19 is contained within Part II of the Act, which consists of sections 17– 23[1] and governs the regulation of service providers in the United Kingdom.[2] Whilst relatively few sections of the Act are concerned with services (relative to the greater number of sections concerned with goods), the extent of the practical significance of Part II of the Act should not be overlooked. Whilst some services are, by their nature, ones that tend to be provided locally, there is a high volume of trade in services between the different parts of the United Kingdom. For example, almost a third of the services consumed in Wales are provided from the rest of the United Kingdom.[3] The services sector dominates the UK economy, accounting for over 80 per cent of both total UK economic output and total numbers of jobs.[4]

4.04 This chapter answers four overarching questions. What is the mutual recognition rule? In what circumstances does the rule apply? When is the rule excluded? What effect does it have in practice?

B. THE MUTUAL RECOGNITION RULE FOR SERVICES

4.05 Section 19(1) of the Act provides that:

> An authorisation requirement in relation to the provision of services in one part of the United Kingdom does not apply to a person who is authorised to provide those services in another part of the United Kingdom.

4.06 The effect of the mutual recognition rule is that a service provider who has obtained, from a regulator in respect of one part of the United Kingdom, an authorization to provide a particular service in that part, can then rely on that authorization when providing that service in the other parts of the United Kingdom.

4.07 Thus, once a service provider has obtained a relevant authorization in one part of the United Kingdom, the service provider may also provide the service in other parts of the United Kingdom without complying with any authorization requirement arising under legislation applicable in those parts. That is so even where those other parts of the United Kingdom require compliance with different or more stringent standards or requirements before they will themselves grant an authorization to provide the service. The service provider will, however, have to comply with any legislation applicable in those parts which requires the service provider to register with a regulator in that part and to provide proof of the existing authorization (s. 17(5)(e)–(d)).

---

[1] Each of these provisions commenced at 11 p.m. on 31 December 2020 (defined as 'IP completion day' in Schedule 1 to the Interpretation Act 1978 by reference to section 39 of the European Union (Withdrawal Agreement) Act 2020): see Regulation 2 of the United Kingdom Internal Market Act 2020 (Commencement No. 1) Regulations 2020.

[2] See section 17(1) of the Act.

[3] EUREGIO dataset (2010), cited in Command Paper 278, *UK Internal Market* (July 2020), at p. 68.

[4] Office for National Statistics, *Index of Services—UK*, March 2021.

It is important to note that the mutual recognition rule applies to a service provider that has obtained a relevant authorization in one part of the United Kingdom regardless of whether the service provider is based in, or is otherwise closely connected with, that part. Accordingly, there is potential for service providers to engage in 'regulatory forum shopping' by choosing to seek authorization in the part of the United Kingdom in which such authorization can most easily be obtained. It may therefore be futile for one part of the United Kingdom to act unilaterally to raise the standards it requires intending service providers to satisfy as a precondition for being granted authorization to provide certain services, since providers may be able to avoid complying with the raised standards by choosing to seek authorization in another part of the United Kingdom instead. **4.08**

The mutual recognition rule applies only where the service provider has obtained a relevant authorization from a regulator in a part of the United Kingdom. Accordingly, a service provider lawfully providing a service in a part of the United Kingdom in which no authorization is required in order to provide the service cannot rely on that entitlement so as to avoid having to obtain an authorization in a part of the United Kingdom in which provision of the service is restricted to authorized persons. **4.09**

The scope of application of the mutual recognition rule is fixed largely by section 17(5) which lists various types of requirements which 'are neither authorisation requirements nor regulatory requirements for the purposes of this Part'. Section 19(1) disapplies only 'authorisation requirements' and therefore does not affect the application of any other requirements. **4.10**

Exclusions from the mutual recognition rule are set out in Parts 1 and 3 of Schedule 2 to the Act. Part 1 sets out a list of *services* to which the rule does not apply. Part 3 sets out a list of *authorization requirements* to which the rule does not apply. **4.11**

A lawyer advising in relation to the lawfulness of prior permission requirements for providers of services, which do not apply on a United Kingdom-wide basis, should consider not only Part II of the Act, but also the Provision of Services Regulations 2009.[5] Part III of the Regulations places limitations on the powers of 'competent authorities'[6] to introduce prior permission requirements for service providers, in order to ensure that such requirements are imposed only if they are 'justified by an overriding reason relating to the public interest' and 'the objective pursued cannot be attained by means of a less restrictive measure'.[7] Part III also lays down certain rules concerning the way in which competent authorities consider and grant applications for such authorizations. Those rules include requirements for mutual recognition to be afforded to equivalent or comparable authorizations already granted to the service provider in the United Kingdom.[8] **4.12**

C. THE APPLICABILITY OF THE MUTUAL RECOGNITION RULE

The mutual recognition rule applies in circumstances where the person providing a service is 'authorised to provide services [of the relevant type] in a part of the United Kingdom'. **4.13**

[5] SI 2009/2999, as amended.

[6] The concept of 'competent authorities' in the Regulations is not limited to governmental bodies but also includes professional bodies, professional associations, and other professional organizations that regulate access to, or the exercise of, a service activity (reg. 3).

[7] Regulation 14.

[8] Regulation 15.

The effect of the rule is that such a person may provide the service in all parts of the United Kingdom without needing also to comply with any 'authorisation requirement' imposed in the other parts (i.e. those parts in which the person is not authorized). A proper understanding of the circumstances in which the mutual recognition rule applies therefore requires an understanding of the meanings of the statutory expressions 'authorised to provide services in a part of the United Kingdom' and 'authorisation requirement'.

1. The Definition of 'authorised to provide services'

4.14 As noted above, the mutual recognition rule benefits persons who are 'authorised to provide services in a part of the United Kingdom'. Section 19(2) defines what is meant by this:

> A person is authorised to provide services in a part of the United Kingdom if they have the permission of a regulator that exercises regulatory functions in relation to the whole of that part to carry on a business of providing those services in that part.

4.15 The term 'regulator' is defined as meaning 'a person exercising regulatory functions' and includes a Minister of the Crown, the Scottish Ministers, the Welsh Ministers, and a Northern Ireland department (s. 23(1)). It is apparent from the wording of section 19(2), however, that the reference therein to 'the permission of a regulator' is limited to regulators that exercise regulatory functions 'in relation to the whole of [a] part' of the United Kingdom. Thus, a licence granted by a local authority for a particular city, county, or region, permitting the licensee to provide certain services within that area, cannot be a relevant authorization for the purposes of section 19(1).

4.16 The wording of section 19(2) appears, however, to be sufficiently wide to include an authorization granted by a regulator on a United Kingdom-wide basis or in relation to multiple parts of the United Kingdom. For example, if a regulator with jurisdiction across England and Wales granted a person an authorization to provide a particular service, then this could, in principle, be relied on as affording mutual recognition so as to disapply either: (a) an additional prior permission requirement imposed in relation to Wales by Welsh legislation; or (b) a prior permission requirement imposed in relation to Scotland by Scottish legislation. That is because the authorization granted by the regulator would entitle the authorized person to provide the service throughout the whole of England.

4.17 Notably, whilst the term 'authorisation requirement' is defined in section 17(3) in a way that confines the meaning of that term to requirements arising under *legislation*, the expression 'authorised to provide services' and the term 'regulator' are not similarly confined (at least not expressly). It may therefore be arguable that an authorization granted by a *non-statutory* or *non-governmental* body could, in some circumstances, be relied on as conferring on the person so authorized the status of being 'authorised to provide services in a part of the United Kingdom'. This could arguably be the position where, for example, a self-regulatory body has been established pursuant to an understanding between the government of a part of the United Kingdom and a trade association representing a particular industry, without any legislative underpinning, and the government effectively relies on the self-regulatory body to grant authorizations to provide certain services.[9]

[9] For an example of a factual situation in which a non-statutory body was being relied on by the UK government to regulate a particular activity which would otherwise have been regulated under legislation, see *R v Panel on Take-overs and Mergers, ex parte Datafin plc* [1987] QB 815.

As the 'authoris[ation] to provide services' must be a 'permission ... to carry on a business of providing those services', it follows that a permission to operate facilities, or to carry on certain activities, relating to the provision of a service will not suffice as a relevant authorization for the purposes of section 19(1). Rather, the authorization must, if it is to trigger mutual recognition, be a permission to carry on a business or providing services of a certain kind. **4.18**

A person cannot, for the purposes of section 19, claim to be 'authorised to provide services' in a part of the United Kingdom based on a permission to provide services which relates to their provision only in relation to particular premises or to a particular place or piece of infrastructure: section 19(3). For example, a person who has been granted licences to sell alcohol at specific pub or shop premises in England could not rely on those licences as affording any mutual recognition under section 19(1). **4.19**

Section 23(4) of the Act provides that 'Any effect of section 5, 20 or 21 (direct and indirect discrimination for goods and services) is to be disregarded when considering whether a person is authorised to provide services in another part of the United Kingdom for the purposes of section 19 (mutual recognition for services)'. Accordingly, any effect of the non-discrimination rules in disapplying a regulatory requirement imposed in a part of the United Kingdom cannot affect whether a person who does, or does not, hold the status of being authorized in that part of the United Kingdom to provide the relevant services. This promotes simplicity: a person needs actually to hold an authorization granted by a regulator which entitles that person to provide the services in (at least) the whole of one part of the United Kingdom, in order to then rely on mutual recognition of that authorization when providing services in other parts of the United Kingdom. **4.20**

2. The Definition of 'authorisation requirement'

Section 19(1) operates to disapply an 'authorisation requirement in relation to the provision of services in one part of the United Kingdom'. The Act defines the term 'authorisation requirement' as meaning 'a *legislative requirement* that a *service provider* must have the permission of a *regulator* before carrying on a business of providing particular services' (s. 17(3), emphasis added). **4.21**

The expression 'legislative requirement' is defined in the Act as meaning 'a requirement imposed by, or by virtue of, legislation' (s. 23(1)). The term 'legislation' is, in turn, defined as meaning 'primary legislation, subordinate legislation and retained direct EU legislation' (s. 58). The words 'by virtue of' are important, since a requirement for prior permission which has not been imposed by legislation, but rather by a person or body exercising a power arising from legislation, may nevertheless constitute an 'authorisation requirement'.[10] **4.22**

[10] Where the prior permission requirement is imposed by a non-governmental entity, such as a professional association or industry self-regulation body, other than in exercise of powers or responsibilities granted to it by legislation, the requirement will fall outside the scope of the mutual recognition rule in the Act. The situation may, however, fall within the scope of the Provision of Services Regulations 2009 (including the provision in reg. 15 thereof for mutual recognition of authorizations). That is because Regulations apply to authorizations granted by 'competent authorities', a term which includes not only governmental bodies but also professional bodies, professional associations, and other professional organizations that regulate access to, or the exercise of, a service activity (reg. 3). That term would not, of course, include situations where a professional association or self-regulation body is granting 'authorisations' that are not in fact *required* by persons wishing to provide particular services. It is, however, possible to envisage circumstances in which it may be arguable that an authorization by a particular body is a requirement (at least *de facto*), even if such requirement is not imposed by, or by virtue of, any legislation.

4.23 The definition of the term 'service provider' is considered below at paragraphs 4.26–4.27 below.

4.24 The term 'regulator' is, as already noted above, defined in the Act as meaning 'a person exercising regulatory functions' and includes a Minister of the Crown, the Scottish Ministers, the Welsh Ministers, and a Northern Ireland department (s. 23(1)). That functions-based definition is capable of catching local authorities and other bodies that exercise regulatory functions in relation to a geographical area that is smaller than a 'part' of the United Kingdom. Although section 19(1) refers to an 'authorisation requirement in relation to the provision of services *in one part of the United Kingdom*' (emphasis added), those words do not appear to limit the concept of an 'authorisation requirement' to a requirement that applies across *the whole* of the relevant part of the United Kingdom. Accordingly, section 19(1) can operate to disapply an authorization requirement imposed in respect of a particular geographical area within a part of the United Kingdom. For example, a requirement imposed by Glasgow City Council requiring all persons providing bicycle repair services in its local authority area to be authorized in advance by the Council would be of no application to a bicycle repair company that had already been granted an authorization to carry out that activity by a regulator in Wales.

4.25 The term 'authorisation requirement' does not include a requirement that applies, not only to service providers, 'but . . . also . . . to persons who do not provide services (for example, a requirement imposing duties on employers)' (s. 17(5)(d)). Accordingly, the mutual recognition rule is of no application to such a requirement.

3. Limitation of the Mutual Recognition Rule to 'service providers'

4.26 The definition of 'authorisation requirement' in section 17(3) refers to 'a legislative requirement that a *service provider* must have the permission of a regulator before carrying on a business of providing particular services' (emphasis added). It is thus beyond doubt that a requirement for prior permission to be obtained can only be an 'authorisation requirement' for the purposes of section 19(1) if and insofar as it requires a 'service provider' to obtain such permission.

4.27 Section 17(1) of the Act provides that Part II of the Act 'governs the regulation of service providers in the United Kingdom'. The concept of a 'service provider' is defined in section 17(9) so that it applies only to persons who have a permanent establishment in the United Kingdom through which they carry on relevant business:

> 'service provider' means a person—
> (a) that provides, or intends to provide, services in the course of the person's business, and
> (b) that has a permanent establishment in the United Kingdom through which that business is wholly or partly carried on;
>
> 'permanent establishment'—
> (a) in relation to a company, is to be read in accordance with Chapter 2 of Part 24 of the Corporation Tax Act 2010, and
> (b) in relation to any other person, is to be read in accordance with that Chapter but as if references in that Chapter to a company were references to that person.

Accordingly, a prior permission requirement applying *only* to persons wishing to provide certain services *who do not have a permanent establishment in the United Kingdom* would not be an 'authorisation requirement'. Such a requirement would therefore not be disapplied in the case of a person holding authorization to provide those services in another part of the United Kingdom.

A more difficult question is whether section 19(1) operates to disapply a prior permission requirement that applies to *all* persons wishing to provide certain services within a part of the United Kingdom (i.e. regardless of whether those persons have a permanent establishment in the United Kingdom), in the case of a person who holds an equivalent authorization in another part of the United Kingdom *but who does not have a permanent establishment in the United Kingdom*. The correct answer seems likely to be that mutual recognition could not benefit such a person, since that person would not be a 'service provider' as defined in section 17(9), and Part II of the Act is concerned with the regulation of 'service providers'. In other words, a person who does not have a permanent establishment in the United Kingdom cannot benefit from the mutual recognition rule. Such a person may therefore have to obtain prior permissions in each of the parts of the United Kingdom in which it provides its services. This appears to have been the intention of the UK government when drafting the legislation, as deduced from the Explanatory Notes to the Act.[11] **4.28**

Such result is not, however, unambiguously required by a natural language interpretation of section 19(1), and therefore the contrary view may also be arguable. In that regard, it is possible to read section 19(1) as being capable of availing a person who does not have a permanent establishment in the United Kingdom, since such a person may be 'a person who is authorised to provide those services in another part of the United Kingdom'. Although such a person would not be a 'service provider' as defined in section 17(9), the prior permission requirement would be an 'authorisation requirement' since it applies to persons who have a permanent establishment within the United Kingdom (as well as to persons who do not). As noted in the preceding paragraph, however, the intention of the UK government in drafting the legislation appears to have been to exclude persons who do not have a UK permanent establishment from benefiting from the mutual recognition rule. In order to achieve that intended result, it may be appropriate to read the words 'authorisation requirement' in section 19(1) as referring to a prior permission requirement *insofar as* it applies to a 'service provider', so that any prior permission requirement is disapplied *only to that extent* (i.e. to the extent it applies to 'service providers'). **4.29**

The concept of 'permanent establishment' in section 17(9) expressly borrows from UK corporation tax legislation but applies the tests for identifying a permanent establishment not only to companies but also to other persons *mutatis mutandis*.[12] This book cannot accommodate a detailed treatment of the concept of 'permanent establishment' in corporation tax law; however, the principal provision of Chapter 2 of Part 24 of the Corporation Tax Act 2010 is **4.30**

[11] *United Kingdom Internal Market Act 2000—Explanatory Notes*, paragraph 194: 'a service provider will only be within scope of [Part II of the Act] if it is a person that ... has a permanent establishment in the UK.' See also paragraph 35: 'This mutual recognition principle ensures that *a service provider* who has been authorised to access or exercise a service activity by a regulator whose functions relate only to a part of the UK, is able to exercise that service activity throughout the whole of the UK' (emphasis added).

[12] The concept of 'permanent establishment' in the Act is not identical to the concept of 'establishment' in the Provision of Services Regulations 2009. Under the Regulations, a business is 'established' in the United Kingdom if it is pursuing an economic activity for an indefinite period and through a stable infrastructure from where the business of providing services is actually carried out (reg. 4). The benefit of the mutual recognition provision made in the Regulations is restricted to individuals who are UK nationals and 'business undertakings', i.e. economic entities 'incorporated or formed under the law of any part of the United Kingdom' (reg. 5(4)–(5)).

section 1141. In simplified terms, a company has a 'permanent establishment' in the United Kingdom if either: (a) 'it has a fixed place of business there through which the business of the company is wholly or partly carried on'; or (b) 'an agent acting on behalf of the company has and habitually exercises their authority to do business on behalf of the company'. The concept of a 'fixed place of business' is a broad one and can be satisfied by, for example, an office, branch, factory, workshop, or a building site or construction or installation project.[13]

4.31 The word 'service' is not itself defined in the Act; however, the term 'goods' is defined in section 16(2) of the Act as 'any tangible movable, or corporeal moveable, thing (including any packaging or label), but not water or gas that is not offered for sale in a limited volume or set quantity'. It seems reasonable to assume that the concept of a 'service' includes any supply in return for payment which is not a supply of 'goods' as defined.

4. The Partial Exclusion of Authorization Requirements Existing Prior to Commencement

4.32 As explained above, the mutual recognition rule in section 19(1) operates to disapply an 'authorisation requirement' in circumstances where the person providing the services already holds a relevant authorization from a regulator in another part of the United Kingdom. Section 17(5)(c) provides that a requirement is not an 'authorisation requirement' if it is:

> a requirement that—
> (i) is in force, or otherwise has effect, on the day before the day on which this section comes into force and has not been substantively changed after that day, or
> (ii) comes into force, or otherwise takes effect, on or after the day on which this section comes into force if it re-enacts or replicates (without substantive change) a legislative requirement in force or having effect immediately before that day.

4.33 The practical effect of section 17(5)(c) is that the mutual recognition rule does not disapply a prior permission requirement imposed in a part of the United Kingdom where that requirement was already in force, or otherwise had effect, prior to 31 December 2020. (This is, however subject to the exception in section 17(6) discussed at paragraph 4.36 below.) The mutual recognition rule therefore operates to limit the scope for individual parts of the United Kingdom to, *after that date*, create *new* obstacles to trade in services within the UK internal market. The rule is not intended to remove obstacles created by prior authorization requirements already existing before that date.

4.34 It is apparent from section 17(5)(c) that the determination of whether a particular prior authorization requirement already existed prior to 31 December 2020 is one of substance rather than form. Legislation re-enacting or replicating a pre-existing requirement *without substantively changing it* will not render a prior authorization requirement subject to the mutual recognition rule.

4.35 The same principle is reinforced by section 17(8), which provides that 'an authorisation requirement is substantively changed if a legislative requirement that would, if not satisfied, prevent a service provider from satisfying the authorisation requirement is substantively changed'. In other words, even if a prior permission requirement was already in force prior to 31 December 2020, it will be regarded as 'substantively changed' if there is, after that date, a substantive change to the conditions for obtaining an authorization. If, for example, a

[13] Corporation Tax Act 2010, section 1141(2).

prior authorization requirement was already in force in a part of the United Kingdom prior to 31 December 2020, but the conditions for obtaining such prior authorization are, after that date, made tougher, or the procedure for obtaining the authorizations is made more cumbersome or expensive, then this could constitute a 'substantive change'. The consequence of making any changes in relation to an existing prior authorization requirement which constitutes a 'substantive change' is to render that requirement thereafter subject to the mutual recognition rule, so that it will no longer be applicable to service providers holding a relevant authorization from another part of the United Kingdom.

Section 17(6) creates a significant exception to the general position arising under section 17(5)(c) that the mutual recognition rule does not apply to a prior permission requirement that was already in force in the relevant part of the United Kingdom before 31 December 2020. The exception applies where 'a corresponding authorisation requirement in another part of the United Kingdom is substantively changed' on or after that date. Section 17(7) defines the term 'corresponding authorisation', explaining that 'an authorisation requirement corresponds to another authorisation requirement if it relates to the same, or substantially the same, services'. 4.36

The practical effect of section 17(6) is that, even if a prior authorization requirement imposed in a part of the United Kingdom is not itself changed, that requirement may nevertheless become subject to the mutual recognition rule in consequence of *another part of the United Kingdom* making a change to its prior authorization requirement relating to the same services. For example, if (hypothetically) a prior authorization requirement for providing a particular type of service was already in force in all parts of the United Kingdom prior to 31 December 2020, but after that date the Scottish Parliament legislated to relax the conditions for obtaining such an authorization, then the mutual recognition rule would apply to the prior authorization requirements relating to that service in all parts of the United Kingdom. As a result, a service provider that was authorized in Scotland under the relaxed conditions would be able to provide the service in other parts of the United Kingdom in reliance on that authorization. 4.37

One area of uncertainty created by the drafting of section 17(6)–(7) is whether the exception provided for in section 17(6) is triggered where, after 31 December 2020, one part of the United Kingdom introduces a prior authorization requirement for providing a particular service, whereas previously it did not impose any requirement for prior authorization relating to that service. It appears to follow from the wording of section 17(7) that the introduction of such a new requirement would not render pre-31 December 2020 prior permission requirements in other parts of the United Kingdom subject to the mutual recognition rule. That is because the introduction of a new prior permission requirement for services that were not previously subject to any prior permission requirement in that part of the United Kingdom could not be a *change* to a corresponding authorization requirement. Whilst this distinction may seem difficult to justify in terms of policy and principle, it is unlikely to be problematic in practice, given the harmonizing impact of EU legislation applying across the United Kingdom up to 31 December 2020. It is difficult to identify any examples of services that were, prior to 31 December 2020, subject to prior permission requirements in some, but not other, parts of the United Kingdom. 4.38

In circumstances where a requirement for prior permission applied in one part of the United Kingdom is, by reason of section 17(5)(c), not an 'authorisation requirement' for the purposes of the Act, mutual recognition of a prior permission granted to the service provider by a UK regulator or in another part of the United Kingdom may nevertheless be 4.39

required by UK law. That is because regulation 15 of the Provision of Services Regulations 2009 may require mutual recognition, albeit subject to the exception that a refusal to afford mutual recognition is permissible where 'justified by an overriding reason relating to the public interest'.[14]

D. EXCLUSIONS FROM THE MUTUAL RECOGNITION RULE

1. Out of Scope

4.40 This chapter has already discussed various situations that are outside the scope of the mutual recognition rule. These are not exclusions as such, but rather are situations that simply do not engage the mutual recognition rule in the first place. It is nonetheless helpful to have them in mind again here.

4.41 First, it appears that the mutual recognition rule can never be relied on by persons who do not have a permanent establishment in the United Kingdom, since such persons are not 'service providers': see paragraphs 4.26–4.27 above.

4.42 Secondly, the mutual recognition rule is of no application to the provision of services *otherwise than in the course of a business*. The definition of 'authorisation requirement' in section 17(3) is confined to requirements to obtain permission 'before carrying on a business of providing particular services'. Further, the definition of 'service provider' in section 17(9) is limited to a person 'that provides, or intends to provide, services in the course of the person's business'.

4.43 Thirdly, the mutual recognition rule generally does not apply to prior permission requirements that were already in force, or otherwise had effect, before 31 December 2020: see paragraphs 4.32–4.38 above.

4.44 Fourthly, requirements that apply, not only to service providers, but also to persons who do not provide services (e.g. a requirement imposing duties on employers), fall outside the scope of the mutual recognition rule: see paragraph 4.25 above.

4.45 Fifthly, the mutual recognition rule does not apply to a requirement to notify, or register with, a regulator (s. 17(5)(e)), or to provide evidence of being authorized in another part of the United Kingdom (s. 17(5)(f)). A part of the United Kingdom which is legislating to create or modify prior permission requirements to which the mutual recognition rule will apply may therefore wish to consider laying down, at the same time, requirements for persons relying on such mutual recognition to: (a) register with the local regulator; and (b) provide proof of the authorization granted by a regulator in another part of the United Kingdom on which the service provider is relying.

4.46 Sixthly, the mutual recognition rule does not apply to requirements that are 'relevant requirements as defined for the purposes of the mutual recognition principle for goods' in section 3 of the Act (s. 17(5)(a)) or 'provision of the sought described in section 24(1) or 28(1) (professional qualifications and regulation) to the extent it has the effect described there' (s. 17(5)(b)). This ensures that the mutual recognition rule, which relates to authorizations to

[14] Provision of Services Regulations 2009, reg. 15(5D). The benefit of the mutual recognition provision made in the Regulations is restricted to individuals who are UK nationals and 'business undertakings', i.e. economic entities 'incorporated or formed under the law of any part of the United Kingdom' (reg. 5(4)–(5)).

provide services, does not overlap with the provisions elsewhere in the Act relating to mutual recognition for goods and for professional qualifications.

2. Public Health Emergency

Section 19(4) of the Act provides that the mutual recognition rule 'does not apply to an authorisation requirement to the extent it can reasonably be justified as a response to a public health emergency'. The expression 'public health emergency' is defined in section 23(1) as meaning 'an event or a situation that is reasonably considered to pose an extraordinary threat to human health'. 4.47

The phrase 'to the extent it can reasonably be justified' is interesting. It implicitly makes clear that a claim by a part of the United Kingdom that a purported abrogation of the mutual recognition rule is justified by a public health emergency will be subject to scrutiny by the courts. The question for the courts would not, however, be simply whether the abrogation was justified, but rather whether it could 'reasonably be justified'. This suggests that the standard of scrutiny of the justification put forward by the government of the relevant part of the United Kingdom could be less intense than the judicial scrutiny that EU law requires EU Member States' domestic courts to apply when assessing whether an interference with 'EU free movement rights' is necessary and proportionate.[15] 4.48

Legal uncertainty may arise in circumstances where a part of the United Kingdom responds to a public health situation by laying down prior permission requirements that *prima facie* apply to all persons providing a particular service, but without stating expressly in the relevant legislation that the mutual recognition rule is being negated. In this scenario, service providers holding an authorization from another part of the United Kingdom may be uncertain as to whether they may rely on that authorization, or whether they must also seek authorization under the new local requirement on the basis that the mutual recognition rule is disapplied by operation of section 19(4). 4.49

If, in such a scenario, a court is called upon to decide the matter, the court may have to do more than answer yes or no to the question whether the public health emergency justifies disapplying the mutual recognition rule. In that regard, the phrase 'to the extent it can reasonably be justified' suggests that the court may have to consider the detail of how the new local prior permission requirement applies to service providers already holding an authorization from another part of the United Kingdom. For example, if one other part of the United Kingdom is applying similar enhanced authorization requirements in response to the public health emergency, then arguably this should be taken into account in the application of the local authorization requirement to a service provider that has also satisfied an enhanced authorization requirement. 4.50

3. Exclusion of Certain Services (Part 1 of Schedule 2)

Section 18(1) of the Act gives effect to Schedule 2. Part 1 of Schedule 2 sets out a table listing services to which section 19 (the mutual recognition rule) does not apply. The excluded services are listed in the left-hand column of the table, whilst the right-hand column sets out examples of those services. 4.51

[15] As to the standard of scrutiny applied by the UK courts under EU law prior to Brexit, see *R (Lumsdon) v Legal Services Board* [2015] UKSC 41.

4.52 The list of excluded services in Part 1 of Schedule 2[16] includes the following:

a. Audiovisual services;
b. Debt collection services;
c. Electronic communication services and networks, and associated facilities and services;
d. Financial services;
e. Gambling services;
f. Healthcare services;
g. Legal services;
h. Notarial services;
i. Private security services;
j. Services provided by persons exercising functions of a public nature or by a person acting on behalf of such a person in connection with the exercise of functions of a public nature;
k. Services of temporary work agencies;
l. Social services relating to social housing, childcare, adult social care, and support of families and persons permanently or temporarily in need; and
m. Transport services.

4. Exclusion of Certain Authorization Requirements (Part 3 of Schedule 2)

4.53 Part 3 of Schedule 2 lists authorization requirements to which section 19 (the mutual recognition rule) does not apply. At present only one category of authorization requirement is listed: 'Any authorisation requirement in connection with taxation'.

4.54 This exclusion is not worded as clearly as it might have been, and there is room for arguments as to the exclusion's true scope in practice. The essential reason for the exclusion seems likely to have been a desire to reflect the Provision of Services Regulations 2009 in excluding 'the field of taxation' from its scope of application.[17] A desire by the UK government, when drafting the Act, to avoid impeding tax collection functions in any part of the United Kingdom is understandable, given that the devolved legislatures have taxation powers and may need to impose certain authorization requirements in connection with tax collection.

4.55 It remains to be seen whether any part of the United Kingdom will seek to take mischievous advantage of this exclusion to impose authorization requirements that are 'in connection

[16] This list of excluded services largely replicates, albeit it is not identical to, the services excluded from the scope of the Provision of Services Regulations 2009. The 2009 Regulations were, when originally made, made for the purpose of implementing in the United Kingdom the EU Services Directive (Directive 2006/123/EC).

[17] Regulation 5(2) of the Regulations provides: 'Nothing in these Regulations applies in respect of the field of taxation.' That exclusion from scope reflects Article 2(3) of the EU Services Directive (Directive 2006/123/EC), which the 2009 Regulations were originally made in order to implement in the United Kingdom. Recital 29 to the Directive explained that the exclusion was appropriate because 'the Treaty provides specific legal bases for taxation matters and given the Community instruments already adopted in that field, it is necessary to exclude the field of taxation from the scope of this Directive'. It is questionable whether the same, or a similar, reason exists to justify the exclusion of '[a]ny authorisation requirement in connection with taxation' from the scope of the mutual recognition rule in the Act.

with taxation' but go beyond what is truly necessary for taxation purposes. If they do so, it will be interesting to see how the courts respond.

5. Future Regulations Amending the Lists of Exclusions

Pursuant to section 18(2), the Secretary of State has power to amend Schedule 2 by regulations so as to alter or add to the exclusions.[18] 4.56

Section 18(3) provides an example of a reason for which the power may be exercised, namely to give effect to an agreement that forms part of a common framework agreement;[19] but the Secretary of State may also exercise the power for other reasons. 4.57

There is a requirement on the Secretary of State to seek the consent of the devolved administrations before exercising the power: section 18(8). If consent is not given by any of the devolved administrations within a month, the Secretary of State may still exercise the power: section 18(9). Before doing so, however, the Secretary of State must publish an explanation for proceeding in the absence of consent: section 18(10). 4.58

At the time of writing of this chapter (July 2021) it appears that the UK government is already actively considering potential amendments to Schedule 2, even though the Act has been in force for only a short time. In February 2021 the UK government published a consultation paper seeking views on whether any exclusions should be removed from, or added to, Schedule 2.[20] The consultation paper recognized that the existing exclusions are largely a replication of the exclusions in the Provision of Services Regulations 2009, which in turn set out the exclusions from the scope of application of the EU Services Directive. Those exclusions were included in the Act in circumstances where it was being drafted under considerable time pressure. It is reasonable to question whether those same exclusions are appropriate in legislation directed at protecting an internal market in services within the United Kingdom. Any proposals to amend Schedule 2 are, however, likely to be politically controversial, given their practical impacts on the powers of the devolved legislatures to set and enforce their own regulatory rules and standards. 4.59

[18] The making of regulations under section 18 is subject to the affirmative resolution procedure (s. 18(7)). The affirmative procedure is a type of parliamentary procedure that applies to statutory instruments ('SIs'). Its name describes the form of scrutiny that the SI receives from Parliament. An SI laid under the affirmative procedure must be actively approved by both Houses of Parliament.

[19] A common framework agreement is a consensus between a Minister of the Crown and one or more devolved administrations as to how devolved or transferred matters previously governed by EU law are to be regulated after IP completion day (s. 18(4)). IP completion day is defined as 11 p.m. on 31 December 2020: see Schedule 1 to the Interpretation Act 1978 by reference to section 39 of the European Union (Withdrawal Agreement) Act 2020). When determining whether a matter is a devolved or transferred matter for the purposes of section 10(4), section 30A of the Scotland Act 1998, section 109A of the Government of Wales Act 2006, and section 6A of the Northern Ireland Act 1998 are to be ignored (s. 18(6)). Those sections each relate to restrictions on legislative competence relating to retained EU law as defined by the European Union (Withdrawal) Act 2018. See, further, the Joint Ministerial Committee (EU Negotiations) communiqué (16 October 2017).

[20] Department for Business, Energy & Industrial Strategy, Consultation paper, 'UK internal market: the continuity of exclusions from the principles of mutual recognition and non-discrimination for services', 25 February 2021. The consultation period, as extended, closed on 7 May 2021.

E. THE EFFECT OF THE MUTUAL RECOGNITION RULE AND HOW IT IS ENFORCED

4.60 The mutual recognition rule does not place a limitation on the legislative competence of any part of the United Kingdom (albeit that the devolved legislatures may not repeal the Act). Rather, the mutual recognition rule operates by simply disapplying authorization requirements in the cases of service providers already holding a relevant authorization from another part of the United Kingdom. In other words, a part of the United Kingdom can legislate for whatever authorization requirements it wishes and need not make any express provision for excluding service providers exercising their right to mutual recognition under section 19(1). A service provider that already holds a relevant authorization from another part of the United Kingdom will be entitled simply to rely on that authorization across the whole of the United Kingdom, save for complying with any local requirements to register with a local regulator and provide proof of holding a UK authorization.

4.61 There are two ways in which a dispute may arise in court to enforce the mutual recognition rule.

4.62 The first is where a business or individual takes the initiative to bring the matter before a court. Such a person may, for example, seek a declaration that a particular requirement imposed by legislation in a part of the United Kingdom constitutes an 'authorisation requirement' and therefore does not apply to a person holding an authorization granted by a regulator in another part of the United Kingdom relating to provision of services of the relevant type.

4.63 The second way a dispute may come before a court is where a regulator pursues a criminal prosecution or other enforcement action against a person for providing certain services within a part of the United Kingdom without holding an authorization granted by a regulator in that part. The person against whom such enforcement action is taken may seek to rely on the mutual recognition rule as a shield, contending that the local legislative requirement to hold an authorization is of no application in its case, since it already held an authorization from a regulator in another part of the United Kingdom permitting it to provide the relevant services.

5
THE NON-DISCRIMINATION RULES FOR SERVICES

Blackstone's Guide to the UK Internal Market Act 2020. Alan Bates, Brendan McGurk, George Peretz QC, and Jack Williams, Oxford University Press.

DOI: 10.1093/oso/9780192856203.003.0005

A. INTRODUCTION

5.01 This chapter examines the application and effect of sections 20 and 21 of the Act. The effect of those sections is, broadly speaking, to render regulatory requirements imposed under the legislation applicable in one part of the United Kingdom 'of no effect' in relation to a service provider that has a 'relevant connection' to another part of the United Kingdom if those requirements directly or indirectly discriminate against that service provider. The concepts of 'direct discrimination' and 'indirect discrimination' are respectively defined in sections 20 and 21.

5.02 Section 20 is concerned with regulatory requirements that are *directly discriminatory*. Sub-section (2) of that section provides that a regulatory requirement directly discriminates against a service provider if it 'has, or would have, the effect of treating the service provider less favourably than other service providers' and 'the reason for that less favourable treatment is the service provider's relevant connection, or lack of relevant connection, to a part of the United Kingdom'.

5.03 Section 21 is concerned with regulatory requirements that are *indirectly discriminatory*. Sub-section (2) of that section provides that a regulatory requirement indirectly discriminates against an incoming service provider if 'it puts the incoming service provider at a relevant disadvantage' and 'has an adverse market effect', and 'cannot reasonably be considered a necessary means of achieving a legitimate aim'.

5.04 Thus, whilst service providers cannot be subjected to regulatory requirements that treat them less favourably *by reason of* their connection with another part of the United Kingdom, service providers may be subjected to regulatory requirements that put incoming service providers at a disadvantage *if the requirement can be justified* as necessary for pursuing a legitimate aim. Sections 20 and 21 of the Act therefore follow the familiar pattern in UK and EU legislation whereby 'directly discriminatory' measures are unacceptable, but other measures may be permissible if they are objectively justified.

5.05 In this chapter, the term 'non-discrimination rules' is used to refer to the rules laid down in sections 20 and 21 which render directly and indirectly discriminatory regulatory requirements relating to provision of services 'of no effect'. The term 'non-discrimination *principle*' is not used in this chapter in relation to those sections, since the 'market access principles' in section 1(2) of the Act are in relation to trade in goods, not services. The word 'rules' anyway seems more appropriate in relation to sections 20 and 21 since those sections lays down specific rules rather than a broader 'principle'.

5.06 Sections 20 and 21 are contained within Part II of the Act, which consists of sections 17–23[1] and governs the regulation of service providers in the United Kingdom.[2] Whilst relatively few sections of the Act are concerned with services (relative to the greater number of sections concerned with goods), the extent of the practical significance of Part II of the Act should

---

[1] Each of these provisions commenced at 11 p.m. on 31 December 2020 (defined as 'IP completion day' in Schedule 1 to the Interpretation Act 1978 by reference to section 39 of the European Union (Withdrawal Agreement) Act 2020): see Regulation 2 of the United Kingdom Internal Market Act 2020 (Commencement No. 1) Regulations 2020.

[2] See section 17(1) of the Act.

not be overlooked. Whilst some services are, by their nature, ones that tend to be provided locally, there is a high volume of trade in services between the different parts of the United Kingdom. For example, almost a third of the services consumed in Wales are provided from the rest of the United Kingdom.[3] The services sector dominates the UK economy, accounting for over 80 per cent of both total UK economic output and total numbers of jobs.[4]

This chapter answers four overarching questions. What are the non-discrimination rules relating to provision of services? In what circumstances does each of the rules apply? When are the rules excluded? What effect do the rules have in practice? **5.07**

B. THE NON-DISCRIMINATION RULES FOR SERVICES

The scope of application of the non-discrimination rules is fixed largely by the definition given by section 17 to the term 'regulatory requirement'. A regulatory requirement 'is a legislative requirement that would if not satisfied (whether at a particular point or on a continuing basis) prevent a service provider from carrying on a business of providing particular services' (s. 17(4)). Section 17(5) then lists various types of requirements which 'are neither authorisation requirements nor regulatory requirements for the purposes of this Part'. **5.08**

Exclusions from the non-discrimination rules are set out in Parts 2 and 4 of Schedule 2 to the Act. Part 2 sets out a list of *services* to which the rules do not apply. Part 4 sets out a list of *regulatory requirements* to which the rules do not apply. **5.09**

1. Directly Discriminatory Regulatory Requirements

Section 20(1)–(2) of the Act provides as follows: **5.10**

(1) A regulatory requirement that directly discriminates against a service provider is of no effect in relation to that service provider.
(2) A regulatory requirement directly discriminates against a service provider if –
   (a) it has, or would have, the effect of treating the service provider less favourably than other service providers, and
   (b) the reason for that less favourable treatment is the service provider's relevant connection, or lack of relevant connection, to a part of the United Kingdom.

The term 'relevant connection', *as it is used in section 20*, is defined in section 20(4). There are multiple bases on which a service provider may have a 'relevant connection' to a part of the United Kingdom. These include (amongst others) having a registered office or place of business in that part, or providing services from that part, or having members, officers, or staff who have a residence in that part. **5.11**

The essence of a directly discriminatory regulatory requirement is that it treats a service provider less favourably than other service providers *by reason of* that service provider having, or not having, a relevant connection to a part of the United Kingdom. Whilst legislation **5.12**

[3] EUREGIO dataset (2010), cited in Command Paper 278, *UK Internal Market* (July 2020), at p. 68.
[4] Office for National Statistics, *Index of Services—UK*, March 2021.

imposing or purporting to impose such a regulatory requirement is not *unlawful* as such, the requirement will be 'of no effect' in relation to that service provider.

2. Indirectly Discriminatory Regulatory Requirements

5.13 Section 21(1)–(2) of the Act provides as follows:

(1) A regulatory requirement that indirectly discriminates against an incoming service provider is of no effect in relation to that incoming service provider.
(2) A regulatory requirement indirectly discriminates against an incoming service provider if –
  (a) it does not directly discriminate against the incoming service provider (within the meaning of section 20),
  (b) it puts the incoming service provider at a relevant disadvantage,
  (c) it has an adverse market effect, and
  (d) it cannot reasonably be considered a necessary means of achieving a legitimate aim.

5.14 An 'incoming service provider' is a service provider that does not have a 'relevant connection' to the part of the United Kingdom in which the regulatory requirement applies: section 21(6)(a). The term 'relevant connection', *as it is used in section 21*, is defined in section 21(6)(c). The bases on which a service provider will have a 'relevant connection' to a part of the United Kingdom are not as numerous as those provided for in relation to section 20 (see paragraphs 5.36 and 5.37 below). For the purposes of section 21, a service provider has a 'relevant connection' to a part of the United Kingdom only if 'it has a registered office, place of business or residence in that part', or 'provides the services from that part'.

5.15 The restriction of the benefit of section 21 to 'incoming service providers' (as opposed to 'service providers') constitutes an important difference between sections 20 and 21. The disapplication of indirectly discriminatory regulatory requirements under section 21 benefits only service providers that both: (a) do not have a registered office, place of business, or residence in the part of the United Kingdom in which the regulatory requirement applies; and (b) are providing the relevant services from another part of the United Kingdom.

5.16 The essence of an indirectly discriminatory regulatory requirement is that it places an incoming service provider at a 'relevant disadvantage' as compared with 'local service providers' (i.e. providers having a 'relevant connection' to the part of the United Kingdom in which the regulatory requirement applies but not to any other part of the United Kingdom: s. 21(6)(b)). The concept of 'relevant disadvantage' is defined broadly in section 21(4): a regulatory requirement puts a service provider at a disadvantage 'if it makes it in any way more difficult, or less attractive, for the service provider to provide the services in that part'.

5.17 Whilst legislation imposing or purporting to impose such a regulatory requirement is not *unlawful*, the requirement will be 'of no effect' in relation to that service provider.

C. THE APPLICABILITY OF THE NON-DISCRIMINATION RULES

5.18 The non-discrimination rules concern 'regulatory requirements' applying to 'service providers'. A proper understanding of the circumstances in which the non-discrimination rules apply therefore requires an understanding of the meanings of the statutory expressions 'regulatory requirement' and 'service provider'.

1. The Definition of 'regulatory requirement'

The term 'regulatory requirement' is defined in section 17(4): 5.19

A regulatory requirement is a legislative requirement that would if not satisfied (whether at a particular point or on a continuing basis) prevent a service provider from carrying on a business of providing particular services.

Accordingly, the non-discrimination rules are applicable to potentially a very wide range of measures, including restrictions, prohibitions, and conditions that govern whether, or how, services may be provided (whether generally or by a particular person or category of persons). For example, a legislative provision requiring suppliers of home decorating services to ensure that their operatives have training in fire prevention would be a 'regulatory requirement', since compliance with that requirement would be necessary (at least absent the effect of ss 20 and 21) in order for such suppliers lawfully to carry on the business of supplying such services. Likewise, a legislative provision requiring suppliers of home decorating services to provide customers with written quotations before commencing work would be a 'regulatory requirement'. 5.20

It is strongly arguable that the definition of 'regulatory requirement' should be interpreted so as to catch a legislative requirement that would, if not satisfied, 'prevent a service provider from carrying on a business of providing particular services' where the prevention would be *de facto* but not *de jure*. Otherwise it would be possible for the non-discrimination rules to be avoided by sophisticated legislative drafting whereby the consequence of non-compliance with a local requirement was to make the activity of providing the services impracticable but not unlawful. 5.21

The definition of 'regulatory requirement' refers specifically to 'a legislative requirement', meaning that other requirements are outside the scope of the non-discrimination rules. The term 'legislative requirement' is defined in Part II of the Act as meaning 'a requirement imposed by, or by virtue of, legislation' (s. 23(1)). The term 'legislation' is, in turn, defined as meaning 'primary legislation, subordinate legislation and retained direct EU legislation' (s. 58). The words 'by virtue of' are important, since a requirement that has not been imposed by legislation, but rather by a person or body exercising a power arising from legislation, may nevertheless constitute a 'regulatory requirement'.[5] 5.22

The term 'regulatory requirement' does not include a requirement that applies, not only to service providers, 'but ... also ... to persons who do not provide services (for example, a requirement imposing duties on employers)' (s. 17(5)(d)). Accordingly, the non-discrimination rules are of no application to such a requirement. 5.23

Where legislation confers a function that may only be exercised in a way that would impose a 'regulatory requirement', that function is itself to be treated as though it were a 'regulatory requirement' for the purposes of the non-discrimination rules: section 23(2). It follows that the function may itself be found to be directly or indirectly discriminatory against certain service providers and thus rendered 'of no effect' in relation to those service providers. 5.24

[5] Where the requirement in question is imposed by a non-governmental entity, such as a professional association or industry self-regulation body, other than in exercise of powers or responsibilities granted to it by legislation, however, the requirement will fall outside the scope of the non-discrimination rules. A service provider wishing to challenge such a requirement will therefore have to look to other sources of law, such as the Provision of Services Regulations 2009, section 2 of the Competition Act 1998, or general principles of administrative law.

2. Limitation of the Rules to 'service providers'

5.25 Section 17(1) of the Act provides that Part II of the Act 'governs the regulation of service providers in the United Kingdom'. The non-discrimination rules are concerned specifically with requirements applying to 'service providers'. The definition of 'regulatory requirement' in section 17(4) refers to 'a legislative requirement that would if not satisfied ... prevent a *service provider* from carrying on a business of providing particular services' (emphasis supplied). Accordingly, a requirement can only be a 'regulatory requirement' for the purposes of the non-discrimination rules if and insofar as it applies to a 'service provider'.[6]

5.26 Further, the non-discrimination rules set out in sections 20(1) and 21(1) concern regulatory requirements that discriminate against 'a service provider'. Those rules provide that a discriminatory regulatory requirement will be of no effect in relation to that service provider. As noted above, section 17(5)(d) makes plain that a requirement that 'applies to a service provider, but which also applies to persons who do not provide services', is not a 'regulatory requirement'.

5.27 The concept of a 'service provider' is defined in section 17(9) so that it applies only to persons who have a permanent establishment in the United Kingdom through which they carry on relevant business.

Section 17(9) provides as follows:

'service provider' means a person—
(a) that provides, or intends to provide, services in the course of the person's business, and
(b) that has a permanent establishment in the United Kingdom through which that business is wholly or partly carried on;

'permanent establishment'—
(a) in relation to a company, is to be read in accordance with Chapter 2 of Part 24 of the Corporation Tax Act 2010, and
(b) in relation to any other person, is to be read in accordance with that Chapter but as if references in that Chapter to a company were references to that person.

Accordingly, a legislative requirement applying *only* to persons wishing to provide certain services *who do not have a permanent establishment in the United Kingdom* would not be a 'regulatory requirement'. Such a requirement would therefore fall outside the scope of the non-discrimination rules.

5.28 The definition of 'permanent establishment' in section 17(9) expressly borrows from UK corporation tax legislation but applies the tests for identifying a permanent establishment not only to companies but also to other persons *mutatis mutandis*.[7] This book cannot accommodate a detailed treatment of the concept of 'permanent establishment' in corporation tax law;

---

[6] See also section 17(1) which provides that Part II of the Act 'governs the regulation of service providers in the United Kingdom'.

[7] The concept of 'permanent establishment' in the Act is not identical to the concept of 'establishment' in the Provision of Services Regulations 2009. Under the Regulations, a business is 'established' in the United Kingdom if it is pursuing an economic activity for an indefinite period and through a stable infrastructure from where the business of providing services is actually carried out (reg. 4). The benefit of the mutual recognition provision made in the Regulations is restricted to individuals who are UK nationals and 'business undertakings', i.e. economic entities 'incorporated or formed under the law of any part of the United Kingdom' (reg. 5(4)–(5)).

however, the principal provision of Chapter 2 of Part 24 of the Corporation Tax Act 2010 is section 1141. In simplified terms, a company has a 'permanent establishment' in the United Kingdom if either: (a) 'it has a fixed place of business there through which the business of the company is wholly or partly carried on'; or (b) 'an agent acting on behalf of the company has and habitually exercises their authority to do business on behalf of the company'. The concept of a 'fixed place of business' is a broad one and can be satisfied by, for example, an office, branch, factory, workshop, or a building site or construction or installation project.[8]

The word 'service' is not itself defined in the Act; however, the term 'goods' is defined in section 16(2) of the Act as 'any tangible movable, or corporeal moveable, thing (including any packaging or label), but not water or gas that is not offered for sale in a limited volume or set quantity'. It seems reasonable to assume that the concept of a 'service' includes any supply in return for payment which is not a supply of 'goods' as defined. 5.29

3. Exclusion of Regulatory Requirements Existing Prior to Commencement

As explained above, the non-discrimination rules in sections 20(1) and 21(1) operate to disapply discriminatory 'regulatory requirements'. Section 17(5)(c) provides that a requirement is not a 'regulatory requirement' if it is: 5.30

a requirement that—
(i) is in force, or otherwise has effect, on the day before the day on which this section comes into force and has not been substantively changed after that day, or
(ii) comes into force, or otherwise takes effect, on or after the day on which this section comes into force if it re-enacts or replicates (without substantive change) a legislative requirement in force or having effect immediately before that day.

The practical effect of section 17(5)(c) is that the non-discrimination rules do not apply to any legislative requirement imposed in a part of the United Kingdom where that requirement was already in force, or otherwise had effect, prior to 31 December 2020. The non-discrimination rules therefore operate to limit the scope for individual parts of the United Kingdom to, *after that date*, create *new* obstacles to trade in services within the UK internal market. The rules are not intended to remove obstacles created by requirements already in force before that date. 5.31

It is apparent from section 17(5)(c) that the determination of whether a particular authorization requirement already existed prior to 31 December 2020 is one of substance rather than form. Accordingly, legislation re-enacting or replicating a pre-existing requirement *without substantively changing it* will not render that requirement subject to the non-discrimination rules. 5.32

[8] Corporation Tax Act 2010, section 1141(2).

D. DIRECTLY DISCRIMINATORY REGULATORY REQUIREMENTS

1. The Definition of 'directly discriminates'

5.33 Section 20(2) of the Act provides that:

> A regulatory requirement directly discriminates against a service provider if—
> (a) it has, or would have, the effect of treating the service provider less favourably than other service providers, and
> (b) the reason for that less favourable treatment is the service provider's relevant connection, or lack of relevant connection, to a part of the United Kingdom.

5.34 The assessment of whether a regulatory requirement directly discriminates against a service provider therefore involves:

a. identifying the service provider's 'relevant connections' to parts of the United Kingdom;

b. assessing whether the regulatory requirement has, or would have, the effect of treating the service provider 'less favourably' than some other service providers; and

if the requirement has, or would have, that effect,

c. whether this difference in treatment would be by reason of the service provider's relevant connection, or lack of relevant connection, to a part of the United Kingdom.

2. The Definition of 'relevant connection'

5.35 Sections 20 and 21 each define the term 'relevant connection' differently from one another. For the purposes of section 20 (direct discrimination), 'relevant connection' is defined in section 20(4) as follows:

> For the purposes of this section, a service provider has a relevant connection to a part of the United Kingdom if the service provider—
> (a) has a registered office, place of business or residence in that part,
> (b) provides services from that part, or
> (c) has members, partners, officers or staff with a registered office, place of business, or residence in that part.

5.36 A service provider may have multiple 'relevant connections' to one or more parts of the United Kingdom. For example, a service provider may have a 'relevant connection' to England because its registered office is located there, to Scotland and Wales because it has offices there, and also in all of England, Scotland, Wales, and Northern Ireland because its members, officers, and staff include individuals living in those parts of the United Kingdom.

5.37 A regulatory requirement may be directly discriminatory, and thus rendered 'of no effect' by section 20(1), even in the case of a service provider that has a 'relevant connection' to the part of the United Kingdom in which that requirement applies. By way of (hypothetical) examples:

a. A legislative requirement in England requiring cleaning services providers to display their office addresses on their vans if they have any UK offices located outside England would be directly discriminatory against a service provider that had a branch office in Wales. That would be so even if the service provider had its registered office in England and provided its cleaning services only in England. The service provider would be being treated less favourably because it has a 'relevant connection' with Wales.

b. A legislative requirement in Scotland requiring cleaning services providers employing only staff living in Scotland to refrain from providing such services on Sundays would be directly discriminatory against a service provider that employed only Scottish residents. That is because the service provider would be being treated less favourably because it did *not* have a particular 'relevant connection' to another part of the United Kingdom (namely, not having staff members who live outside Scotland). This result would be obtained even if the service provider had no 'relevant connection' to any part of the United Kingdom other than Scotland. Thus, as this example illustrates, section 20(1) can avail even a service provider that has no relevant connection to a part of the United Kingdom other than the part in which the regulatory requirement applies.

3. The Meaning of 'less favourable treatment'

The terms 'less favourably' and 'less favourable treatment', used in section 20(2), are not defined in the Act. **5.38**

It is implicit in those terms, however, that the making of any assessment as to whether a regulatory requirement has, or would have, the effect of treating the service provider 'less favourably than other service providers' necessarily requires a comparison. The comparison will be between the treatment of the first service provider and the treatment of actual or hypothetical 'other service providers' (i.e. comparators). **5.39**

Further, if it is to be shown that *the reason for* the less favourable treatment is the first service provider having, or not having, a particular 'relevant connection' to a part of the United Kingdom, the comparators need to be *relevantly* comparable. In other words, the comparators need to have materially similar circumstances to those of the first service provider, save for either having, or not having, a particular 'relevant connection' to a part of the United Kingdom. **5.40**

The need for, and use of, such comparators is a familiar approach in the context of UK and EU equality legislation. For the purposes of the prohibitions of direct discrimination in the Equality Act 2010, 'less favourable treatment' is a broad concept: any disadvantage will constitute 'less favourable treatment'; there is no need for the person complaining of such treatment to have suffered, or be liable to suffer, a tangible or material loss.[9] **5.41**

---

[9] See Robinson and others (eds), *Blackstone's Guide to The Equality Act 2010* (4th edn, Oxford University Press 2021), paragraphs 3.04–3.08. For the purposes of prohibitions of direct discrimination in equality legislation, depriving or restricting a person's choices, whilst actual or hypothetical relevant comparators enjoy greater choice, can itself constitute 'less favourable treatment' even if this gives rise to no tangible or material loss: *Bahl v The Law Society* [2004] IRLR 799. The Equality Act specifies, in section 13(5), that segregation of people from a racial group from other persons constitutes 'less favourable treatment' regardless of whether the segregation is shown to lead to that group suffering any specific disadvantage.

4. Regulatory Requirements for Responding to a Public Health Emergency

5.42 Section 20 identifies regulatory requirements as being directly discriminatory, and renders such requirements 'of no effect', without any need to consider whether the requirement is objectively justified. The general rule, therefore, is that regulatory requirements that treat a service provider less favourably by reason of its either having, or not having, a 'relevant connection' to a part of the United Kingdom cannot be objectively justified. Section 20(3) provides, however, what might be seen as an exception to that general position, albeit a narrow one:

> A regulatory requirement is not to be taken to directly discriminate against a service provider to the extent the requirement can reasonably be justified as a response to a public health emergency.

5.43 The expression 'public health emergency' is defined in section 23(1) as meaning 'an event or a situation that is reasonably considered to pose an extraordinary threat to human health'. Accordingly, the expression is limited to threats to human health. Thus, directly discriminatory regulatory requirements are liable to be rendered 'of no effect' by section 20(1) even where those requirements might reasonably be regarded as necessary and proportionate in response to an emergency relating to animal or plant health.

5.44 The phrase 'to the extent the requirement can reasonably be justified' is interesting. It implicitly makes clear that question as to whether, and to what extent, the requirement can be justified by a public health emergency will be subject to scrutiny by the courts. The courts would focus on, in particular, whether the treatment of service providers less favourably by reason of their having, or not having, a particular 'relevant connection' to a part of the United Kingdom could be justified. The question for the courts would not, however, be simply whether the requirement was, in the court's own view, justified, but rather whether it could 'reasonably be justified'. This suggests that the standard of scrutiny of the justification put forwards by the government of the relevant part of the United Kingdom could be less intense than the judicial scrutiny that EU law requires EU Member States' domestic courts to apply when assessing whether an interference with 'EU free movement rights' is necessary and proportionate.[10]

E. INDIRECTLY DISCRIMINATORY REGULATORY REQUIREMENTS

1. The Definition of 'indirectly discriminates'

5.45 Section 21(2) of the Act provides that:

> A regulatory requirement indirectly discriminates against an incoming service provider if—
> (a) it does not directly discriminate against the incoming service provider (within the meaning of section 20),
> (b) it puts the incoming service provider at a relevant disadvantage,
> (c) it has an adverse market effect, and

[10] As to the standard of scrutiny applied by the UK courts under EU law prior to Brexit, see *R (Lumsdon) v Legal Services Board* [2015] UKSC 41.

(d) it cannot reasonably be considered a necessary means of achieving a legitimate aim.

Pursuant to section 21(1), a regulatory requirement that indirectly discriminates against an incoming service provider is 'of no effect in relation to that incoming service provider'. Accordingly, an indirectly discriminatory requirement is rendered 'of no effect' only in relation to incoming service provider that would otherwise be placed at a 'relevant disadvantage'. The assessment of whether a regulatory requirement is 'of no effect' in relation to a service provider, on account of the requirement being indirectly discriminatory, therefore involves: 5.46

a. determining whether that service provider is an 'incoming service provider';
b. assessing whether the requirement puts that service provider at a 'relevant disadvantage';
c. assessing whether the regulatory requirement has an 'adverse market effect'; and
d. assessing whether the regulatory requirement can 'reasonably be considered a necessary means of achieving a legitimate aim'.

Each of those aspects is considered in turn below. 5.47

2. The Definitions of 'incoming service provider' and 'relevant connection'

The term 'incoming service provider' is defined in section 21(6)(a): 5.48

an 'incoming service provider' is a service provider that—
(i) provides the services in the part of the United Kingdom in which the regulatory requirement applies, but
(ii) does not have a relevant connection to that part.

Accordingly, the benefit of section 21 is restricted to service providers that do not have a 'relevant connection' to the part of the United Kingdom in which the regulatory requirement applies. This is an important distinction between section 21 (indirect discrimination) and section 20 (direct discrimination). Section 20 is capable of assisting a service provider even if that provider's 'relevant connections' are all to the same part of the United Kingdom as the part in which the regulatory requirement in question applies (see example b. in paragraph 5.37 above). 5.49

As already noted above, sections 20 and 21 each define the term 'relevant connection' differently from one another. For the purposes of section 21 (indirect discrimination), 'relevant connection' is defined in section 21(6)(c) as follows: 5.50

a service provider has a 'relevant connection' to a part of the United Kingdom if the service provider—
(i) has a registered office, place of business or residence in that part, or
(ii) provides the services from that part.

This definition of 'relevant connection' is narrower than the definition of that term in section 20 (direct discrimination). In particular, the definition of that term for the purposes of section 21 is narrower in the following two ways: 5.51

a. First, a 'relevant connection' to a part of the United Kingdom will arise on the basis that the service provider is providing services from that part, only if that service provider is providing from that part not merely 'services' but rather '*the* services' (emphasis added).

In other words, it is necessary that the service provider is providing *the particular services* in relation to which it is being placed at a disadvantage *from a part of the United Kingdom other than the part in which the regulatory requirement applies.*[11]

b. Secondly, a 'relevant connection' to a part of the United Kingdom cannot arise based on the location of a registered office, place of business, or residence of the service provider's members, partners, officers, or staff.

5.52 A single service provider may have 'relevant connections' to more than one part of the United Kingdom. For example, a service provider may have its registered office in England, and places of business in Scotland and Northern Ireland. As already noted above, if any of the parts of the United Kingdom to which the service provider has a 'relevant connection' is the part in which the regulatory requirement applies, section 21 cannot assist that service provider. That is because such a service provider will not be an 'incoming service provider'. The policy behind this rule appears to be to limit section 21 to services being supplied into a part of the United Kingdom from one or more other parts of the United Kingdom. A service provider that has an established a place of business in a part of the United Kingdom is required to comply with the regulatory requirements applicable in that part and cannot rely on section 21 so as to avoid those requirements.[12]

3. The Definitions of 'relevant disadvantage' and 'local service provider'

5.53 Pursuant to section 21(2), a regulatory requirement indirectly discriminates against an incoming service provider only if it 'puts the incoming service provider at a relevant disadvantage'. The term 'relevant disadvantage' is then defined in sub-sections (3) and (4):

(3) A regulatory requirement puts an incoming service provider at a relevant disadvantage if—
 (a) it puts the incoming service provider at a disadvantage in relation to the provision of services in the part of the United Kingdom in which the requirement applies, and

---

[11] The drafting of section 21 is ambiguous as to whether the regulatory requirement will be indirectly discriminatory, and therefore 'of no effect', *only if and insofar as the services directly affected by the regulatory requirement are themselves actually being provided from the other part of the United Kingdom.* The alternative view is that it suffices that the service provider is providing services *of the same type* from the other part of the United Kingdom. Of those two views, the first seems most likely to be correct. In that regard, it seems appropriate to bear in mind that this basis for identifying a 'relevant connection' will need to be relied on only where the service provider does not anyway have a 'relevant connection' to that other part of the United Kingdom by reason of having a registered office, place of business, or residence in that part. This further basis could thus be seen as a 'fall-back' that assists service providers that do not have a registered office or any places of business in the United Kingdom, but nevertheless qualify for protection under section 21, in the interests of the UK internal market, insofar as they are providing their services affected by the requirement from another part of the United Kingdom. Reliance on this basis for having the status of an 'incoming service provider' is likely to be rare, given that the term 'service provider' is anyway limited to persons having a 'permanent establishment' in the United Kingdom: see paragraphs 5.27–5.28 above.

[12] This is a point that service providers are likely to wish to consider before establishing branch offices or other fixed facilities. A service provider that is keen to avoid the application to its services of regulatory requirements applicable in a particular part of the United Kingdom which it considers have discriminatory effects, may wish to avoid establishing a place of business in that part.

(b) it does not put, or would not put, each local service provider at that disadvantage in relation to the provision of those services in that part (at all or to the same extent).

(4) A regulatory requirement puts a service provider at a disadvantage in relation to the provision of services in a part of the United Kingdom if it makes it in any way more difficult, or less attractive, for the service provider to provide the services in that part.

It follows from those sub-sections that: 5.54

a. A 'disadvantage' does not need to involve causing the incoming service provider to suffer any loss in trade or to incur additional costs. For example, a service provider would be being 'disadvantaged' if it were restricted from advertising its services in a particular way or had to comply with certain inconvenient bureaucratic formalities. That is because a regulatory requirement imposing such a restriction or formalities would make it more difficult, or less attractive, to provide services in the part of the United Kingdom where the regulatory requirement applies. This suffices to establish that the regulatory requirement puts a service provider at a 'disadvantage': the concept of a 'disadvantage' does not require any comparison between the effect on incoming service providers vis-à-vis local service providers.

b. However, a 'disadvantage' will put an incoming service provider to a '*relevant* disadvantage' (emphasis added) only if the disadvantage: (i) is in relation to the provision of services in the part of the United Kingdom in which the requirement applies; and (ii) does not affect local service providers at all or to the same extent. In other words, a determination as to whether a regulatory requirement gives rise to a 'relevant disadvantage' requires a comparison to be made between, on the one hand, the disadvantage to the incoming service provider, and on the other hand, the disadvantage (if any) to 'local service providers', in relation to the provision of services in that part. Since section 21(3)(b) refers to '*each* local service provider' (emphasis added), the fact that the disadvantage affects some, but not all, local service providers to a similar extent to the incoming service provider will not suffice to prevent a conclusion that the incoming service provider is being put to a 'relevant disadvantage'.

The term 'local service provider' is defined in section 21(6)(b): 5.55

'local service provider' is a service provider that—

(i) provides the services in the part of the United Kingdom in which the regulatory requirement applies,

(ii) has a relevant connection to that part, and

(iii) does not have a relevant connection to another part of the United Kingdom.

It will, of course, often be the case that an indirectly discriminatory regulatory requirement disadvantages not only incoming service providers, but also some service providers that have certain 'relevant connections' both to the part of the United Kingdom in which the regulatory requirement applies and to one or more other parts of the United Kingdom. Disadvantages to such service providers are, however, irrelevant for the purposes of section 21. Such service providers are not 'incoming service providers' and therefore cannot benefit from section 21(1); but neither are they 'local service providers', and so they are excluded from being relevant comparators for the purpose of assessing whether the regulatory requirement puts an incoming service provider at a 'relevant disadvantage'. 5.56

4. The Definition of 'adverse market effect'

5.57 Pursuant to section 21(2), a regulatory requirement indirectly discriminates against an incoming service provider only if it 'has an adverse market effect'. The term 'adverse market effect' is defined in sub-section (5) as follows:

A regulatory requirement has an adverse market effect if, by putting an incoming service provider (or incoming service providers) at a relevant disadvantage in relation to the provision of services, it has a significant adverse effect on competition in the market for those services in the United Kingdom.

5.58 This definition of 'adverse market effect' is largely circular in that the concept of an 'adverse effect' is not itself defined.[13] Drawing on analogies with UK and EU competition law, however, it seems reasonable to suppose that the concept of 'adverse effect on competition' includes any potential harm to, or reduction or weakening of, competition in an economic market[14] (as compared with the counterfactual situation in which incoming service providers were not being placed at a relevant disadvantage by the regulatory requirement), especially if this could potentially give rise to detriment to consumers.

5.59 An adverse effect will not suffice to constitute an 'adverse market effect' for the purposes of section 21(2) unless it is 'significant'. The word 'significant' is not defined in the Act, but again an analogy might reasonably be drawn with competition law, which includes concepts of an 'appreciable' effect on competition.[15]

5. The Definition of 'legitimate aim'

5.60 Section 21(7) provides an exhaustive list of potential 'legitimate aims':[16]

In this section 'legitimate aim' means one, or a combination of any, of the following aims—
(a) the protection of the life or health of humans, animals or plants;
(b) the protection of public safety or security;
(c) the efficient administration of justice.

---

[13] Section 21 of the Act does not replicate section 8(5) which provides, in relation to the identification of a requirement that indirectly discriminates against incoming goods, that the assessment of whether a requirement has an 'adverse market effect' is 'to be determined with regard both to the content of the requirement and to the way in which it operates, or is administered, in practice (as a whole or in particular classes of case)'. Notwithstanding that section 21 does not replicate section 8(5), it seems appropriate that any assessment of whether a regulatory requirement affecting the provision of services 'has a significant adverse effect on competition' take into account not only the content of the requirement, but also the way it operates and is administered in practice.

[14] For the purposes of competition law, an economic market is defined by reference to a consideration of both 'supply-side substitutability' and 'demand-side substitutability'. The parameters of the economic market are defined in terms both of the products (i.e. which products are competing with each other in the same market) and geography (i.e. what is the geographical area within which competition is taking place). See further D. Bailey and L. E. John (eds), *Bellamy & Child European Union Law of Competition* (8th edn, Oxford University Press 2019), chapter 4 ('Market Definition').

[15] See e.g. European Commission, 'Commission Notice on agreements of minor importance which do not appreciably restrict competition under Article 101(1) of the Treaty on the Functioning of the European Union (De Minimis Notice)' (August 2014), EU Official Journal 2014 C291/1.

[16] These 'legitimate aims' echo, to a degree, the bases on which restrictions on the intra-EU free movement of goods and/or services may be imposed by an EU Member State compatibly with EU law.

Section 21(8) provides that the Secretary of State may by regulations amend sub-section (7) so as to 'add, vary or remove a legitimate aim'. The making of regulations under sub-section (8) is subject to the affirmative resolution procedure (s. 21(9)).[17] The Secretary of State must seek the consent of each of the devolved administrations before exercising the power to make such regulations (s. 21(10)), but the exercise of the power is not conditional on such consent being given (s. 21(11)–(12)). 5.61

In order for a regulatory requirement to avoid being indirectly discriminatory, by reason of its being in pursuance of a legitimate aim, the requirement must be one that can 'reasonably be considered a necessary means of achieving' such aim (s. 21(2)(d)). Sub-section (13) provides that a determination as to whether a regulatory requirement meets that condition is to be made: 5.62

> ... with regard, in particular, to—
> (a) the effects of the requirement in all the circumstances, and
> (b) the availability of alternative means of achieving the aim in question.

F. EXCLUSIONS FROM THE NON-DISCRIMINATION RULES

1. Out of Scope

This chapter has already discussed various situations that are outside the scope of the non-discrimination rules. These are not exclusions as such, but rather are situations that simply do not engage the non-discrimination rules in the first place. It is nonetheless helpful to have them in mind again here. 5.63

First, the non-discrimination rules can never be relied on by persons who do not have a permanent establishment in the United Kingdom, since such persons are not 'service providers': see paragraphs 5.25–5.28 above. 5.64

Secondly, the non-discrimination rules are of no application to the provision of services *otherwise than in the course of a business*. The definition of 'regulatory requirement' in section 17(4) is confined to requirements that would, if not satisfied, 'prevent a service provider from carrying on a business of providing particular services'. Further, the definition of 'service provider' in section 17(9) is limited to a person 'that provides, or intends to provide, services in the course of the person's business'. 5.65

Thirdly, the non-discrimination rules do not apply to requirements that were already in force, or otherwise had effect, before 31 December 2020: see paragraphs 5.31 and 5.32 above. 5.66

Fourthly, requirements that apply, not only to service providers, but also to persons who do not provide services (e.g. a requirement imposing duties on employers), fall outside the scope of the non-discrimination rules: see paragraph 5.23 above. 5.67

Fifthly, the non-discrimination rules do not apply to a requirement to notify, or register with, a regulator (s. 17(5)(e)), or to provide evidence of being authorized in another part of the United Kingdom (s. 17(5)(f)). It appears that such requirements were regarded by Parliament as unlikely to give rise to material obstruction to the UK internal market. 5.68

[17] The affirmative procedure is a type of parliamentary procedure that applies to statutory instruments ('SIs'). Its name describes the form of scrutiny that the SI receives from Parliament. An SI laid under the affirmative procedure must be actively approved by both Houses of Parliament.

5.69 Sixthly, the non-discrimination rules do not apply to requirements that are 'relevant requirements as defined for the purposes of the mutual recognition principle for goods' in section 3 of the Act (s. 17(5)(a)) or 'provision of the sought described in section 24(1) or 28(1) (professional qualifications and regulation) to the extent it has the effect described there' (s. 17(5)(b)). This ensures that the non-discrimination rules, which relate to regulatory requirements in relation to the provision of services, does not overlap with the provisions elsewhere in the Act relating to mutual recognition for goods and for professional qualifications.

2. Exclusion of Certain Services (Part 2 of Schedule 2)

5.70 Section 18(1) of the Act gives effect to Schedule 2. Part 2 of Schedule 2 sets out a list of services to which sections 20 and 21 (the non-discrimination rules) do not apply. Part 2 is in the format of a table in which the excluded services are listed in the left-hand column, whilst the right-hand column sets out examples of those services.

5.71 The list of excluded services in Part 2 of Schedule 2[18] includes the following:

a. Audiovisual services;
b. Debt collection services;
c. Electronic communication services and networks, and associated facilities and services;
d. Financial services;
e. Gambling services;
f. Healthcare services;
g. Notarial services;
h. Postal services;
i. Private security services;
j. Services connected with the supply of natural gas through pipelines or production or storage of natural gas;
k. Services connected with the supply or production of electricity;
l. Services of a statutory auditor within the meaning of Part 42 of the Companies Act 2006;
m. Services of temporary work agencies;
n. Services provided by a person exercising functions of a public nature or by a person acting on behalf of such a person in connection with the exercise of functions of a public nature;
o. Social services relating to social housing, childcare, adult social care, and support of families and persons permanently or temporarily in need;
p. Transport services;
q. Waste services; and
r. Water supply and sewerage services.

[18] This list of excluded services largely replicates, albeit it is not identical to, the services excluded from the scope of the Provision of Services Regulations 2009. The 2009 Regulations were, when originally made, made for the purpose of implementing in the United Kingdom the EU Services Directive (Directive 2006/123/EC).

3. Exclusion of Certain Authorization Requirements (Part 4 of Schedule 2)

Part 4 of Schedule 2 lists authorization requirements to which the non-discrimination rules do not apply. At present only one category of authorization requirement is listed: 'Any regulatory requirement in connection with taxation'. 5.72

This exclusion is not worded as clearly as it might have been, and there is room for arguments as to the exclusion's true scope in practice. The essential reason for the exclusion seems likely to have been a desire to reflect the Provision of Services Regulations 2009 in excluding 'the field of taxation' from its scope of application.[19] A desire by the UK government, when drafting the Act, to avoid impeding tax collection functions in any part of the United Kingdom is understandable, given that the devolved legislatures have taxation powers and may need to impose certain regulatory requirements in connection with tax collection. 5.73

It remains to be seen whether any part of the United Kingdom will seek to take mischievous advantage of this exclusion to impose regulatory requirements that are 'in connection with taxation' but go beyond what is truly necessary for taxation purposes. If they do so, it will be interesting to see how the courts respond. 5.74

4. Future Regulations Amending the Lists of Exclusions

Pursuant to section 18(2), the Secretary of State has power to amend Schedule 2 by regulations so as to alter or add to the exclusions.[20] 5.75

Section 18(3) provides an example of a reason for which the power may be exercised, namely to give effect to an agreement that forms part of a common framework agreement;[21] but the Secretary of State may also exercise the power for other reasons. 5.76

There is a requirement on the Secretary of State to seek the consent of the devolved administrations before exercising the power: section 18(8). If consent is not given by any of the devolved administrations within a month, the Secretary of State may still exercise the 5.77

[19] Regulation 5(2) of the Regulations provides: 'Nothing in these Regulations applies in respect of the field of taxation'. That exclusion from scope reflects Article 2(3) of the EU Services Directive (Directive 2006/123/EC), which the 2009 Regulations were originally made in order to implement in the United Kingdom. Recital 29 to the Directive explained that the exclusion was appropriate because 'the Treaty provides specific legal bases for taxation matters and given the Community instruments already adopted in that field, it is necessary to exclude the field of taxation from the scope of this Directive'. It is questionable whether the same, or a similar, reason exists to justify the exclusion of '[a]ny regulatory requirement in connection with taxation' from the scope of the mutual recognition rule in the Act.

[20] The making of regulations under section 18 is subject to the affirmative resolution procedure (s. 18(7)). The affirmative procedure is a type of parliamentary procedure that applies to statutory instruments ('SIs'). Its name describes the form of scrutiny that the SI receives from Parliament. An SI laid under the affirmative procedure must be actively approved by both Houses of Parliament.

[21] A common framework agreement is a consensus between a Minister of the Crown and one or more devolved administrations as to how devolved or transferred matters previously governed by EU law are to be regulated after IP completion day (s. 18(4)). IP completion day is defined as 11 p.m. on 31 December 2020: see Schedule 1 to the Interpretation Act 1978 by reference to section 39 of the European Union (Withdrawal Agreement) Act 2020). When determining whether a matter is a devolved or transferred matter for the purposes of section 10(4), section 30A of the Scotland Act 1998, section 109A of the Government of Wales Act 2006, and section 6A of the Northern Ireland Act 1998 are to be ignored (s. 18(6)). Those sections each relate to restrictions on legislative competence relating to retained EU law as defined by the European Union (Withdrawal) Act 2018. See, further, the Joint Ministerial Committee (EU Negotiations) communiqué (16 October 2017).

power: section 18(9). Before doing so, however, the Secretary of State must publish an explanation for proceeding in the absence of consent: section 18(10).

5.78 At the time of writing of this chapter (July 2021) it appears that the UK government is already actively considering potential amendments to Schedule 2, even though the Act has been in force for only a short time. In February 2021 the UK government published a consultation paper seeking views on whether any exclusions should be removed from, or added to, Schedule 2.[22] The consultation paper recognized that the existing exclusions are largely a replication of the exclusions in the Provision of Services Regulations 2009, which in turn set out the exclusions from the scope of application of the EU Services Directive. Those exclusions were included in the Act in circumstances where it was being drafted under considerable time pressure. It is reasonable to question whether those same exclusions are appropriate in legislation directed at protecting an internal market in services within the United Kingdom. Any proposals to amend Schedule 2 are, however, likely to be politically controversial, given their practical impacts on the powers of the devolved legislatures to set and enforce their own regulatory rules and standards.

G. THE EFFECT OF THE NON-DISCRIMINATION RULES AND HOW THEY ARE ENFORCED

5.79 The non-discrimination rules do not place a limitation on the legislative competence of any part of the United Kingdom (albeit that the devolved legislatures may not repeal the Act). Rather, the non-discrimination rules operate by simply rendering regulatory requirements 'of no effect' in relation to the service providers against which those requirements would be directly or indirectly discriminatory. Thus, a part of the United Kingdom can legislate for whatever regulatory requirements it wishes, without making any express provision for avoiding direct or indirect discrimination against service providers having a 'relevant connection' to another part of the United Kingdom. If and to the extent that the new regulatory requirements are directly or indirectly discriminatory (as defined in the non-discrimination rules) against certain service providers, those requirements will simply be 'of no effect' in the cases of those service providers.

5.80 There are two ways in which a dispute may arise in court to enforce the non-discrimination rules.

5.81 The first is where a business or individual takes the initiative to bring the matter before a court. Such a person may, for example, seek a declaration that a particular requirement imposed by legislation in a part of the United Kingdom is directly or indirectly discriminatory against certain service providers and therefore does not apply to those service providers.

5.82 The second way a dispute may come before a court is where a regulator pursues a criminal prosecution or other enforcement action against a service provider for infringing a regulatory requirement applicable in a part of the United Kingdom. The service provider against which such enforcement action is taken may seek to rely on the non-discrimination rules as a shield, contending that the local requirement is, by operation of those rules, of no effect in its case.

[22] Department for Business, Energy & Industrial Strategy, Consultation paper, 'UK internal market: the continuity of exclusions from the principles of mutual recognition and non-discrimination for services', 25 February 2021. The consultation period, as extended, closed on 7 May 2021.

6
PROFESSIONAL QUALIFICATIONS AND REGULATION

A. INTRODUCTION

This chapter examines the provisions in Part 3 of the Act, which is entitled 'UK Market Access: Professional Qualifications and Regulations'. Part 3 contains sections 24–29 of the Act. The provisions in respect of professional qualifications and professional regulation are a very obvious application of the principles of mutual recognition and non-discrimination embodied within the Act.[1] The Explanatory Notes to the Act state that the main objective of this part of the Act is to avoid new barriers to the movement of professionals within the UK internal market, by making provision for an overarching system of mutual recognition of professional qualifications that applies across the United Kingdom.[2] 6.01

The objectives of Part 3 of the Act were set out in the UK Internal Market White Paper which observed that even in areas where specific EU powers were not being repatriated, 'the absence of EU rules could make it easier for new barriers to arise ... For example, if different qualifications or other regulations on professionals working in [a certain field] emerged in England and Wales, this could deter workers from qualifying for the smaller Welsh market, 6.02

[1] However, the Act does not address employment law in the United Kingdom and the UK internal market beyond the rights and entitlements that Part 3 confers on professionals who are 'qualified UK residents' for the purposes of section 24 and who are 'externally qualified UK practitioners' for the purposes of section 28.

[2] Explanatory Notes to the United Kingdom Internal Market Act 2020, paragraph 48 (hereafter, 'Explanatory Notes').

Blackstone's Guide to the UK Internal Market Act 2020. Alan Bates, Brendan McGurk, George Peretz QC, and Jack Williams, Oxford University Press. © Alan Bates, Brendan McGurk, George Peretz QC, and Jack Williams 2021.
DOI: 10.1093/oso/9780192856203.003.0006

limiting growth and investment there.'[3] It further observed that a shared UK marketplace 'helps professionals move across the UK with ease so that they can provide services closer to their customers and develop business in those parts of the UK that offer the best conditions'.[4]

6.03 In its policy statement on the recognition of professional qualifications ('the Policy Statement'), the government recognized that there is 'currently no overarching system that allows for professionals who are qualified to practise in one part of the UK to move and practise in another if the qualification requirements to do so are different. Without putting in place a way for professionals to have their qualifications recognised in different parts of the UK, barriers may emerge within the UK internal market. This could prevent UK qualification holders from being able to work in all parts of the UK and restrict their economic competitiveness or life choices.'[5]

6.04 Specifically in relation to professional qualifications, the White Paper explained that 'mutual recognition of professional qualifications means that compliance with regulation required to access a profession in one territory can be used to demonstrate compliance towards the access of that profession in another territory. Where access requirements in the other territory differ, a process will be implemented to enable professionals to demonstrate compliance.'[6]

6.05 There are two systems by which professional qualifications obtained in one part of the United Kingdom may be recognized in another part of the United Kingdom: (i) the automatic system and (ii) the alternative system. The Policy Statement explains those two systems as follows:

> The automatic system will mean that if you have the qualifications or experience required to practise a profession in one part of the UK, or specific qualifications are not required to practise the profession in a part of the UK, you will be treated as meeting the qualification requirements in all other parts of the UK. The automatic recognition system will apply by default unless a decision is made by the relevant authority to replace it with the alternative system.
>
> If an alternative system is put in place, it must meet with certain principles . . . This will ensure that the alternative recognition system is suitable and ensures that professionals and their qualifications are treated fairly when applying for recognition.
>
> Combined, these recognition systems will ensure that professionals are able to be recognised and practise across the whole UK with relative ease, whilst protecting devolved administrations ability to set and maintain their own standards.

B. ACCESS

1. The Right of Access: Automatic Recognition

6.06 Section 24 of the Act is entitled 'Access to professions on grounds of qualifications or experience' and provides:

[3] UK Internal Market White Paper, paragraph 18 (hereafter, the 'White Paper').

[4] ibid, paragraph 66.

[5] Policy Paper: Recognition of professional qualifications' 17 November 2020, accessed on 23 May 2021 https://www.gov.uk/government/publications/uk-internal-market-bill-2020-policy-statements/recognition-of-professional-qualifications#:~:text=UK's%20internal%20market.-,What%20are%20we%20introducing%3F,of%20the%20UK%20when%20necessary.

[6] ibid, paragraph 133(b).

(1) Subsection (2) applies in relation to provision applying in a part of the United Kingdom ('the relevant part') that limits the ability to practise a profession in that part to individuals who have certain qualifications[7] or experience.[8]
(2) A qualified UK resident[9] (see section 25) is to be treated for the purposes of the provision (and any related provision) as if the qualified UK resident had the qualifications or experience required to be able to practise the profession.[10]
(3) Provision does not fall within subsection (1) by making the ability of an individual to continue to practise a particular profession, having started to do so on a fully qualified basis, subject to continuing requirements as to training, learning or other forms of experience.
(4) Subsections (1) and (2) are subject to sections 26 and 27.'

Section 24 thus embodies the principle of mutual recognition in the context of professional services on the basis that a 'qualified UK resident', as defined, will have a right of access to, and is thus enabled to practise within, the relevant part of the United Kingdom where the relevant provision applies. It is a form of 'home state authorisation', whereby a qualified UK resident permitted to practise a profession in one part of the United Kingdom will be permitted to practice in all other parts of the United Kingdom. Section 24 in effect contains a presumption of automatic recognition for anyone who is legally able to practise their profession in one part of the United Kingdom who seeks to work in that profession in another part of the United Kingdom. **6.07**

An important exception to the right to automatic recognition in section 24(2) is contained in sections 27(1)–(2) which provide: **6.08**

(1) Section 24(2) does not apply to existing provision (subject to subsection (3)).
(2) In subsection (1) '*existing provision*' means—
    (a) provision that is in force on the date that this Act is passed, or

---

[7] Section 29(8) defines 'qualification' to mean: 'any record, issued by a body whose ordinary activities include the issuing of such records, of having attained a particular standard following a course of study or training'.

[8] Section 29(2) of the Act provides: 'Provision that limits the ability referred to in subsection (1)(a) to individuals with certain qualifications or experience falls within section 24(1) only if the activities affected by the provision are, in a significant number of cases, essential to the practice of the profession in question'. Therefore, the provision that limits the ability to undertake activities that comprise the practice of a profession must be one that applies to activities that are central to the pursuit of the professional activity. Section 29(2) will therefore not catch a provision that regulates a peripheral or ancillary aspect of the practice of the profession where it does not otherwise limit the ability to pursue activities that are central to the profession.

[9] Section 29(8) defines a 'UK resident' to mean 'an individual who is lawfully resident in the United Kingdom; and for this purpose an individual is not lawfully resident in the United Kingdom if the individual requires leave to enter or remain in the United Kingdom but does not have it'.

[10] Section 24(2) is a deeming provision. The classic approach to the treatment of statutory deeming provisions was set out in *East End Dwellings Co. Ltd. v Finsbury BC* [1952] AC 109. Lord Asquith indicated that the approach to be adopted to the application of a statutory provision was as follows: 'If you are bidden to treat an imaginary state of affairs as real, you must surely, unless prohibited from doing so, also imagine as real the consequences and incidents which, if the putative state of affairs had in fact existed, must inevitably have flowed from or accompanied it ... The statute says that you must imagine a certain state of affairs; it does not say that having done so, you must cause or permit your imagination to boggle when it comes to the inevitable corollaries of that state of affairs.' That approach was reiterated by Peter Gibson LJ in the Court of Appeal in *Marshall v Kerr* [1993] STC 360: 'I further bear in mind that because one must treat as real that which is only deemed to be so, one must treat as real the consequences and incidents inevitably flowing from or accompanying that deemed state of affairs, unless prohibited from doing so.'

(b) provision that comes into force after that date so far as it is, in substance, a re-enactment or replication of provision within paragraph (a).

6.09 Thus existing provisions for the recognition of professional qualifications as between different parts of the United Kingdom fall outside the scope of the right of automatic recognition under section 24(2) of the Act. However, section 27(3) provides that section 27(1) will not apply (such that the right in section 24(2) accordingly will apply) if, after the date on which the Act is passed, 'provision comes into force in a part of the United Kingdom other than the relevant part that changes the circumstances in which individuals are qualified in relation to the profession concerned'.[11] Section 27(3) thus operates on the presumption that any new regulation governing entry into a profession in one part of the United Kingdom will be treated as imposing sufficient requirements on professionals in that part of the United Kingdom such that the professional qualification thereby conferred should be automatically recognized in every other part of the United Kingdom.

6.10 It follows that the right of automatic recognition in section 24(2) applies to the regulation of a new profession or changes to existing systems of professional regulation after the commencement of the Act. However, as will be seen below, insofar as professions that are governed by existing provisions which operate as gateways to the practice of a profession in a part of the United Kingdom will be subject to alternative systems of recognition, section 26 sets out principles by which those systems of alternative recognition must operate.

2. What Professions and Professional Activities Will Fall Within the Scope of Section 24?

6.11 Section 25 of the Act provides a definition of a 'qualified UK resident'. Sections 25(1)–(2) provide:

(1) A UK resident is '*qualified*' in relation to a profession for the purposes of section 24(2) if, in any part of the United Kingdom other than the relevant part ('the other part'), the resident is qualified (within the meaning of subsections (3) to (5)) to undertake the full range of corresponding activity.

(2) In this section—

(a) '*corresponding activity*' means activity that is the same as, or substantially corresponds to, relevant professional activity;

(b) '*the full range*' of corresponding activity is a range of corresponding activity that substantially corresponds to the full range of relevant professional activity;

(c) '*relevant professional activity*' means activity that, in the relevant part, ordinarily comprises the practice of the profession in question.

6.12 The further conditions for a UK resident to be 'qualified' are contained in sections 25(3)–(5) and provide as follows:

(3) To the extent that—

(a) corresponding activity is ordinarily undertaken by practitioners of a particular profession in the other part, and

[11] Section 27(4) provides that 'In subsection (3)–(a) "*relevant part*" is to be read in accordance with section 24(1); (b) "*qualified*" is to be read in accordance with section 25'.

(b) provision applying in the other part limits the ability to practise that profession to individuals who have certain qualifications or experience, a UK resident is qualified to undertake the corresponding activity if the resident has the qualifications or experience required to be able to practise the profession in the other part.[12]

(4) To the extent that—
(a) the position is not as described in subsection (3)(a) and (b), and
(b) provision applying in the other part limits the ability to undertake corresponding activity to individuals who have certain qualifications or experience, a UK resident is qualified to undertake the corresponding activity if the resident has the qualifications or experience required to do so in the other part.

(5) To the extent that the position is not as described in subsection (3)(a) and (b) or (4)(b), any UK resident is qualified to undertake corresponding activity in the other part.

By way of clarification, section 25(7) provides that, for the purposes of sub-sections (3) and (4): **6.13**

(a) qualifications may be relied on only if they were obtained in the United Kingdom, and
(b) experience may be relied on only if it was obtained mainly in the United Kingdom.

It follows that professionals who hold non-UK qualifications will not be able to benefit from the recognition systems, even if their qualification has been recognized by a UK body. The Act makes no provision for the recognition of foreign-qualified professionals. **6.14**

A qualification is 'obtained' in the place where the issuing body is based. This is where the body's registered office is located or, if the body does not have a registered office, where its head office or principal place of operation is located.[13] **6.15**

While section 24 refers to provisions which limit 'the ability to practise a profession', it is clear that the Act is not adopting a narrow or traditional meaning of what constitutes professional activity.[14] That is clear from section 25 where the touchstone is the relevant activity—and corresponding activity—to which any provision purporting to limit those entitled to undertake that activity applies. Section 25(3) and (4) thus applies to activities that may not be formally regulated as professional activities by professional bodies and/or which are not confined to persons holding or having certain professional qualifications or experience. In that regard, section 29 (which governs the interpretation of Part 3 of the Act) relevantly provides: **6.16**

(1) References in this Part to the ability to practise a profession include reference to the ability—
(a) to undertake activities that comprise the practice of a profession,
(b) to use a particular professional title, or

[12] Section 25(3) is qualified by section 25(6) which provides:
'For the purposes of subsection (3)—

(a) it does not matter that corresponding activity may also be undertaken by individuals who are not practitioners of a profession;
(b) to the extent that corresponding activity is ordinarily undertaken by practitioners of more than one profession regulated as mentioned in subsection (3)(b), a UK resident is qualified in relation to that activity only if the resident has qualifications or experience required to be able to practise whichever of those professions most closely corresponds to the profession in the relevant part.'

[13] Section 29(6) of the Act.

[14] As to which, see the discussion in J. Powell and R. Stewart, *Jackson & Powell on Professional Liability* (8th edn, Sweet & Maxwell 2016), paragraphs 1-001–1-007.

(c) to be registered, licensed or similarly authorised, where that is required in order to undertake such activities or use such a title.

. . .

(8) In this Part—

'*profession*' includes—
(a) an occupation or trade, and
(b) any subdivision of, or distinct specialism within, a profession;

'*provision*' means—
(a) provision contained in legislation, or
(b) provision not of a legislative character but made under, and given effect by, legislation.

6.17 The definition of 'profession' (which includes an occupation or trade and thus gives the concept of 'profession' a broader scope than traditional formulations[15]) and the definition of 'provision' thus makes clear that only professions (broadly defined) that are regulated by law will be in scope of Part 3 of the Act (i.e. where access to a profession is limited by legislation to individuals who hold specific professional qualifications or experience). Professions that are self-regulated through voluntary membership of a professional body or institution therefore do not fall within the scope of the Act.

6.18 Sections 29(3)–(4) seek to clarify the scope of the right, by clarifying when the right of automatic recognition in section 24 will apply. Those sub-sections provide:

(3) Subsection (4) applies if provision applying in a part of the United Kingdom—
  (a) enables individuals to practise a profession—
    (i) on the basis of certain qualifications or experience, or not on the basis of any particular qualifications or experience, only following an individual assessment,[16] and
    (ii) on the basis of certain qualifications or experience, without the need for an individual assessment, or
  (b) generally enables individuals to practise a profession only following an individual assessment, but provides for a less demanding assessment in some cases than in others according to what qualifications or experience an individual has.
(4) References in section 24 to the ability to practise a profession are to be read, in relation to the profession to which the provision relates, as references to the ability to practise the profession—
  (a) if the provision is within subsection (3)(a), without the need for an individual assessment, or
  (b) if the provision is within subsection (3)(b), following an individual assessment of the least demanding sort provided for.

6.19 The purpose of those sub-sections is to require section 24 to be read in a way that broadens the applicable scope of the right of automatic recognition under section 24 and reduces the

[15] The UK Internal Market Bill Impact Assessment noted (at footnote 16) that there were approximately 120 generic professions listed as regulated in the United Kingdom on the European Commission's regulated professions database. Source: The European Commission, 2020, European Commission's Regulated Professions Database. The impact assessment is here: https://publications.parliament.uk/pa/bills/cbill/58-01/0177/UK%20Internal%20Market%20Bill%20Impact%20Assessment%2008092020.pdf

[16] Section 95(5) defines 'individual assessment' to mean 'an assessment of the individual's qualifications, experience, knowledge or skills'.

burden that may permissibly be imposed under an alternative system of recognition applied in accordance with section 26 (discussed in paragraphs 6.23–6.33 below) as follows:

a. where the provision in question can be satisfied (i) by reference to certain qualifications or experience or (ii) following an individual assessment,[17] that provision is to be read as only requiring the person to have certain qualifications or experience (and thus precluding the provision from being read as requiring an individual assessment to be imposed). That enables the qualified UK resident to be automatically recognized since if the person has the relevant qualifications or experience, they are entitled to be recognized without any further assessment; and
b. where the provision in question can only be satisfied by undertaking an individual assessment (i.e. under an alternative system of recognition), the assessment must be read as meaning the least onerous form of assessment that the body or measure otherwise imposing the provision otherwise provides for. Thus insofar as a person may still have to undergo further assessment by way of an alternative system of recognition (and notwithstanding that they have relevant qualifications or experience), that assessment must be the least onerous consistent with those qualifications or experience.

Section 24(2) thus provides that automatic recognition of qualifications will be the default 6.20
position when a new profession is regulated or when changes are made to existing qualification or experience requirements in a part of the United Kingdom (as explained in paragraphs 6.23–6.25 below, section 24 does not apply to alternative systems by which professional qualifications from one part of the United Kingdom may be recognized in another part of the United Kingdom and which therefore fall outside the scope of the right of automatic recognition in section 24).[18]

Section 24(3) makes clear that regulator in the relevant part of the United Kingdom can 6.21
nevertheless impose continuing professional development obligations on the qualified UK resident where that person had begun to provide professional services in that relevant part of the United Kingdom on a 'fully qualified basis'. That is, the presumption of automatic recognition in section 24(2) will not bypass any administrative measures required to register or practise those professions.

C. EXCEPTIONS

There are exceptions to the right of access contained within section 24 of the Act in both 6.22
sections 26 and 27:

a. Section 26 disapplies the automatic recognition principle in section 24 where individual assessments are offered; and
b. Section 27 sets out other exceptions from the right of access contained in section 24, including (i) those where existing provision is already made for the recognition of qualifications obtained in another part of the United Kingdom and (ii) those pertaining to the legal profession and school teaching.

[17] That is, a provision that is within section 29(3)(a).

[18] And see paragraph 49 of the Explanatory Notes.

1. The Section 26 Exceptions: Disapplication of Section 24—Alternative Systems of Recognition

6.23 Section 26(1) provides:

> (1) Section 24(2) does not apply in a case where the qualified UK resident—
> (a) is able to seek, or has sought, to be able to practise the profession in the relevant part by way of a process that satisfies the requirements of this section, and
> (b) has not lawfully practised the profession in the relevant part at any time before being able to seek that ability by way of that process.

6.24 That is, a qualified UK resident will not be able to rely on the automatic right of recognition in section 24(2) of the Act where there is a process enabling such a person to meet a provision that would otherwise preclude them from practising in the relevant part of the United Kingdom.[19] Such a process amounts to an alternative system of recognition. However, the qualified UK resident cannot be required to undergo further assessment of their qualification, knowledge, experience, or skills under such an alternative system of recognition unless that system complies with the requirements of section 26.[20]

6.25 It follows that competent authorities may derogate from automatic recognition in administering provisions that restrict access to a profession in the relevant part of the United Kingdom. Where it is determined that two professional qualifications from different parts of the United Kingdom cannot be considered equivalent, given substantial differences in the level of training and qualification required, it will be permissible to disapply the right of automatic recognition by the profession in question in the relevant part of the United Kingdom. Administrators will in such circumstances be able to provide for an alternative means of recognition which allows differences in the requirements to be considered and a decision to be taken as to whether, and on what basis, a person should be allowed access to the professional in that relevant part of the United Kingdom. In this regard, the Policy Statement observes: '[i]t is our expectation that the alternative recognition process will be used where there are sufficient differences in professional standards between UK nations to justify a case-by-case assessment of incoming professionals'.

6.26 Whether to impose an alternative recognition process will thus be at the discretion of the relevant government or regulator.[21] To that end, the Policy Statement further noted that:

> Where the UK government or a UK regulator[22] is directly responsible for the regulation of a profession, either the UK government or the regulator will decide whether an alternative recognition process should be used instead of the default automatic recognition principle.
>
> Where the profession is regulated separately in a part of the UK, the devolved government or the relevant devolved regulator will be responsible for deciding whether to apply an alternative recognition process.

---

19 Section 26(2)(a).

20 Section 26(2)(b) read with sections 26(3)–(4). Section 26 does not, though, affect the position of any individual who has practised the profession in a part of the United Kingdom before the process was available (who will still be able to rely on automatic recognition).

21 Although as the Policy Statement notes, '[U]nder an alternative recognition process, the relevant authorities will be obliged to recognise professionals who meet the required standards in their jurisdictions. This means that, if the alternative system was applied when there was no difference in standards, professionals would have to be recognised.'

22 That is, where there is uniform or United Kingdom-wide regulation of a profession.

Thus, if any changes to qualification or experience requirements are made after the Act came into force, automatic recognition would apply unless a compliant alternative recognition process is put in place by the relevant government or regulator. The Explanatory Notes to the Act thus observe that this Part of the Act 'allows for the disapplication of the automatic recognition process, provided that an alternative process for recognition is instituted that complies with specific principles set out in the Act. The process will have to have legislative backing and will be administered by the relevant professional regulator (or, if there is not one, whichever of the UK Government or devolved administrations is responsible for the profession).'[23] 6.27

The principles against which an alternative system of recognition will be assessed are those set out in section 26(4):[24] 6.28

(4) The principles are that, in connection with the ability to practise a profession in the relevant part—
  (a) qualifications or experience obtained in any other part of the United Kingdom should have the same effect as qualifications or experience obtained in the relevant part, to the extent that the former demonstrate the like knowledge and skills to substantially the same standard as the latter;
  (b) the applicant should be able to rely on any qualifications or experience obtained in any other part of the United Kingdom in order to demonstrate the necessary knowledge and skills, so far as those qualifications or experience are reasonably capable of demonstrating them;
  (c) to the extent that the applicant cannot, on application of the principles set out in paragraphs (a) and (b), demonstrate the necessary knowledge and skills to the satisfaction of the regulatory body, the applicant should (subject to subsection (5)) have an opportunity to do so by way of a test or assessment the demands of which are proportionate to the deficiency;
  (d) if the applicant can, on application of the principles set out in paragraphs (a) to (c), demonstrate the necessary knowledge and skills to the satisfaction of the regulatory body, the regulatory body should decide as mentioned in subsection (2).

Paragraph 51 of the Explanatory Notes summarizes the section 26(4|) principles as follows: 6.29

The principles that must be complied with for the alternative process include that: for the purposes of accessing a profession, qualifications or experience obtained in another part of the UK have to be taken into account and are to be treated the same as 'like' qualifications or experience obtained in the relevant part (where the individual is seeking recognition). If the qualifications or experience do not meet the required standard, an assessment should be offered to allow the professional the opportunity to demonstrate the required knowledge and skills. If the knowledge and skills required can be demonstrated either by qualifications or experience or the assessment, the individual must be recognised and permitted to practise that profession in the relevant part of the UK.[25]

The qualification to section 26(4)(c) in section 26(5) permits the regulatory body[26] to decline the qualified UK resident's application without the applicant first being offered a 6.30

---

[23] Ibid, paragraph 50.

[24] Pursuant to section 26(3).

[25] Although, consistent with sections 29(3)–(4), it would appear that where knowledge and skills may be demonstrated either by qualifications or experience or an individual assessment, section 24 should be read as though such knowledge and skill could be sufficiently demonstrated by qualifications and experience, such that an assessment should not be required.

[26] '*Regulatory body*' is defined in section 26(10) as meaning '(a) the person, if any, responsible for determining whether a person has the qualifications or experience referred to in section 24(1), or (b) if there is

test or assessment without contravening section 24(4). Rejecting an application without first offering a test will be permissible where it is plain from the face of the application that the qualified UK resident does not have the skills, knowledge, experience, or qualifications to have any real prospect of passing the test.[27]

6.31 The regulatory body must inform the qualified UK resident of its decision on their application within a reasonable time after their receipt of the application.[28] It is likely that this provision will require the regulatory body to give the applicant reasons for any decision rejecting the application or refusing to offer the applicant a test in the event that section 26(5) is applicable.

6.32 In the event that the qualified UK resident is not provided with a decision on their application within a reasonable time, and if the regulatory body accepts that it has not provided the applicant with a timely decision or a court determines that no timely decision has been given, section 26(1) is disapplied whereby the applicant can avail of the automatic right of recognition conferred by section 24(2) if it otherwise applies.[29]

6.33 Section 29(9) provides that a regulatory body that administers a process to which this section applies must publish information about (a) the procedure for making an application within the process, and (b) the way in which the principles set out in section 26(4) will be given effect in the context of the profession concerned. However, it further states that a failure to comply with the duty to publish does not mean that the process does not comply with the requirements of this section. It would appear to follow that a body's failure to publish information about the relevant procedure or how the principles in section 26(4) are given effect to, would not be a basis on which the applicant might seek to disapply section 26(1) such as to avail of section 24(2) by default.

2. The Remaining Section 27 Exceptions

a) *The exceptions for specific professions*

6.34 As the Policy Statement observes, 'there are exceptions for specific professions ... This is to reflect some long-standing differences concerning these professions across the United Kingdom, such as in the case of legal professions.' Thus section 27(5)–(6) provides:

(5) Section 24(2) does not apply in relation to provision that limits the ability to practise a legal profession.
(6) In subsection (5) 'legal profession' means—
  (a) in relation to England or Wales, the profession of barrister, solicitor, notary, chartered legal executive, costs lawyer, licensed conveyancer or licensed CLC practitioner (see section 53 of the Courts and Legal Services Act 1990);
  (b) in relation to Scotland, the profession of advocate, solicitor, notary, conveyancing practitioner (see section 17 of the Law Reform (Miscellaneous Provisions) (Scotland) Act 1990), executry practitioner (see section 18 of that Act) or commercial attorney;

---

no such person, the responsible administration'. The responsible administration is defined for each of the devolved administrations, at section 26(10)(a)–(c). In default, the responsible administration for England is the Secretary of State (s. 26(10)(d)).

[27] Which appears to be the implication of section 26(6).

[28] Section 26(7).

[29] Section 26(8).

(c) in relation to Northern Ireland, the profession of barrister, solicitor or notary;
(d) in relation to any part of the United Kingdom, the profession of patent attorney or trade mark attorney.

Legal services have traditionally been dealt with completely separately in each jurisdiction in the United Kingdom, reflecting the diverse legal systems in those jurisdictions.[30] Section 27(5)–(6) reflects the government's commitment in the White Paper and throughout the legislative process, that the Act would not interfere with the longstanding differences between the legal systems in each part of the United Kingdom. One obvious difference, alluded to in chapter 1 above, was the greater reception of civil law (based on Roman law) by the Scottish legal system, which in many respects has a starkly different approach to the system of common law that operates in the rest of the United Kingdom. In addition, different procedural rules apply to the process of litigation across the United Kingdom, one obvious difference being that whereas civil procedure in England and Wales is governed by the civil procedural rules adopted to give effect to the Woolf reforms, the Rules of the Supreme Court (RSC) still apply in Northern Ireland. 6.35

Finally, section 27(7) provides that: '[s]ection 24(2) does not apply in relation to provision that limits the ability to practise the profession, or any profession, of school teaching'. 6.36

D. PROFESSIONAL REGULATION AND EQUAL TREATMENT

As the Policy Statement notes, '[q]ualification recognition is not the only barrier that might emerge in the internal market. It would be possible for unfair or discriminatory measures to be put in place to act as a further barrier to professionals practising their profession. Therefore, we have put in place provisions to ensure equal treatment of professionals regardless of where in the UK they obtained their qualifications or experience.' 6.37

This has echoes of the approach taken under EU law of the freedom of individuals to provide and receive services. Article 56 of the Treaty on the Functioning of the European Union (TFEU) provides that restrictions on freedom to provide services within the Union shall be prohibited in respect of nationals of Member States who are established in a Member State other than that of the person for whom the services are intended. Article 57 TFEU defines services and applies the principle of equal treatment to the service provider. Article 61 TFEU further provides that: 6.38

> As long as restrictions on freedom to provide services have not been abolished, each Member State shall apply such restrictions without distinction on grounds of nationality or residence to all persons providing services within the meaning of the first paragraph of Article 56.[31]

The concern is that unless professionals are entitled to be treated in the same way and in accordance with the same domestic provisions governing service providers in the Member State of establishment, the exercise of the freedom to establish would be quickly undermined. 6.39

[30] As discussed in further detail in chapter 1 above.

[31] Specific provision for the mutual recognition of professional qualifications was contained in Directive 2005/36 on the recognition of professional qualifications. The current consolidated version of 24 April 2020 can be found here: https://eur-lex.europa.eu/legal-content/EN/TXT/?uri=CELEX%3A02005L0036-20200424.

6.40 Similarly, and with regard to the same concerns, the Policy Statement thus observes that the principle of equal treatment contained within Part 3 of the Act 'prevents professionals being treated differently on the basis of where in the UK they obtained their qualifications or experience. This means that where there are ongoing requirements to practise a profession, incoming professionals cannot be treated less favourably because of where in the UK their qualifications or experience were obtained or the type of qualifications they have (unless this is justified). For example, they could not be required to pay a higher annual fee than a locally qualified professional. Equal treatment will mean that professionals cannot be disadvantaged and can practise their profession on the same basis as a locally qualified professional.'[32]

6.41 The provision imposing the requirement for the equal treatment of UK professionals is contained in section 28 of the Act which, in broad terms, makes it unlawful for one nation to regulate in any way that affords less favourable treatment to professionals, at least not without objective justification (where that defence is available), to that afforded to its own professionals. Section 28(1) sets out the scope of the type of requirements to which the equal treatment obligation applies as follows:

(1) This section applies in relation to provision that—
  (a) is not of the sort described in section 24(1),
  (b) makes the ability to practise a particular profession in a part of the United Kingdom ('the relevant part') subject to a requirement or restriction, and
  (c) applies differently to individuals according to—
  (i) where any qualifications or experience of an individual were obtained, or
  (ii) what qualifications or experience an individual has.

6.42 Section 28(1) therefore does not apply to provisions that would otherwise operate to preclude qualified UK residents practising in the relevant part of the United Kingdom; rather, it applies to those ongoing administrative and professional obligations that are ancillary to the practice of a profession. The phrase 'requirement or restriction' in section 28(1)(b) makes this clear insofar as it is defined in section 28(2) to include 'for example, a requirement as to registration, monitoring, insurance or continuing professional development, or a restriction on the undertaking of particular activities in the course of practising the profession'.

6.43 In a situation where a relevant 'requirement or restriction' has the differential effect as described in section 28(1)(c)(i) and where that differential effect imposes 'a more onerous requirement or restriction on an externally qualified UK practitioner[33] than it would have the effect of imposing on a locally qualified practitioner',[34] section 28(4) will then apply. Section 28(4) provides that '[t]he externally qualified UK practitioner is to be treated for

---

[32] The Explanatory Notes similarly state: 'Professionals also benefit from provisions ensuring equal treatment in respect of the ongoing practice of a profession under this part of the Act. Professionals qualified in another part of the UK cannot be treated less favourably in respect of ongoing practice requirements than those qualified in the relevant part, based on where in the UK their qualifications or experience were obtained or the type of qualifications they have (unless this is justified). This means that professionals cannot be required to meet higher ongoing requirements than locally qualified professionals as part of their ongoing practise, such as continuing professional development or insurance requirements.'

[33] Section 28(8) defines an '*externally qualified practitioner*' to mean 'a UK resident any of whose qualifications or experience was obtained in a part of the United Kingdom other than the relevant part'.

[34] Section 28(3). Section 28(8) defines a '*locally qualified practitioner*' to mean 'a UK resident all of whose qualifications and experience were obtained in the relevant part'.

the purposes of the provision (and any related provision) as if the practitioner's external UK qualifications or experience had been obtained in the relevant part'.[35]

In a situation where a relevant 'requirement or restriction' has the differential effect as described in section 28(1)(c)(ii), and where that differential effect (i) imposes a more onerous requirement or restriction on an externally qualified UK practitioner than it would on a locally qualified practitioner, and (ii) the external UK qualifications or experience are of a sort that cannot be obtained in the relevant part, section 28(6) will apply. In that regard: 6.44

a. Section 28(6) provides that in such a situation, '[t]he externally qualified UK practitioner is to be treated for the purposes of the provision (and any related provision) as if the practitioner's external UK qualifications or experience were the nearest equivalent qualifications or experience that can be obtained in the relevant part'.
b. However, section 28(7) provides that sub-section (6) will not apply if the more onerous requirement or restriction can reasonably be justified on the grounds of differences between the external UK qualifications or experience and the nearest equivalent qualifications or experience.

However, the equal treatment provisions are not subject to the same exceptions as apply to the recognition system provisions and accordingly, will apply to all professionals with UK qualifications or experience regardless of whether they have been recognized under the automatic or alternative systems. 6.45

[35] Section 28(8) defines 'external UK qualifications or experience' to mean 'the qualifications or experience by virtue of which a UK resident is an externally qualified UK practitioner'.

7

MONITORING OF THE UK INTERNAL MARKET

A. INTRODUCTION

7.01 The parts of the Act covered by this chapter concern what might be called the administration of the Act, as opposed to its application by courts in legal proceedings (a matter covered in preceding chapters).

7.02 The bulk of this chapter deals with the advisory and reporting role, and associated information-gathering powers, given to the Competition and Markets Authority (CMA) in Part 4 of the Act. The decision to give the CMA this role may well be another example of unacknowledged lessons being drawn from the EU model: a model which is driven not just by the creation of legal remedies enforceable by private parties before courts, but also by the European Commission, with its powers of review and enforcement. That said, the role given to the CMA under the Act differs in fundamental respects from that of the Commission in the EU system—the obvious and critical difference being the absence of any power by the CMA itself to bring enforcement proceedings in relation to any regulation that engages the principles laid down by the Act. But the role given to the CMA does recreate some of the important functions of the Commission in the EU system, including functions which are not capable of being exercised by courts, such as the ability to give a view on regulatory proposals and the ability to report on the operation of the UK internal market, or aspects of it, as a whole and without being confined to a particular case.

7.03 The final sections of this chapter deal with sections 12 and 13, which confer powers and duties on the Secretary of State in relation to guidance and review of the use of the Secretary of State's powers of amendment.

Blackstone's Guide to the UK Internal Market Act 2020. Alan Bates, Brendan McGurk, George Peretz QC, and Jack Williams, Oxford University Press.
DOI: 10.1093/oso/9780192856203.003.0007

B. THE CMA'S REPORTING, ADVISING, AND MONITORING FUNCTIONS

1. The CMA

Part 4 confers various functions on the CMA. The CMA is a body corporate, created by section 25 of the Enterprise and Regulatory Reform Act 2013 (ERRA 2013). It performs its functions on behalf of the Crown.[1] It consists of a chair, a chief executive, a CMA Board (which is the principal decision-maker within the CMA), and a CMA panel,[2] all appointed by the Secretary of State.[3] 7.04

The CMA is, primarily, a successor to two bodies which (under different names) dated back several decades before the creation of the CMA in 2013: the Competition Commission[4] and the Office of Fair Trading[5] (OFT). Its main responsibilities are in the area of competition law and consumer law, where it has extensive powers and functions.[6] 7.05

The CMA's structure bears traces of its origins. In many areas of UK competition law,[7] the pattern of regulation was, before 2013, one in which the OFT conducted an initial analysis and then, if it considered that there was a significant competition issue, referred that issue to the Competition Commission for a detailed report, which report contained recommendations that could trigger statutory powers to intervene. The Competition Commission exercised its powers through an ad hoc group, appointed in each case from a general panel of people with business experience and leading experts in various disciplines. When the CMA was set up by ERRA 2013, the two-stage process, with the second stage conducted by an ad hoc group, was maintained, though with both stages now being carried out within the same body, and the ad hoc group now being drawn from the CMA panel.[8] 7.06

The CMA's functions as a competition regulator require it to maintain a core of economic and regulatory expertise: that expertise in legal and economic analysis, as well as its reputation for independence, made it a natural candidate for the role given to it under the Act.[9] That said, the debates on the Bill revealed some concern as to whether the CMA was the right body to be undertaking that task, to which concerns the government responded by proposing an amendment to add what is now section 44 of the Act, requiring a review of the CMA's performance of its role under the Act.[10] 7.07

---

[1] Paragraph 8 of Schedule 4 to ERRA 2013.

[2] See paragraph 7.6 below.

[3] Paragraphs 1 and 9 of Schedule 4 to ERRA 2013: these and subsequent paragraphs deal with terms of office, re-appointment, and eligibility.

[4] Formerly, until the Competition Act 1998, the Monopolies and Mergers Commission.

[5] The successor, as from the coming into force of the Enterprise Act 2002, of the Director General of Fair Trading, an office that dates back to the Fair Trading Act 1973.

[6] For a brief and non-technical explanation of the history and functions of the CMA, and an analysis of the challenges it faces, see G Peretz, 'The Competition and Markets Authority: a powerful body faces an uncertain future', 4 November 2020, https://www.prospectmagazine.co.uk/economics-and-finance/brexit-law-competition-markets-authority.

[7] Merger control (Part 3 of the Enterprise Act 2002) and market investigations (Part 4 of that Act).

[8] See Part 3 of Schedule 4 to ERRA 2013.

[9] The Minister stated, on the second reading of the Bill in the House of Commons, that '[t]he CMA has a strong reputation for independence and impartiality, which the Government have striven to preserve in setting out the functions of the office for the internal market' (Hansard HC, 15 September 2020, col. 266).

[10] See paragraphs 7.48ff below.

7.08 Nonetheless, the point that the CMA is appointed entirely by the Secretary of State (i.e. by the UK government) attracted some attention during debates on the Bill. In particular, an amendment was made by the House of Lords that would have given the devolved administrations the right to appoint one member each of the CMA Board[11], but that amendment was rejected by the House of Commons[12] and the House of Lords did not insist on it.

7.09 However, a more successful Lords amendment, accepted by the government, requires the Secretary of State to seek the consent of the devolved administrations to appointments to the Office of the Internal Market (OIM) panel.[13]

7.10 The OIM panel, together with 'OIM task groups', is a new structure within the CMA established in order to exercise the CMA's functions under the Act: it is created by section 32 of, and Schedule 3 to, the Act.[14] Section 32(1) provides that the CMA may authorize an OIM task group to do anything required or authorized to be done by the CMA under the Act. An OIM task group consists of at least three members chosen by the OIM panel chair from among members of the OIM panel to carry out particular functions of the CMA under the Act.[15] The OIM panel chair (who is *ex officio* a member of the CMA Board[16]), and members of the OIM panel, are appointed by the Secretary of State: as noted above, he must, before appointing them, seek the consent of the devolved administrations, though, if any of those administrations do not consent within one month, the Secretary of State may make the appointment without its consent, giving his reasons to the non-consenting administration.[17] In making his appointments, the Secretary of State must have regard to the desirability of securing that a variety of skills, knowledge, and experience is available among the members of the OIM panel, and that 'there is an appropriate balance among the members of that panel of persons who have skills, knowledge or experience relating to the operation of the United Kingdom internal market in different parts of the United Kingdom'.[18] Appointment to the OIM panel is for a non-renewable term of no more than eight years.[19] In exercising its functions, an OIM task group is required to act independently of the CMA Board.[20]

7.11 In discharging its functions under the Act, the CMA must have regard to the objective of 'support[ing], through the application of economic and other technical expertise, the

---

[11] See paragraph 2(3) of Schedule 3 to the Bill as amended at report stage in the House of Lords.

[12] The Minister objected to the Lords' amendment on the basis that 'changing the wider CMA governance structures would be wholly inappropriate. The CMA board ensures that the organization operates effectively and fulfils its statutory duties, which have fallen entirely within reserved competence. It would create a deeply unhelpful precedent, therefore, to have devolved Administrations' appointees on the CMA Board' (Hansard HC, 7 December 2020, col. 604). The Act does however require the CMA's annual plan, proposals for annual plan, and performance report now to be laid before the devolved legislatures as well as each House of the UK Parliament: section 40 (amending Schedule 4 to ERRA 2013).

[13] Paragraph 1(2B)–(2D) of Schedule 4 to ERRA 2013, inserted by paragraph 2 of Schedule 3 to the Act.

[14] Schedule 3 makes various amendments to Schedule 4 to ERRA 2013, which contains provisions dealing with the constitution of the CMA. Both it and section 32 came into force on IP completion day.

[15] Paragraphs 58B and 58C of Schedule 4 to ERRA 2013. Paragraphs 58A–58M of Schedule 4 to ERRA 2013 contained detailed provisions for the constitution and operation of OIM task groups.

[16] Paragraph 1(1)(b)(iv) of Schedule 4 to ERRA 2013.

[17] Paragraph 1(1)(b)(iv) and (v), and (2B)–(2D), of Schedule 4 to ERRA 2013.

[18] Paragraph 1(2A) of Schedule 4 to ERRA 2013.

[19] Paragraphs 3(2A) and 4(1A) of Schedule 4 to ERRA 2013: a term may be extended only in order to enable panel members to complete their service on any ongoing OIM task group to which they have been appointed.

[20] Paragraph 58K(1) of Schedule 4 to ERRA 2013: cf. paragraph 49 of that Schedule, which makes the same provision in relation to the work of CMA groups exercising certain of the CMA's competition functions, such as conducting 'phase 2' reports into mergers.

effective operation of the internal market in the United Kingdom (with particular reference to the purposes of Parts 1, 2 and 3)'.[21] That objective includes in particular 'supporting the operation of the internal market (a) in the interests of all parts of the United Kingdom, and (b) in the interests of consumers of goods and services as well as other classes of person with an interest in its operation'.[22] The CMA is also required to have regard to the need to operate even-handedly between the relevant national authorities.[23]

In order to ensure that there is no confusion between the pre-existing powers of the CMA under its competition and consumer law functions and those conferred upon it by the Act,[24] in exercising its functions under the Act the CMA's general objective of promoting competition, laid down in section 25(3) of ERRA 2013, is disapplied, along with its functions under the Enterprise Act 2002 of giving advice and information to the public and Ministers.[25] Instead, the CMA has a power under the Act to give advice or information to the Secretary of State on matters relating to any of its functions under the Act.[26] 7.12

Reports of, and advice by, the CMA under the Act attract absolute privilege for the purposes of defamation law.[27] The published reports may exclude information which the CMA thinks is contrary to the public interest, commercial information that the CMA thinks might significantly harm legitimate business interests, or information relating to the private affairs of an individual the disclosure of which the CMA thinks might significantly harm the individual's interests.[28] 7.13

The CMA must prepare and publish general advice and information about how it expects to approach the exercise of its advice and reporting functions under sections 33–36 (as described in the following paragraphs). That advice or information may include advice or information about the factors the CMA may take into account in considering whether to exercise those reporting and advice functions.[29] 7.14

2. Ad Hoc and Annual/Quinquennial Reports

The CMA may from time to time review any matter[30] that it considers relevant to assessing or promoting the effective operation of Parts 1–3 of the Act or of the internal market generally, and to publish a report on any such matter if it thinks it appropriate.[31] It can do so of its own volition or after being requested to do so by others.[32] 7.15

---

[21] Section 31(1) and (2).

[22] Section 31(3).

[23] Section 31(4).

[24] See the Minister's comment in Hansard HL, 2 November 2020, col. 516: 'Distinct objectives will prevent any operationally problematic blurring of functions.'

[25] Section 31(5).

[26] Section 31(6).

[27] Section 30(7).

[28] Section 38.

[29] Section 39. See https://www.gov.uk/government/organisations/office-for-the-internal-market (which contains a link to current Guidance).

[30] The Explanatory Notes, paragraph 280, state that the matters that the CMA may wish to review under this section include 'matters, whether about particular sets of regulations, sectors or regions, that either are relevant to the continuing effectiveness of an integrated internal market or relate to concerns about this effectiveness and extend to the provisions of Parts 1 to 3. The areas this monitoring may consider include but are not limited to cross-border competition, cross-border investment, nature and levels of trade between different parts of the UK and access to goods and services.'

[31] Section 33(1)–(4).

[32] Section 33(2).

7.16 The CMA must prepare, by 31 March 2023 and then at least once in every 12-month period thereafter, a report covering the operation of the internal market in the United Kingdom and developments as to the effectiveness of the operation of that market.[33] By the same date, and at least once in every five-year period after that date, it must also prepare a report into the effectiveness of the operation of provisions of Parts 1–3, the impact of the operation of those Parts on the operation and development of the internal market in the United Kingdom, any interaction between the operation of those Parts and common framework agreements,[34] and the impact of common framework agreements on the operation and development of the internal market in the United Kingdom.[35] Such reports, so far as they are concerned with the effective operation of the internal market in the United Kingdom, may consider (among other things) developments in the operation of the internal market, for example as regards competition, access to goods and services, volumes of trade (or of trade in any direction) between participants in different parts of the United Kingdom, and the practical implications of differences of approach embodied in regulatory provisions, falling within the scope of Part 4,[36] that apply to different parts of the United Kingdom.[37] Those reports must be laid before each House of the UK Parliament and the devolved legislatures.[38]

3. Advice and Reports at the Request of National Authorities

7.17 Sections 34–37 deal with advice and reports that the CMA may give or make to national authorities at the request of those national authorities.

7.18 In each case, the CMA's advice or report must relate to regulatory provisions (or proposed regulatory provisions) within the scope of Part 4, as provided by section 30.[39] A regulatory provision must be one that is in legislation, or is not of a legislative character but made under and given effect by legislation.[40] To be within scope, the (proposed) regulatory provision must impose[41] a 'relevant requirement' for the purposes of the mutual recognition or non-discrimination principles,[42] impose an authorization requirement within the meaning

[33] Section 33(5). The Explanatory Notes, paragraph 283, state that this will be 'an annual health of the market assessment [that] will set out broad trends and developments in the UK internal market, including levels of integration across different sectors, regions and nations'.

[34] See paragraph 2.87 above.

[35] Section 33(6). The Explanatory Notes, paragraph 284, state that this quinquennial report 'will be expected to include an assessment of the effectiveness of and levels of familiarity with the mutual recognition and non-discrimination principles, including whether improvements may be necessary. This will also be expected to consider the views of all relevant stakeholders to present an overview of how well the internal market is serving interested parties across the UK. The multi-year report will also review any interaction between the operation of Parts 1 to 3 of the Act and common framework agreements, and the impact of common framework agreements on the operation and development of the internal market in the UK.'

[36] See paragraph 7.18 below. Note that the effect of section 30(9) is that regulatory provisions in force as a result of the Northern Ireland Protocol are excluded.

[37] Section 33(8).

[38] Section 33(7).

[39] That definition of 'regulatory provisions' applies across Part 4: see section 45(4).

[40] Section 30(8).

[41] In relation to proposed provisions, proposals that vary or revoke regulatory provisions are also covered: section 30(3).

[42] See chapters 2 to 4, above.

of section 17(3),[43] impose a regulatory requirement within the meaning of section 17(4),[44] or comprise provisions described in section 24(1) or to which section 28 applies.[45,46] In essence, that means that it must be a regulatory provision of the kind covered by Parts 1–3. A second condition is that the regulatory provision must apply to one or more nations within the United Kingdom but not to the whole of the United Kingdom: regulations that apply across the whole United Kingdom are therefore not in scope.[47]

Provisions that contain anything necessary to give effect to the Northern Ireland Protocol are also not 'regulatory provisions' within the scope of Part 4:[48] the CMA is therefore unable to exercise its section 34–36 powers to advise or report on regulatory provisions that apply in Northern Ireland as a result of the Protocol. 7.19

Section 34 deals with proposed regulatory provisions. A relevant national authority (the Secretary of State, Scottish or Welsh Ministers, or a Northern Ireland department),[49] or more than one national authority acting jointly,[50] may ask the CMA to advise or report[51] on a 'qualifying proposal': a qualifying proposal is a proposal to pass or make a regulatory provision[52] that applies to the relevant part of the United Kingdom.[53] A qualifying proposal must be a proposal of the requesting authority, or of a person on whose behalf it is acting (e.g. a statutory body having powers to make regulatory provision under its own powers):[54] it would not be possible for one national authority (such as the Secretary of State[55]) to invoke section 34 in relation to a proposal being made by a different national authority. The CMA has power to advise or report only where it appears to the requesting authority that the regulatory provision at issue is within the scope of Part 4 and within relevant competence[56] and that it should be further considered in the light of the significance of its potential effects on the 7.20

[43] See paragraph 4.01 above. Section 30(5) provides that the reference to an authorization requirement does not include an authorization requirement to which section 19 does not apply by virtue of section 18(1)(c).

[44] See paragraph 5.19 above. Section 30(6) provides that the reference to a regulatory requirement does not include a regulatory requirement to which sections 20 and 21 do not apply by virtue of section 18(1)(d).

[45] See paragraph 6.41 above.

[46] Section 30(2).

[47] Section 30(4).

[48] Section 30(9).

[49] See section 45(6).

[50] Section 34(5): this would cover the case where two or three national authorities are each proposing the same or similar regulatory provisions. When it completes its report or advises in such a case, or if it declines to act, the CMA must give its advice, report, or reasons for not acting to each of the requesting authorities simultaneously: section 30(8).

[51] Apart from sub-section (10) on publication (see n. [*59] below), there does not seem to be any difference between 'advice' and a 'report' under this section.

[52] In this context, a regulatory provision includes a provision that varies or revokes an existing provision: see n. 41 above.

[53] Scotland for the Scottish Ministers, Wales for the Welsh Ministers, Northern Ireland for a Northern Ireland Department, the United Kingdom for the Secretary of State.

[54] Section 34(2).

[55] For national authorities other than the Secretary of State, a further reason why they could not make a request under section 34 in relation to a proposal by a different national authority is that that other national authority would be making provision for an area that was not in the requesting authority's 'relevant part of the United Kingdom' (see n. 53 above).

[56] See the somewhat tortuous provisions of section 45(5) and (7)–(11) for the precise definition of 'relevant competence'.

operation of the internal market in the United Kingdom.[57] The requesting authority must set out the reasons for asking for the CMA's advice or report,[58] and if it rejects the request the CMA must also set out, and publish, its reasons.[59]

7.21 The CMA's advice or report may consider among other things the potential economic effects of the proposed regulatory provision on the effective operation of the internal market in the United Kingdom,[60] including: indirect or cumulative effects; distortion of competition or trade; and impacts on prices, the quality of goods and services, or choice for consumers.[61] Any advice or report must be provided to the national authorities who did not make the request within two weeks of provision to the requesting authority or, if sooner, as soon as reasonably practical after the requesting authority gives permission for the report to be provided to them,[62] and (in the case of a report), the CMA must publish it as soon as possible thereafter.[63]

7.22 There is no requirement on the requesting authority to follow the CMA's report or advice, though it may well be that a court would hold that the authority should, as a matter of public law, have regard to the report or advice in deciding whether or how to proceed. In any event, the CMA's report or advice may also contain material that is of considerable relevance to the application of the market access principles to the regulatory provision at issue—for example, in relation to the question of whether the provision has an 'adverse market effect' under section 8(3):[64] a report or advice that provided powerful support for a contention that a provision would have such an effect is likely in many cases to dissuade the requesting authority from proceeding with the proposal, at least without modification. Nonetheless, there is nothing to stop a requesting authority that disagreed with an adverse assessment by the CMA on a question of relevance to the application of the market access principles from proceeding on the basis that it would seek to persuade the court in the event of any dispute as to the application of those principles that the CMA's assessment was incorrect or based on incomplete facts.

7.23 Section 35 of the Act makes provision for the CMA to report,[65] at the request of the national authority[66] concerned, on any regulatory provisions within the scope of Part 4[67] and passed or made after the section comes into force.[68] The CMA may report only if the provision is within competence and if it applies to the relevant part of the United Kingdom

---

[57] Section 34(1) and (3).

[58] Section 34(6).

[59] Section 34(7).

[60] Note that section 45(3) provides that references in Part 4 of the Act to the 'operation of the internal market in the United Kingdom' are to be read as including a reference to aspects of its operation, e.g. its operation in relation to a particular description of goods or services or in a particular area or region of the United Kingdom.

[61] Section 34(4).

[62] Section 34(9).

[63] Section 34(10): there is no requirement to publish 'advice' under this section, although in practice such advice would generally be obtainable on request from the requesting authority or from the CMA itself under the Freedom of Information Act 2000, absent the application of one of the exemptions in that Act. It is also likely that such advice would in many cases be disclosable, or (in Scotland) subject to recovery, in legal proceedings under the Act.

[64] See paragraph 3.69 above.

[65] Sections 35 and 36 make no provision for 'advice' as an alternative to a 'report'.

[66] Or authorities acting jointly: section 35(3).

[67] See paragraphs 7.18 and 7.19 above.

[68] Section 35(1)(a) and (b).

(i.e. the part over which the requesting authority has jurisdiction—see s. 35(7)).[69] However, it appears that the Secretary of State would be able to make a valid request to the CMA under this section even if the regulatory provision at issue affected only a part of the United Kingdom other than England: that is because section 35(7) provides that, as far as he is concerned, the relevant part of the United Kingdom is not just England, but 'any part of the United Kingdom'.[70]

The requesting authority may not make such a request unless it has considered whether any other person or body is qualified to provide an independent report on the matter,[71] although there does not seem to be any obstacle to the requesting authority making such a request of the CMA even if it has determined that there is such an alternative (though, presumably, the CMA may well refuse to provide a report in such circumstances, if it considers that the alternative is better placed). The requesting authority must provide reasons for the request,[72] and the CMA must provide reasons for refusing it, and publish such reasons,[73] 7.24

If it does decide to report, the CMA must provide the report to the requesting authority and then publish it as soon as practicable.[74] The points made in paragraph 7.22 above as to the legal effect of reports or advice under section 34 apply equally to reports under section 35 (or, indeed, under s. 36). 7.25

Section 36 makes further provision for the CMA to report on regulatory provisions within the scope of Part 4[75] and passed or made after the section comes into force.[76] However, unlike section 35, it allows any national authority—including the devolved administrations—to request a report on a regulatory provision applying to any part of the United Kingdom, including a part of the United Kingdom over which it has no jurisdiction: the requesting national authority just needs to take the view that the operation of the provision at issue is or may come to be detrimental to the effective operation of the internal market in the United Kingdom.[77] Section 36 is therefore, in essence, a provision that allows a national authority concerned that regulatory provisions imposed by another national authority may detrimentally affect the internal market to get the CMA to consider and report on the matter. 7.26

The CMA may report in response to such a request even if it has already, under section 34(1), reported or advised on the proposal for the regulation at issue:[78] although there is nothing to prevent the CMA taking the fact of its previous work into account in deciding whether or not to decline the request. 7.27

Section 36 contains provisions that have the same effect as those in section 35 discussed at paragraph 7.24 above.[79] However, in relation to publication of the report, section 36(7) 7.28

---

69 Section 35(1)(c).

70 That said, it is not obvious why he should make a request of that kind under section 35 rather than section 36 (see the following paragraph), given that he is unlikely to want to take such a course unless he considers that the provision at issue may be detrimental to the operation of the internal market.

71 Section 35(2): the Minister stated during consideration of the Bill that that provision 'is simply intended to make it clear that the OIM is not intended to displace other bodies that might in theory provide more relevant advice on the same matter and, in doing so, make the best possible use of public funds' (Hansard HL, 2 November 2020, col. 606).

72 Section 35(4).

73 Section 35(5).

74 Section 35(6).

75 See paragraphs 7.18 and 7.19 above.

76 Section 36(1).

77 Section 36(1)(b).

78 Section 36(2).

79 See section 36(3)–(6).

requires the CMA to provide the report simultaneously to all the national authorities, and section 36(8) and (9) requires it to lay the report before each House of the UK Parliament and all the devolved legislatures, as soon as practicable after each national authority has told the CMA that it needs no further time for private consideration of the report (or, if earlier, six months after provision of the report to the national authorities). The CMA must then publish the report.[80]

7.29 Section 37 contains somewhat tortuous provisions that require the authority that requested a section 36 report, and the authority responsible for the provision that was the subject of the report, to make a statement to their respective legislatures after the report has been laid. The statement will presumably set out the action that each relevant authority proposes to take as a result of the report.

7.30 As a general comment on reports and advice under sections 34–36, it may be noted that there is no requirement that the CMA's report or advice contain any recommendations nor any provision that imposes a duty on, or gives a power to, either the CMA or the relevant authorities to take action as a result of the report or advice.[81] The CMA's role is purely advisory: though, as already noted, its reports and advice may well contain material that is of considerable assistance to parties seeking to demonstrate that market access principles have (or have not) been engaged, and therefore may well result in action being taken in order to amend regulation which appears, as a result of the report, to be difficult to reconcile with the market access principles, or to forestall litigation invoking those principles which appears as a result of the CMA's report or advice to be unlikely to succeed. For that reason, national authorities may well seek to use the power to obtain reports from the CMA under sections 34 and 35 as a way of establishing whether proposed or actual legislation that is being said to engage the market access principles actually does so without the risks and expense of litigation, though it should be noted that the CMA's task on such a report is to advise on broader public policy questions rather than on the application of the market access principles in any particular situation. It is also quite possible that these provisions (especially s. 36) will be used as a way of resolving political disputes between different national authorities as to the implications of a proposed measure for the internal market.

C. THE CMA'S INFORMATION-GATHERING POWERS

7.31 Sections 41–43 of the Act set out provisions for the CMA to have power to require persons to produce documents or information to the CMA and powers for the CMA to impose penalties if those requirements are not complied with.

7.32 Section 41(1) provides that the CMA's powers to require documents or information to be produced may be exercised either for the purposes of preparing a report under sections 33–36 or, more generally, for its general function of obtaining, compiling, and keeping under review information about matters relating to in relation to which the CMA proposes to undertake a review, prepare a report, or give advice under any of those sections.[82] The CMA may therefore

[80] Section 36(10).

[81] Contrast the market investigation provisions of Part 4 of the Enterprise Act 2002, which give the CMA wide powers to impose remedies as a result of findings made by it in a market investigation report.

[82] Section 41(1)(b), read with section 5 of the Enterprise Act 2002.

use its powers not just in relation to reports (etc.) it is actually preparing, but also in relation to reports that it is proposing to prepare.

Section 41(2) contains a power to require by notice the production of documents that may be exercised against any person who has that document in their custody or control. 7.33

Section 41(3) contains a power to require by notice the production of 'estimates, forecasts, returns or other information'—that is to say information that may not be in an existing document but which the recipient may be asked to create. That power may only be exercised against a person who carries on a business (and so could not be used to obtain information from a public authority not engaged in any business activity). 7.34

In either case, the notice: must specify (or identify or describe) the documents or information concerned;[83] may specify the time, place,[84] form, manner, or person at, in, or to which the document or information is to be provided;[85] and may require the provision of a legible and intelligible copy of information recorded otherwise than in legible form.[86] The notice must also state the purpose for which the notice is given (stating which function mentioned in s. 41(1) is relevant) and must include information about the consequences of non-compliance.[87] The person to whom the notice requires a document to be produced may copy the document.[88] 7.35

A notice may not require a person to produce documents or information that they could not be compelled to produce or give in evidence in civil proceedings before the High Court (or, in Scotland, the Court of Session).[89] That provision would, for example, preclude any requirement to produce documents covered by lawyer/client privilege. 7.36

Information obtained by the CMA under the Act is covered by the general restrictions on disclosure by the CMA set out in Part 9 of the Enterprise Act 2002.[90] 7.37

Under section 42(1), the CMA may impose a penalty on any person who, without reasonable excuse, has failed to comply with a section 41 notice.[91] 7.38

In deciding whether or not to do so, the CMA must[92] have regard to the version of its statement of policy on enforcement in force at the time. The CMA is required to publish such a statement,[93] and must consult the national authorities and any other person it thinks appropriate before doing so.[94] The statement must also set out the considerations relevant to the determination of the nature and amount of any penalty imposed.[95] 7.39

---

[83] Section 41(2)(a) and (3).

[84] Note that a person may not be required to go to a place more than 10 miles from his place of residence unless an offer is made to pay his travelling expenses: section 41(8)(b).

[85] Section 41(4).

[86] Section 41(5).

[87] Section 41(6).

[88] Section 41(7).

[89] Section 41(8)(a) and (9).

[90] See section 41(10), which adds the Act to the list of legislation set out in Schedule 14 to the Enterprise Act 2002 and to which Part 9 of that Act applies (by virtue of its being 'specified information' under s. 238(1)(b)). In general, such information may not be disclosed during the lifetime of the individual concerned or the existence of the business, save for 'gateways' provided for under the Act, such as consent, discharge of a statutory function, civil and criminal proceedings, and certain overseas disclosures.

[91] Or on any person who has obstructed or delayed the making of copies under section 41(7).

[92] Section 42(3). The current statement of policy is at https://www.gov.uk/government/organisations/office-for-the-internal-market.

[93] Section 42(6): section 42(8) gives it power to vary the published statement.

[94] Section 42(9).

[95] Section 42(7).

7.40 A penalty may not be imposed[96] after four weeks have elapsed from the completion of the report.[97]

7.41 A penalty is of such amount as the CMA considers appropriate: it may be a fixed sum, or calculated as a daily rate, or a combination of the two.[98] However, the level of penalty cannot exceed amounts set out in regulations made by the Secretary of State,[99] which levels may not exceed £30,000 for a fixed penalty and £15,000 a day.[100] If penalty is set by reference to a daily rate, no account is to be taken of days before the service of notice of the penalty and the penalty ceases to accumulate after the earlier of the date on which the notice is complied with or the completion of the report.[101]

7.42 By section 43(11), the procedural and appeals provisions set out in sections 112–115 of the Enterprise Act 2002 apply to penalties under section 42. Section 112 of that Act sets out the requirements for a notice of penalty, section 113 provides for interest, and section 114 provides for appeals against the imposition or amount of a penalty to the Competition Appeal Tribunal: on such an appeal, that Tribunal may quash the penalty or substitute a different penalty as it considers appropriate.

D. GUIDANCE AND REVIEWS BY THE SECRETARY OF STATE

7.43 Section 12 of the Act is the result of a government amendment at committee stage in the House of Commons.[102] It gives the Secretary of State the power to issue[103] guidance on any matter relating to the practical operation of the UK market access principles, or to the effect of any provision of Part 1. The guidance may be aimed at the public generally or at any description of persons, such as traders, or persons with enforcement functions in relation to legislative provisions that may be subject to the market access principles for goods.[104] Any guidance must be published.[105]

7.44 The Secretary of State must consult the devolved administrations before issuing, varying, or withdrawing guidance under section 12.[106]

---

[96] Though this provision does not apply to the variation or substitution of a penalty following an appeal: see sections 42(5) and 43(11).

[97] Section 42(4) sets out all the various ways in which reports may be said to be completed.

[98] Section 43(1) and (2). A penalty imposed for obstructing the making of copies may only be a fixed rate: section 43(3).

[99] Section 43(4) and (5): such regulations are subject to the negative resolution procedure (s. 43(7)). The current Regulations are the United Kingdom Internal Market Act 2020 (Maximum Penalty) Regulations (SI 2021/1056). Section 43(8) requires the Secretary of State to consult the CMA, the devolved governments and others before making such regulations.

[100] Section 43(6).

[101] Section 43(9) and (10).

[102] Hansard HC, 22 September 2020, col. 903.

[103] Or vary or withdraw: section 12(4).

[104] Section 12(2) and (3). Paragraph 158 of the Explanatory Notes states that '[g]uidance will be needed to explain how the existing enforcement framework will work to give effect to the new market access principles, including how this affects the roles and responsibilities of regulators and what it means for traders in terms of regulatory compliance'.

[105] Section 12(6).

[106] Section 12(5).

There is no provision requiring either devolved administrations or courts to have regard to, let alone be bound by, guidance under section 12. There is no equivalent provision to section 12 in either Part 2 or Part 3 of the Act (services and professions). 7.45

Section 13 of the Act is the result of a government amendment at report stage in the House of Lords, responding to concerns as to the scope of the regulation-making powers given by the Bill to the Secretary of State. The Minister explained its purpose as being 'to offer comfort to the House that the powers to make delegated legislation contained in Parts 1 and 2 will be scrutinised not only when they are being laid before Parliament, but in a more holistic way after a suitable period of time has elapsed. This dedicated review will ensure that individual uses of the power can be considered in the round, for example, taking into account cumulative impacts and those that could not have been foreseen prior to the change. The report has to be laid between three and five years after the Bill is passed. This will ensure that enough time has passed for the effect of the powers to be thoroughly and properly considered, while not waiting too long before the House has a chance to consider the evidence.'[107] 7.46

The powers at issue are those in sections 6(5), 8(7), and 10(2) of the Act (respectively, to vary the scope of the non-discrimination principle, to vary the list of legitimate aims for the purposes of indirect discrimination under the non-discrimination principle, and to vary the list of exclusions from the market access principles).[108] The Secretary of State must, at some point between 17 December 2023 and 17 December 2025,[109] carry out a review of any use that has been made of those powers, prepare a report on that review, and lay a copy of that report before Parliament.[110] In carrying out that review, he must consult the devolved administrations, consider any CMA reports or advice under Part 4,[111] and assess the impact and effectiveness of any changes made under the powers at issue.[112] If the powers at issue have not been used by the time the review is carried out, the Secretary of State's report should simply contain a statement to that effect.[113] 7.47

Section 44 of the Act provides for a review of the CMA's discharge of its role under Part 4. As noted above,[114] that provision has its origins in a government amendment responding to concerns about the CMA's suitability for that role. In moving the amendment, the Minister said that the amendment 'will require the Secretary of State to review, after between three and five years and in close consultation with the devolved Administrations, the appropriateness of, effectiveness of and potential alternatives to the CMA carrying out its Part 4 functions. This will allow Ministers from all Administrations to closely consider the CMA's performance and the pros and cons of continuing with the CMA as the delivery vehicle for the Part 4 functions.'[115] 7.48

Under section 44, the Secretary of State is required, at some point between the third and fifth anniversaries of section 32 coming into force,[116] to carry out a review of the 'appropriateness, for the purpose of securing the most effective and efficient performance of the Part 4 7.49

[107] Hansard HL, 18 November 2020, col. 1482.
[108] Section 13(1).
[109] Section 13(4).
[110] Section 13(2).
[111] See section B above.
[112] Section 13(3).
[113] Section 13(5).
[114] Paragraph 7.7 above.
[115] Hansard HL, 9 December 2020, col. 1305.
[116] Section 44(1) and (6).

functions' of the provisions conferring functions on the CMA and of any arrangements made under or in connection with those provisions. He must prepare a report on that review, and lay a copy of that report before Parliament and the devolved legislatures.[117] The review must in particular assess: the way in which Part 4 functions have been carried out by the CMA through OIM task groups; any advantages or disadvantages of continuing with the provisions conferring functions under the Act on the CMA; and the arrangements made under or in connection with that provision or those amendments, as compared with other possible ways of providing for the Part 4 functions to be carried out (including possible arrangements not involving the CMA).[118]

7.50 In carrying out the review, the Secretary of State must consult the devolved administrations, and must, before finalizing the report, send them a draft of it and consider any representations made by them on that draft.[119]

[117] Section 44(1).

[118] Section 44(2).

[119] Section 44(3) and (4): he may, but need not, consult further on any changes made by him in response to such representations (s. 44(5)).

8

NORTHERN IRELAND

A. INTRODUCTION

This chapter examines the provisions in Part 5 of the Act, which seeks to accommodate the Ireland–Northern Ireland Protocol (hereafter, the 'Northern Ireland Protocol') within the parameters of a United Kingdom-wide internal market. Part 5 contains sections 46–49 of the Act. The key purpose of the Northern Ireland Protocol was to avoid the creation of a **8.01**

Blackstone's Guide to the UK Internal Market Act 2020. Alan Bates, Brendan McGurk, George Peretz QC, and Jack Williams, Oxford University Press. © Alan Bates, Brendan McGurk, George Peretz QC, and Jack Williams 2021.
DOI: 10.1093/oso/9780192856203.003.0008

hard land border on the island of Ireland, an outcome that on one view would have violated the Good Friday Agreement.[1] Instead, the Northern Ireland Protocol in substance keeps Northern Ireland within the EU's customs union and single market in respect of goods, such as to create, in effect, a border in the Irish Sea.

8.02 There is, therefore, an evident *prima facie* tension between one part of the United Kingdom continuing to adhere to EU law and permitting trade in goods with the rest of the EU in the same way as trade was conducted before the end of the transition period, while seeking to impose an internal market that governs all parts of the United Kingdom. It was imperative, therefore, for the Act to make provision for how any conflict in those competing provisions might be resolved. However, insofar as the position in Northern Ireland as regards goods is required to give primacy to the still applicable EU laws referred to in Annex 2 to the Protocol, provisions dealing with any internal conflict would have to reflect the continuing supremacy of EU law in Northern Ireland.

8.03 In addition, the Protocol does not seek to codify a permanent solution. As noted by the Department for Business Energy and Industrial Strategy to the Delegated Powers and Regulatory Reform Committee, the Protocol is 'designed to solve a particular set of problems and it can only do this in practice as long as it has the consent of the people of Northern Ireland'.[2]

B. THE NORTHERN IRELAND PROTOCOL

1. The Inherent Tension Within the Protocol

8.04 In December 2019, during an interview on Sky television, Prime Minister Johnson stated: '[T]here's no question of there being checks on goods going NI/GB or GB/NI . . . We're a UK government, why would we put checks on goods going from NI to GB or GB to NI? It doesn't make sense.' He made the same commitment in the House Commons on 22 January 2020: when asked whether the commitment to unfettered access for goods going from Northern Ireland to Great Britain (GB) applied in the opposition direction, Mr Johnson stated: '[e]mphatically it does'.

8.05 Those claims were, however, legally wrong.[3] That was already clear from the face of the Protocol, the implications of which had already been explained in significant detail in,

[1] The incompatibility arises from the section on 'Security' in the Good Friday Agreement and in particular paragraph 2 of that section which states: 'The British Government will make progress towards the objective of as early a return as possible to normal security arrangements in Northern Ireland, consistent with the level of threat and with a published overall strategy, dealing with: (i) the reduction of the numbers and role of the Armed Forces deployed in Northern Ireland to levels compatible with a normal peaceful society; (ii) the removal of security installations; (iii) the removal of emergency powers in Northern Ireland; and (iv) other measures appropriate to and compatible with a normal peaceful society.' Insofar as infrastructure would be needed to facilitate checks on goods moving from North to South and vice versa, that would, it is said, violate the obligation to remove security installations in paragraph 2(ii). The ninth recital to the Protocol recalls 'the commitment of the United Kingdom to protect North-South cooperation and its guarantee of avoiding a hard border, including any physical infrastructure or related checks and controls'.

[2] Memorandum from BEIS dated 8 September 2020, paragraph 10.

[3] Albeit that there was, by November 2020, a long list of Cabinet Ministers who had made incorrect statements about the operation of the Protocol: see Professor Weatherill's article 'The Protocol of Ireland/ Northern Ireland: What it says is not what it does', 17 March 2020, http://eulawanalysis.blogspot.com/2020/03/the-protocol-on-ireland-northern.html.

amongst other places, the report of the House of Lords European Union Committee of 1 June 2020 on 'The Protocol on Ireland/ Northern Ireland'.[4] As the Committee noted, the Protocol contained a fundamental tension at its core. On the one hand, Article 4, entitled 'Customs territory of the United Kingdom' provides:

Northern Ireland is part of the customs territory of the United Kingdom.

Accordingly, nothing in this Protocol shall prevent the United Kingdom from including Northern Ireland in the territorial scope of any agreements it may conclude with third countries, provided that those agreements do not prejudice the application of this Protocol.

In particular, nothing in this Protocol shall prevent the United Kingdom from concluding agreements with a third country that grant goods produced in Northern Ireland preferential access to that country's market on the same terms as goods produced in other parts of the United Kingdom.

Nothing in this Protocol shall prevent the United Kingdom from including Northern Ireland in the territorial scope of its Schedules of Concessions annexed to the General Agreement on Tariffs and Trade 1994.

That Northern Ireland is and will remain integral to the wider United Kingdom's internal **8.06** market is reinforced by Article 6 of the Protocol which is entitled 'Protection of the UK internal market' and provides:

1. Nothing in this Protocol shall prevent the United Kingdom from ensuring unfettered market access for goods moving from Northern Ireland to other parts of the United Kingdom's internal market. Provisions of Union law made applicable by this Protocol which prohibit or restrict the exportation of goods shall only be applied to trade between Northern Ireland and other parts of the United Kingdom to the extent strictly required by any international obligations of the Union. The United Kingdom shall ensure full protection under international requirements and commitments that are relevant to the prohibitions and restrictions on the exportation of goods from the Union to third countries as set out in Union law.
2. Having regard to Northern Ireland's integral place in the United Kingdom's internal market, the Union and the United Kingdom shall use their best endeavours to facilitate the trade between Northern Ireland and other parts of the United Kingdom, in accordance with applicable legislation and taking into account their respective regulatory regimes as well as the implementation thereof. The Joint Committee shall keep the application of this paragraph under constant review and shall adopt appropriate recommendations with a view to avoiding controls at the ports and airports of Northern Ireland to the extent possible.[5]
3. Nothing in this Protocol shall prevent a product originating from Northern Ireland from being presented as originating from the United Kingdom when placed on the market in Great Britain.

[4] The Committee's report followed the government's Command Paper of 20 May 2020, a paper that, as the Committee noted, should have provided much needed clarity on the United Kingdom's plans as to how the Protocol would be implemented. However, the Committee noted that the Command Paper had made very little progress in explaining the detail of how the movement of goods, in particular from Northern Ireland to GB and from GB to Northern Ireland, would work.

[5] The Joint Committee is the UK-EU Joint Committee, the committee established by Article 164(1) of the EU Withdrawal Agreement. It is the body charged with overseeing the implementation of the Withdrawal Agreement and the Protocol, and with making key decisions determining the Protocol's operation, including on the criteria for judging which goods brought into Northern Ireland are not at risk of moving on into the EU single market.

4. Nothing in this Protocol shall affect the law of the United Kingdom regulating the placing on the market in other parts of the United Kingdom of goods from Northern Ireland that comply with or benefit from technical regulations, assessments, registrations, certificates, approvals or authorisations governed by provisions of Union law referred to in Annex 2 to this Protocol.

8.07 Thus, Northern Ireland was and would continue to be part of the United Kingdom's own customs union and internal market, for goods and for everything else.

8.08 The tension arises as a result of Article 5 of the Protocol which makes further provision for customs and the movement of goods. In particular, Article 5(4) provides: 'The provisions of Union law listed in Annex 2 to this Protocol shall also apply, under the conditions set out in that Annex, to and in the United Kingdom in respect of Northern Ireland.' Annex 2 contains a lengthy list of EU customs legislation—including the entirety of the Union Customs Code—that will continue to apply in Northern Ireland such as to give effect to the settlement whereby Northern Ireland in substance remains within the customs union and single market of the EU.[6][7]

8.09 As the EU Committee of the House of Lords summarized the position: 'Article 5 thus retains a single regulatory zone for goods on the island of Ireland, achieving the key aim of avoiding a hard border between Ireland and Northern Ireland.' However, in contrast to various members of the government, the Committee immediately recognized that this would require 'the imposition of new customs processes and regulatory checks on goods moving from Great Britain to Northern Ireland'. That is because, as Professor Weatherill has noted:

> [G]iven the absence of commitment to persisting regulatory alignment between the EU and GB, the risk arises that goods originating in GB or imported into it from a third country will be routed through Northern Ireland and over the soft border into the EU's internal market without any payment of tariffs or checks for compliance with EU rules, thereby harming the integrity of the EU's customs union and internal market. Therefore, compliance with EU rules on matters covered by the Protocol such as product composition, safety, technical standards and sanitary and phytosanitary requirements will need to be checked, because GB will no longer be bound by these rules. The Protocol does not say exactly how these checks shall occur, nor exactly how intense they shall be: it is in principle for the UK to implement and apply the EU rules made applicable by the Protocol to the United Kingdom in respect of Northern Ireland, subject to the proviso that EU representatives have the right to be present during any such activities pertaining to implementation and application (Article 12). But it is clear that what the Protocol does is to require that there shall be such checks.[8]

8.10 For these reasons there will have to be customs and other regulatory checks on goods moving from Great Britain to Northern Ireland.

[6] Article 5(5) of the Protocol further provides that 'Articles 30 and 110 TFEU shall apply to and in the United Kingdom in respect of Northern Ireland. Quantitative restrictions on exports and imports shall be prohibited between the Union and Northern Ireland.'

[7] Article 8 of the Protocol makes similar provision in respect of the applicability of EU VAT and excise legislation in Northern Ireland. The first provision of Article 8 thus provides that '[t]he provisions of Union law listed in Annex 3 to this Protocol concerning goods shall apply to and in the United Kingdom in respect of Northern Ireland'. The legislation in Annex 3 includes the Principal VAT Directive (Council Directive 2006/112/EC) and the Excise Directive (Council Directive 2008/118/EC).

[8] Weatherill, 'The Protocol of Ireland/ Northern Ireland', n. 3 above.

2. The Customs Arrangements in Respect of Goods Brought into Northern Ireland

Article 5(1) of the Protocol provides that '[n]o customs duties shall be payable for a good brought into Northern Ireland from another part of the United Kingdom by direct transport, notwithstanding paragraph 3, unless that good is at risk of subsequently being moved into the Union, whether by itself or forming part of another good following processing'. A good brought into Northern Ireland destined for Ireland will of course be a good destined to be moved into the Union. Ireland being within the common customs union, checks would of course be required in relation to goods coming into Northern Ireland from third countries (which, following its withdrawal from the EU, the United Kingdom also now is): insofar as those goods are destined for Ireland, the common customs tariff that would otherwise be exigible at the Northern Ireland land border will instead have to be levied at ports of entry in Northern Ireland. Goods coming into Northern Ireland from third countries will also have to be checked since they may be liable to customs duties applicable in the United Kingdom insofar as those goods are destined for the United Kingdom.[9] 8.11

Article 5(2) of the Protocol provides that a good brought into Northern Ireland from outside the Union shall be considered to be at risk of subsequently being moved into the Union unless it is established that that good: (a) will not be subject to commercial processing in Northern Ireland;[10] and (b) fulfils the criteria established by the Joint Committee in accordance with the fourth sub-paragraph of Article 5(2). Thus, whereas Article 5(1) suggests that the imposition of customs duties will be the exception (for goods at risk of being moved into the EU) not the rule, Article 5(2) effectively creates a presumption that goods brought into Northern Ireland will be considered to be at risk of being moved into the EU unless the two conditions set out above can be established. 8.12

Article 5(2) goes on to provide that before the end of the transition period, 'the Joint Committee shall by decision establish the criteria for considering that a good brought into Northern Ireland from outside the Union is not at risk of subsequently being moved into the Union. The Joint Committee shall take into consideration, inter alia: (a) the final destination and use of the good; (b) the nature and value of the good; (c) the nature of the movement; and (d) the incentive for undeclared onward-movement into the Union, in particular incentives resulting from the duties payable pursuant to paragraph 1.' 8.13

The Joint Committee issued its decision 'on the determination of goods not at risk' on 17 December 2020 (hereafter, 'the Decision').[11] The two key issues to be determined were (i) when a good will not be considered to be subject to commercial processing (dealt with 8.14

---

[9] As the Command Paper of December 2020 noted, anti-avoidance provisions would be introduced 'to tackle any EU businesses who seek to route their goods through Northern Ireland to avoid the UK's customs regime' (paragraph 10).

[10] On the basis that if it is to be subject to further processing, it cannot be assumed that the goods are destined for use or consumption in Northern Ireland, whereas if the goods will not be subject to further processing—such that they are in final form—it may be considered that they are destined for use or consumption in Northern Ireland. Article 5(2) of the Protocol defines 'processing' to mean 'any alteration of goods, any transformation of goods in any way, or any subjecting of goods to operations other than for the purpose of preserving them in good condition or for adding or affixing marks, labels, seals or any other documentation to ensure compliance with any specific requirements'.

[11] https://assets.publishing.service.gov.uk/government/uploads/system/uploads/attachment_data/file/949846/Decision_of_the_Withdrawal_Agreement_Joint_Committee_on_the_determination_of_goods_not_at_risk.pdf.

at Article 2 of the Decision); and (ii) the criteria for considering goods not to be at risk of subsequently being moved into the Union (dealt with at Article 3 of the Decision).

8.15 Article 2 on non-commercial processing thus provides:

A good shall not be considered to be subject to commercial processing where:
(a) the person who lodges a declaration for release for free circulation in respect of that good or on whose behalf such declaration is lodged ('importer') had a total annual turnover of less than GBP 500,000 in its most recent complete financial year; or
(b) the processing is in Northern Ireland and is for the sole purpose of:
(i) the sale of food to an end-consumer in the United Kingdom;
(ii) construction, where the processed goods form a permanent part of a structure that is constructed and located in Northern Ireland by the importer;
(iii) direct provision to the recipient of health or care services by the importer in Northern Ireland;
(iv) not-for-profit activities in Northern Ireland, where there is no subsequent sale of the processed good by the importer; or
(v) the final use of animal feed on premises located in Northern Ireland by the importer.

8.16 If not within the five categories of processing set out in Article 2(b), the import of such goods liable to other forms of processing would mean that customs duties would be payable on those imports. That would catch a potentially wide-ranging number of imports. That risk is obviated by the possibility of lodging a declaration as envisaged in Article 2(a), a potential catch-all solution that removes the spectre of customs duties becoming payable on a wide range of goods imported into Northern Ireland.

8.17 Article 3 establishes the criteria for considering goods not to be at risk of subsequently being moved into the Union and provides:

1. A good shall be considered not to be at risk of subsequently being moved into the Union, where it is not considered to be subject to commercial processing in accordance with Article 2, and where:
(a) in the case of goods brought into Northern Ireland from another part of the United Kingdom by direct transport,
(i) the duty payable according to the Union Common Customs Tariff is equal to zero,[12] or
(ii) the importer has been authorised in accordance with Articles 5 to 7 of this Decision to bring that good into Northern Ireland for its sale to, or final use by, end-consumers located in the United Kingdom, including where that good has been subject to non-commercial processing in accordance with Article 2 before its sale to, or final use by, end-consumers;
(b) in the case of goods brought into Northern Ireland by direct transport other than from the Union or another part of the United Kingdom,
(i) the duty payable according to the Union Common Customs Tariff is equal to or less than the duty payable according to the customs tariff of the United Kingdom,[13] or
(ii) the importer has been authorised in accordance with Articles 5 to 7 of this decision to bring that good into Northern Ireland for its sale to, or final use by, end-consumers

[12] Article 4(a) of the Decision provides that 'the duty payable according to the Union Common Customs Tariff to a good shall be determined in accordance with the rules set out in the Union customs legislation'.

[13] Article 4(b) of the Decision provides that 'the duty payable according to the customs tariff of the United Kingdom to a good shall be determined in accordance with the rules set out in the customs legislation of the United Kingdom'.

located in Northern Ireland (including where that good has been subject to non-commercial processing in accordance with Article 2 before its sale to, or final use by, end-consumers), and the difference between the duty payable according to the Union Common Customs Tariff and the duty payable according to the customs tariff of the United Kingdom is lower than 3% of the customs value of the good.'[14]

It remains to be seen how often goods imported into Northern Ireland in practice comply with the cumulative conditions in Articles 2 and 3 of the Decisions which must be met for a good to be treated as being within the UK customs territory (and thus not liable to customs duties under Article 5(1) of the Protocol) and how often those conditions are not complied with such that they, by default, fall to be treated under the EU's customs rules which may in turn lead to the imposition of the EU's Common Customs Tariff. **8.18**

Article 5 of the Decision makes provision for the authorization of traders for the purposes of Article 3. Article 6 sets out further general conditions for the authorization of traders including, by way of Article 6(b), the requirement that traders who apply for authorization should undertake to bring goods into Northern Ireland solely for sale to, or final use by, end-consumers, including where those goods have been subject to non-commercial processing in accordance with Article 2 before their sale to, or final use by, end-consumers; and, in the case of a sale to end-consumers in Northern Ireland, undertake that the sale will be from one of several physical outlets in Northern Ireland from which physical direct sales are made to end-consumers. **8.19**

Article 7 then sets out some further specific conditions for authorization including the requirement that an applicant trader declares they will declare for release for free circulation goods brought into Northern Ireland in accordance with Article 3(1)(a)(ii) or 3(1)(b)(ii).[15] **8.20**

Goods deemed, pursuant to this Decision, to be at risk of being moved into the EU single market and thus liable to EU Common Customs Tariffs, will be administered through a new UK Trader Scheme that will allow businesses authorized under Articles 5–7 of the Decision to undertake (including by way of the undertakings declarations referred to in Articles 6(b) and 7 of the Decision) that the goods they are moving into Northern Ireland are 'not at risk' of onward movement to the EU, and therefore not liable to EU tariffs. The Command Paper on the Northern Ireland Protocol of December 2020 ("the Command Paper") confirms that the 'scheme will include safeguards to ensure that it is not available to those with serious criminal records or existing compliance issues'. It further states that '[t]he scheme will be focused on goods being sold to, or provided for final use by, end consumers located in Northern Ireland or, for internal UK trade, elsewhere in the UK. The scheme will be open only to businesses established in Northern Ireland, or businesses who meet certain closely linked criteria. It will not be available to businesses established only in the EU.'[16] **8.21**

---

[14] Article 3(2), however, provides that paragraphs 1(a)(ii) and 1(b)(ii) shall not apply to goods subject to trade defence measures adopted by the Union.

[15] Releasing goods for free circulation has echoes of the approach to when excise goods become chargeable to tax in EU law, the question being whether they have been released for consumption: see e.g. Article 7(1) of Directive 2008/118/EC.

[16] Command Paper on the Northern Ireland Protocol of December 2020, paragraph 20. The Command Paper further confirmed that there will be 'a reimbursement scheme for goods that attract a tariff, but which can subsequently be shown to have remained in the UK customs territory' (paragraph 27). The Command

C. ACCESS

1. Section 46: Northern Ireland's Place in the UK Internal Market and Customs Territory

8.22 Section 46 of the Act seeks to enshrine the commitments made in Articles 4 and 6 of the Protocol to, respectively, maintain Northern Ireland in the UK customs union and to ensure that Northern Ireland will have unfettered access for goods moving from Northern Ireland to Great Britain. The Explanatory Notes to the Act state that '[s]ection 46 will streamline the movement of goods between Great Britain and Northern Ireland by placing a duty on all UK authorities, including relevant devolved authorities, administering the Protocol to have the highest possible regard to: (i) Northern Ireland's integral place in the UK's internal market as set out in Article 6(2) of the Protocol; (ii) Northern Ireland's place in the UK customs territory; and (iii) the need to facilitate the free flow of goods between Great Britain and Northern Ireland. It thus seeks to support the streamlining of trade in line with the obligations set out in the Protocol.'[17]

8.23 Section 46 is entitled 'Northern Ireland's place in the UK internal market and customs territory'. Section 46(1) provides:

> (1) An appropriate authority must have special regard to the following matters when exercising any function for a relevant purpose—
> (a) the need to maintain Northern Ireland's integral place in the United Kingdom's internal market;
> (b) the need to respect Northern Ireland's place as part of the customs territory of the United Kingdom; and
> (c) the need to facilitate the free flow of goods between Great Britain and Northern Ireland with the aim of—
> (i) streamlining trade between Great Britain and Northern Ireland, and
> (ii) maintaining and strengthening the integrity and smooth operation of the internal market in the United Kingdom.

8.24 Section 46(2) provides that a 'function' is exercised 'for a relevant purpose' if it is exercised for: (i) the purpose of implementing or otherwise dealing with matters arising out of, or related to the Northern Ireland Protocol; (ii) the purpose of enabling or facilitating a purpose described in paragraph (a) to be achieved; or (iii) a purpose relating to movement of goods within the United Kingdom (including movement that involves movement in a country or territory outside the United Kingdom).

8.25 Section 46(3) provides that an 'appropriate authority' means either a Minister of the Crown, the Scottish Ministers, the Welsh Ministers, the First Minister and deputy First Minister in Northern Ireland acting jointly, Northern Ireland Minister or a Northern Ireland Department, or any other person who exercises functions of a public nature.

Paper is here: https://assets.publishing.service.gov.uk/government/uploads/system/uploads/attachment_data/file/950601/Northern_Ireland_Protocol_-_Command_Paper.pdf

[17] Explanatory Notes to the Act, paragraph 60: https://www.legislation.gov.uk/ukpga/2020/27/pdfs/ukpgaen_20200027_en.pdf.

2. Section 47: Unfettered Access to UK Internal Market for Qualifying Northern Ireland Goods

Section 47 is a detailed provision entitled '[u]nfettered access to UK internal market for Northern Ireland goods'. Section 47 requires appropriate authorities not to exercise their functions in a way that would result in a new check, control, or administrative process on the movement of qualifying Northern Ireland goods from Northern Ireland to Great Britain.[18] Additionally, an exercise of a function should not result in an existing check, control, or administrative process being used for the first time, or for a new purpose or to a new extent. Section 47(1) thus provides that: **8.26**

(1) On or after IP completion day, an appropriate authority[19] must not exercise any function in a way that would—
  (a) result in an existing kind of NI-GB check, control or administrative process being used—
    (i) for the first time, or
    (ii) for a new purpose or to a new extent; or
  (b) result in a new kind of NI-GB check, control or administrative process—
    (i) being introduced, or
    (ii) being used.

Section 47(1) is therefore plainly intended to avoid any *de facto* or *de jure* increase in the regulatory burden on goods coming from Northern Ireland to Great Britain. It does not purport to confer a direct right on traders but rather imposes an obligation on any 'appropriate authority' to so comply. Enforcement of the provision would therefore not be by way of a claim for breach of statutory duty but rather by way of judicial review. **8.27**

An 'NI-GB check, control or administrative process' is defined as one applicable to the direct movement of qualifying Northern Ireland goods from Northern Ireland to Great Britain.[20] Further: **8.28**

a. an 'existing kind' of NI-GB check, control, or administrative process is one that (i) was in use or available for use immediately before IP completion day, or (ii) is the same as, or substantially similar to, one that was in use or available for use immediately before IP completion day (defined as the 'predecessor');[21] and
b. a 'new kind of' NI-GB check, control, or administrative process is one that is not of an existing kind. Section 47(8)(e) provides that such process will be new if the purpose for which, or extent to which, a function would be used is 'new' if it had not been used for that purpose, or to that extent, before IP completion day.

A 'direct movement' is, for these purposes, a movement that does not involve movement by land in a country or territory other than the United Kingdom.[22] So a shipment **8.29**

---

[18] The government's White Paper had earlier confirmed that it would ensure 'that where Northern Ireland traders gain product approvals and certification for the Northern Ireland market from EU authorities and bodies, the UK will recognise those for the purpose of placing goods on Great Britain's market' see paragraph 120 of the White Paper.

[19] An 'appropriate authority' has the same meaning as it has under section 46(3): see section 47(11).

[20] Section 47(8)(a).

[21] Section 47(8)(b). Section 47(8)(d) then provides that 'where an NI-GB check, control or administrative process is of an existing kind because of paragraph (b)(ii), that check, control or administrative process and the predecessor are to be treated as a single function for the purpose of determining whether subsection (1) (a) prevents its exercise'.

[22] Section 47(11).

of qualifying goods from Larne to Stranraer would be a direct movement, whereas it would appear that a shipment from Belfast to Liverpool via Dublin would not. However, section 47(9) provides that a Minister of the Crown may amend section 47 by regulations so that it applies to a type of movement instead of, or in addition to, a type of movement to which it already applies (whether that type of movement is direct movement or another type of movement provided for by the regulations thereby made). That provision was to allow for, for example, indirect movements of qualifying goods from Northern Ireland to Great Britain via Ireland, where it was clear those goods would not and did not undergo any further processing etc. when passing through a non-UK territory (and this would most likely relate to a movement from Northern Ireland to Great Britain via Ireland).[23] In the Command Paper on the Northern Ireland Protocol of December 2020, the government confirmed that '[p]rotections for qualifying businesses on arrival in Great Britain will apply whether goods are moved directly to Great Britain or indirectly via Ireland—meaning unfettered access whether goods leave Belfast for Cairnryan, or Dublin for Holyhead'.[24]

8.30 The concept of 'Qualifying Northern Ireland goods' has the same meaning that it has in the European Union (Withdrawal) Act 2018, including any meaning defined for the purposes of that Act from time to time by regulations made under the power conferred by section 8C(6) of that Act[25] (which power provides that '[a] Minister of the Crown may by regulations define "qualifying Northern Ireland goods" for the purposes of [the European Union (Withdrawal) Act 2018]'. The regulations promulgated under section 8C(6) of the European Union (Withdrawal) Act 2018 were the Definition of Qualifying Northern Ireland Goods (EU Exit) Regulations 2020.[26] Regulations 3 of those Regulations is entitled 'Definition of qualifying Northern Ireland Goods' and regulations 3(1)–(2) provide:

> (1) For the purposes of the European Union (Withdrawal) Act 2018, '*qualifying Northern Ireland goods*' means goods which—
> (a) meet or have met the condition at paragraph (2), or
> (b) are NI processed products.[27]

[23] Section 47(10) provides that any regulations made under section 47(9) are subject to the affirmative resolution procedure.

[24] Command Paper, paragraph 12, with the consequence that UK authorities in Great Britain would be able to subject non-NI traders moving 'non-qualifying goods' to the UK's full process for third country customs and agri-food checks once those checks had been established. By the same token, for goods moving from Great Britain to Northern Ireland via Irish ports, the Command Paper on the Northern Ireland Protocol of December 2020 states that 'the UK Trader Scheme will enable goods to be routed from Great Britain through Irish ports to Northern Ireland without being liable for tariffs, provided these movements are done under transit procedures and goods are under customs supervision until cleared in Northern Ireland. This will support time sensitive routes for Northern Ireland businesses and help Welsh ports such as Holyhead' ibid, paragraph 25.

[25] Section 47(11), wherein the definition goes on to state that if such regulations provide for different meanings to be defined for different purposes of that Act, regulations under section 8C(6) may make provision about the meaning or meanings that are to apply for the purposes of section 47.

[26] SI 2020/1454.

[27] Regulation 3(3) defines 'NI processed products' as 'goods which (a) have undergone processing operations carried out in Northern Ireland only, and (b) incorporate only goods which (i) were not at the time of processing under any form of customs supervision, restriction or control, or (ii) have been domestic goods within the meaning of section 33 of the Taxation (Crossborder Trade) Act 2018'. Regulation 3(3) further defines 'processing operations' to mean any of the following carried out under customs supervision: (a) the working of goods, including erecting or assembling them or fitting them to other goods; (b) the processing of goods; (c) the destruction of goods; (d) the repair of goods, including restoring them and putting them in order; (e) the use of goods which are not to be found in the processed products, but which allow or facilitate

(2) The condition is that the goods are present in Northern Ireland and are not subject to any customs supervision, restriction or control which does not arise from the goods being taken out of the territory of Northern Ireland or the European Union.'

The Command Paper on the Northern Ireland Protocol of December 2020 explained that Northern Irish traders had expressed concern that the definition of qualifying Northern Ireland goods should be tightly drawn so that only genuine Northern Ireland businesses benefit from unfettered access. The Command Paper responded to those concerns by stating that '[t]hat is why we will bring in a long-term regime in the second half of 2021 which focuses its benefits on those businesses established in Northern Ireland. This will identify 'qualifying' traders as they 'check in' in the usual way at ports and airports, meaning that the system will be light-touch - with many traders auto-enrolled in the scheme - while still ensuring that goods are free of checks, controls or tariffs when moving from Northern Ireland to Great Britain. This is crucial to unfettered access.'[28] **8.31**

A limited number of qualifications to the commitment to provide unfettered access to qualifying Northern Ireland goods conferred by section 47(1) are listed in section 47(2) which provides that section 47 will not prevent the exercise of a function which is necessary (a) for the administration of arrangements which have the purpose of facilitating access for qualifying Northern Ireland goods to the internal market in the United Kingdom; (b) to secure compliance with, or to give effect to, any international obligation or arrangement to which the United Kingdom is a party (whenever the United Kingdom becomes a party to it);[29] (c) where goods have been declared for a voluntary customs procedure;[30] (d) for the purposes of VAT or excise duty in consequence of the Northern Ireland Protocol;[31] (e) for the purpose of dealing with a threat to biosecurity in Great Britain;[32] or (f) for the purpose of dealing with a threat to food or feed safety in Great Britain.[33] **8.32**

the production of those products, even if they are entirely or partially used up in the process; (f) the usual forms of handling intended to preserve the goods, improve their appearance or marketable quality or otherwise prepare them for distribution or resale; and (g) any operation on goods intended to ensure their compliance with technical requirements for their release for free circulation in the United Kingdom.

[28] Command Paper, paragraph 18.

[29] In this regard, section 47(3) states that sub-section (2)(b) authorizes (in particular) the exercise of a function in relation to a check, control or administrative process if the exercise is necessary to secure compliance with, or to give effect to, Article 6(1) of the Northern Ireland Protocol. As noted above, Article 6(1) of the Protocol commits to ensuring unfettered access of goods moving from Northern Ireland to Great Britain. But this qualification is really concerned with the second sentence in Article 6(1) which states that '[p]rovisions of Union law made applicable by this Protocol which prohibit or restrict the exportation of goods shall only be applied to trade between Northern Ireland and other parts of the United Kingdom to the extent strictly required by any international obligations of the Union'. That is, Union law that continues to be applicable in Northern Ireland further to Article 5(4) of and Annex 2 to the Protocol and which prohibit or restrict the exportation of goods from Northern Ireland will be interpreted strictly where those goods are in fact destined for Great Britain as opposed to some other third country.

[30] 'Declared for a voluntary customs procedure' means 'declared, in accordance with the Taxation (Cross-border Trade) Act 2018, for a special Customs procedure or temporary storage': section 47(11).

[31] The circumstances in which a function will be necessary for the purposes of VAT or excise duty in consequence of the Northern Ireland protocol are explained in section 47(4).

[32] The circumstances in which a function is necessary for the purpose of dealing with a threat to biosecurity in Great Britain are further detailed in section 47(5) and (6) of and Schedule 1 to the Act.

[33] The circumstances in which a function is 'necessary for the purpose of dealing with a threat to food or feed safety in Great Britain are set out in section 47(7)'.

D. MODIFICATIONS TO THE MARKET ACCESS PRINCIPLES

8.33 Section 11 of the Act is entitled 'Modifications in connection with the Northern Ireland Protocol' and sets out modifications to the market access principles for goods in relation to the sale of goods in parts of Great Britain. Section 11(1) is somewhat asymmetric, applying differently depending on whether goods are to be sold in Great Britain on the one hand, or Northern Ireland on the other. It provides that the UK market access principles for goods apply, in relation to the sale of goods in a part of the United Kingdom other than Northern Ireland, with modifications. However, it further provides, in parentheses, that for provisions affecting the application of those principles in relation to the sale of goods in Northern Ireland, one should consult, in particular, the Northern Ireland Protocol and sections 7A, 7C, and 8C of the European Union (Withdrawal) Act 2018.

1. Modifications to the Mutual Recognition Principle for Goods Moving from Northern Ireland to Great Britain

8.34 Section 11(2) then provides that '[t]he mutual recognition principle for goods applies in relation to all qualifying Northern Ireland goods as if they were produced in, or imported into, Northern Ireland'. The phrase 'qualifying Northern Ireland goods' has the same meaning as in section 47 of the Act, as explained above.[34] However, section 11(3) provides that the mutual recognition principle does not apply in relation to goods produced in, or imported into, Northern Ireland that are not qualifying Northern Ireland goods, unless sub-section (4) applies. The qualification in section 11(4) provides:

> If goods falling within subsection (3) are moved in a way that would, but for the fact that Northern Ireland is a part of the United Kingdom, amount for the purposes of the mutual recognition principle for goods to the importation of the goods into England, Scotland or Wales, the goods are to be regarded for the purposes of that principle as having been so imported.

8.35 In summary, sub-section (4) enables goods falling within sub-section (3) (to which mutual recognition would not otherwise apply) to benefit from mutual recognition if they move from Northern Ireland into England, Scotland, or Wales, in the same way as goods imported into those places from outside the United Kingdom.[35]

2. Modifications to the Mutual Recognition Principle for Goods Moving from Great Britain to Northern Ireland

8.36 To exemplify the potential difference in the application of the mutual recognition principle in relation to goods moving from Great Britain to Northern Ireland, it must be recalled that Northern Ireland continues to be governed—so far as concerns goods—by all of the EU legislation set out in Annex 2 to the Protocol as continues to be applicable in Northern Ireland pursuant to Article 5(4) of the Protocol. It must also be recalled that the approach

---

[34] Section 11(8).

[35] These modifications flow from the first part of section 11(1) which was concerned with goods moving from Northern Ireland to Great Britain.

to the meaning of EU law differs as between the Withdrawal Agreement and the Protocol. In particular:

a. Article 6(1) of the Withdrawal Agreement is an interpretation clause and provides that '[w]ith the exception of Parts Four and Five, unless otherwise provided in this Agreement all references in this Agreement to Union law shall be understood as references to Union law, including as amended or replaced, as applicable on the last day of the transition period'.[36]
b. Article 13(3) of the Protocol, by contrast, contains an interpretative provision that provides: '[n]otwithstanding Article 6(1) of the Withdrawal Agreement, and unless otherwise provided, where this Protocol makes reference to a Union act, that reference shall be read as referring to that Union act as amended or replaced'.[37]

In other words, references to Union law in the Protocol will include references to Union legislation as amended or replaced after the final day of the transitional period. Whereas references to Union law in the Withdrawal Agreement therefore became set in stone on the final day of the transitional period, by virtue of the fact that Northern Ireland remains for the purposes of goods, within the EU customs union and single market, the application in Northern Ireland of the legislation in Annex 2 must necessarily relate to that legislation as it exists and is amended from time to time. 8.37

That in turn means that EU laws applicable in Northern Ireland may impose regulatory standards that cause regulatory divergence between Northern Ireland on the one hand and 8.38

[36] Article 6(3) of the Withdrawal Agreement further provides that '[f]or the purposes of this Agreement, references to provisions of Union law made applicable by this Agreement shall be understood to include references to the relevant Union acts supplementing or implementing those provisions'. So provisions supplementing or implementing a provision of Union law will be encompassed within Article 6(1) but again references to those provisions as supplemented or implemented will only include references to such law as they are applicable on the last day of the transition period.

[37] Article 13(4) of the Protocol further provides that '[w]here the Union adopts a new act that falls within the scope of this Protocol, but which neither amends nor replaces a Union act listed in the Annexes to this Protocol, the Union shall inform the United Kingdom of the adoption of that act in the Joint Committee. Upon the request of the Union or the United Kingdom, the Joint Committee shall hold an exchange of views on the implications of the newly adopted act for the proper functioning of this Protocol, within 6 weeks after the request.' After such notification, it falls to the Joint Committee to either (a) adopt a decision adding the newly adopted act to the relevant Annex to the Protocol; or (b) where an agreement on adding the newly adopted act to the relevant Annex to this Protocol cannot be reached, examine all further possibilities to maintain the good functioning of this Protocol and take any decision necessary to this effect. In this way, the legislation in the Annexes to the Protocol may not itself be exhaustive and may be added to if the Joint Committee agrees it is necessary to do so for the proper functioning of the Protocol. In fact, eight pieces of legislation had, as at December 2020, already been added to Annex 2 of the Protocol albeit via the errors, omissions, and deficiencies mechanism set out in Article 164(d) of the Withdrawal Agreement itself. Pursuant to that mechanism, the EU and the United Kingdom agreed in principle to 13 changes to Annex 2 of the Protocol. In addition to the eight additional pieces of legislation, three new explanatory notes were to be inserted alongside legislation already listed in Annex 2. There are two areas in which the changes in fact remove or limit provisions from the scope of Annex 2: (i) that ensuring that Northern Ireland CO_2 emissions count towards UK rather than EU targets; and (ii) limiting the scope of EU trade defence instruments by excluding Northern Ireland industries from EU calculations on trade remedies investigations, preserving Northern Ireland's place in the United Kingdom's international trade regime. The Decision of the Joint Committee on errors and omissions covering these changes is dated 17 December 2020 and is here: https://assets.publishing.service.gov.uk/government/uploads/system/uploads/attachment_data/file/949847/Decision_of_the_Withdrawal_Agreement_Joint_Committee_on_errors_and_omissions.pdf.

Great Britain on the other. That is because Northern Ireland is subject to the laws set out in Annex 2 of the Protocol as amended from time to time, whereas Great Britain is not. If the EU laws in Annex 2 impose higher regulatory standards on certain goods than are imposed by legislation in relation to the same goods manufactured or imported into Great Britain, what is the implication for the application of the principle of mutual recognition for goods moving from Great Britain to Northern Ireland? In the hypothetical example posited, the goods manufactured in Great Britain would have been manufactured to lower standards than those applicable in Northern Ireland. The application of section 2 of the Act without more would suggest that those goods should be able to be sold in Northern Ireland without having to adhere to 'any relevant requirements that would otherwise apply to the sale'.

8.39 However, section 11(1) indicates that the relevant provisions affecting the application of the market access principles, including the mutual recognition principle, are those contained in the Northern Ireland Protocol itself and sections 7A, 7C, and 8C of the European Union (Withdrawal) Act 2018. In that regard:

a. Insofar as the Protocol itself is said to govern in relation to the application of the market access principles for goods moving from Great Britain to Northern Ireland, the fact that the EU laws set out in Annex 2 as amended from time to time will be binding in Northern Ireland, it would appear that those laws—and the higher standards they may, *ex hypothesi*, impose—will trump section 2 of the Act.

b. Section 7A of the European Union (Withdrawal) Act 2018 applies, *inter alia*, to all 'obligation and restrictions' from time to time created or arising by or under the Withdrawal Agreement. Higher regulatory standards arising as a result of the amendment of a piece of EU legislation listed in Annex 2 would constitute 'obligations and restrictions' for the purposes of section 7A(1). Section 7A(2) makes clear that such obligations and restrictions are to be '(a) recognised and available in domestic law, and (b) enforced, allowed and followed accordingly'. That again suggests that higher regulatory standards that may apply in Northern Ireland pursuant to the subsequent amendment of an EU Act listed in Annex 2 will trump the mutual recognition principle in relation to goods manufactured or imported into Great Britain which might otherwise be sought to be placed on the market in Northern Ireland: insofar as such goods do not comply with the higher EU standards made applicable by the Protocol as implemented by the European Union (Withdrawal) Act 2018, they cannot be placed on the market in Northern Ireland.

c. That conclusion is reinforced by section 7A(3) of the 2018 Act which provides that '[e]very enactment (including an enactment contained in this Act) is to be read and has effect subject to subsection (2)'. The phrase 'every enactment' will include the United Kingdom Internal Market Act.

d. Section 7A(2) has the effect that all rights, powers, liabilities, obligations, restrictions, remedies and procedures from time to time created or arising by or under the withdrawal agreement, are to be recognised and available in domestic law and enforced, allowed and followed accordingly.EU law made applicable in Northern Ireland pursuant to Article 5(4) of the Protocol is thus made domestic law by virtue of section 7A(2). Section 7C(1) provides that any question as to the validity, meaning or effect of 'any relevant separation agreement law is to be decided, so far as they are applicable, (a) in accordance with the withdrawal agreement ...'[38] S.7C(3)(a)(i) defines 'relevant separation agreement law'

[38] Section 7C is entitled 'Interpretation of relevant separation agreement law'.

to include 'any of the following provisions or anything which is domestic law by virtue of them' and lists, inter alia, section 7A of the European Union (Withdrawal) Act 2018. Section 7C(2)(c) specifically refers to Article 13 of the Protocol, which contains the interpretative provision that makes clear that references to EU law in the Protocol includes references to those laws as amended from time to time. Therefore, EU law that amends that EU law referred to in Annex 2 to the Protocol will become domestic law and will govern what can and cannot be placed on the market in Northern Ireland from time to time.

In those circumstances, the principle of mutual recognition will not avail a UK manufacturer of goods who produces those goods to a lower standard than those made applicable in Northern Ireland pursuant to Article 5(4) of the Protocol and section 7A of the European Union (Withdrawal) Act 2018, where that manufacturer seeks to place such goods on the market in Northern Ireland. If they do not comply with those higher EU law standards, they cannot be placed on the Northern Irish market.[39] **8.40**

And that is consistent with the fact that the commitment to unfettered access provided for in section 47 is a commitment to provide such access to the UK internal market specifically for Northern Ireland goods. There is no equivalent commitment in the Act in respect of 'Great Britain goods' having unfettered access to Northern Ireland.[40] **8.41**

3. Modifications to the Non-Discrimination Principle

Section 11(5) then provides that 'goods that are not qualifying Northern Ireland goods do not have a relevant connection with Northern Ireland for the purposes of the non-discrimination principle for goods (despite section 5(4))'. As explained in chapter 3 above, pursuant to section 5(4), goods have 'a relevant connection' with a part of the United Kingdom (and so are 'incoming goods' for the purposes of s. 5(2)(b)) if they or any of their components[41] (i) are produced in that part of the United Kingdom; (ii) are produced by a business based in that part of the United Kingdom; or (iii) come from, or pass through, that part of the United Kingdom before reaching the destination part of the United Kingdom. If the goods in question have a relevant connection with a part of the United Kingdom in one of these ways, section 5(1) operates to prohibit any discrimination in respect of those goods having any such relevant connection. The upshot is that the effect of section 11(5) is that goods that are not qualifying Northern Ireland goods do not have a 'relevant connection' with Northern Ireland such that they will not benefit from the non-discrimination principle for goods. **8.42**

---

[39] This was, indeed, envisaged in the Government's White Paper of July 2020 which observed (at paragraph 120): 'there are some considerations for Northern Ireland that the legislative proposals set out below will take into account. Firstly, Northern Ireland will continue to apply a subset of EU goods rules for the purposes of avoiding a hard border on the island of Ireland. This means that any goods being placed on the Northern Ireland market will need to comply with those rules.' And at paragraph 147 the White Paper further recognized that '[g]oods moving into Northern Ireland from Great Britain will also need to meet the specific requirements set out in the Northern Ireland Protocol. However, where the Northern Ireland Executive sets regulatory requirements outside of the scope of the Protocol, these requirements will be subject to the principles of mutual recognition and non-discrimination ... '.

[40] The tenth recital to the Protocol similarly notes that 'nothing in this Protocol prevents the United Kingdom from ensuring unfettered market access for goods moving from Northern Ireland to the rest of the United Kingdom's internal market'.

[41] The term 'components' includes parts, ingredients, and constituent materials (s. 5(5)(a)).

4. Modifications in Relation to the Operation of Schedule 1 to the Act

8.43 Schedule 1 of the Act contains a number of exclusions from the market access principles. Paragraph 1 of Schedule 1 sets out the conditions for when the market access principles will not apply to legislation aimed at preventing or reducing the movement of a pest or disease into a part of the United Kingdom where it poses, or would pose, a serious threat to the health of humans, animals, or plants.

8.44 The first condition in sub-paragraph 2 is that the aim of the relevant legislation is to prevent or reduce the movement of a pest or disease into the part of the United Kingdom in which the legislation applies ('the restricting part') from another part of the United Kingdom ('the affected part'). In that regard, section 11(6) provides that section 11(7) applies for the purposes of paragraph 1 of Schedule 1 in a case where Northern Ireland is the 'affected part' within the meaning of sub-paragraph (2) of that paragraph.

8.45 The second condition for the disapplication of the market access principles to legislation aimed at preventing or reducing the movement of a pest or disease into the restricting part of the United Kingdom is contained in sub-paragraph (3) of paragraph 1 of Schedule 1; that second condition is that 'it is reasonable to believe that the pest or disease (a) is present in the affected part, and (b) is not present, or is significantly less prevalent, in the restricting part'. Where Northern Ireland is the affected part, section 11(7) applies and provides that in determining whether the condition in sub-paragraph (3) of paragraph 1 of Schedule 1 is met, 'a pest or disease is to be taken to be present in Northern Ireland if it is, or may be, present in qualifying Northern Ireland goods (including when the goods are in Great Britain)'.

8.46 The effect of sub-sections (6) and (7) is that the second condition in paragraph 1 of Schedule 1 (that a pest or disease is present in Northern Ireland) is met even if the pest or disease was merely present in qualifying Northern Ireland goods but not present in Northern Ireland more widely.

E. EXIT PROCEDURES

8.47 There is no mention in the Protocol itself of exit or export declarations regarding goods leaving Northern Ireland. Such need would *prima facie* appear to be inconsistent with the guarantee of unfettered access of Northern Irish goods to the rest of the United Kingdom market. Nor is there any mention of exit or export declarations in the United Kingdom Internal Market Act.[42] Concern was raised by the House of Lords' EU Committee on the lack of certainty as to the need for, and extent of, exit summary declarations further to the government's Command Paper of May 2020. The EU Committee noted in its 1 June 2020 report that the UK government had not adequately addressed the continued uncertainty—and the contradictory statements of Ministers and officials—over whether Northern Ireland businesses will be required to complete exit summary declarations on goods moving to Great Britain.[43]

---

[42] Clause 42(1) if the Bill had provided for a power to disapply or modify declarations and other exit procedures (see the discussion in the BEIS memo of 8 September 2020 to the Delegated Powers and Regulatory Reform Committee at paragraphs 75–83). That provision was not retained in the Act.

[43] See footnote 4 above: House of Lords European Union Committee report of 1 June 2020, , p. 4. And see pp. 40–3 of that report.

That concern arose from the fact that in its technical note on the implementation of the Protocol, the European Commission had stated that the United Kingdom had committed to apply the relevant Union Customs Code formalities in respect of all goods leaving Northern Ireland to either a third country or Great Britain.[44] The concern was, more particularly, that the Union Customs Code imposes requirements to complete export declarations and exit summary declarations, and thus would impose the same requirements on goods moving from Northern Ireland to Great Britain (or third countries), as a 'Safety and Security Declaration', which the EU uses to help enforce its international restrictions and prohibitions.[45] The question arose in practice at a time when there was no clear means of distinguishing goods travelling from Ireland (or the rest of the EU) being exported to Great Britain via Northern Ireland and goods originating from Northern Ireland that would seek to avail of the commitment to unfettered access to the UK internal market (and with which commitment exit summary declarations would be incompatible). 8.48

However, in the Command Paper on the Northern Ireland Protocol published by the Cabinet Office in December 2020, the Chancellor of the Duchy of Lancaster, Mr Gove, stated that the Protocol 'upholds unfettered access for Northern Ireland businesses to their most important market, eliminating any risk of Northern Ireland to Great Britain export declarations'[46] At this stage, the Definition of Qualifying Northern Ireland Goods (EU Exit) Regulations had already come into force, pursuant to which it would now, in principle, be possible to distinguish goods originating in Ireland or the rest of the EU and which may require exit declarations, and qualifying Northern Ireland goods which would not. Section one of that Command Paper further stated that '[w]e have removed the requirement for export declarations for Northern Ireland traders moving their goods from Northern Ireland to Great Britain'.[47] More specifically, the Command Paper recorded that: 8.49

The agreement in principle reached by the Co-Chairs achieves this: proposed declarations in the Joint Committee with legal standing will confirm that the Protocol does not require export or exit declarations for those internal UK movements. At the same time, we will ensure that the relevant authorities have access to equivalent information and reciprocal data sharing on Northern Ireland to Great Britain movements, drawing on data sources such as shipping manifests and enabling the UK to meet our obligations. This will mean we can maintain a seamless flow of goods from Northern Ireland to its most critical market in Great Britain, while maintaining our capacity for effective enforcement and tackling smuggling.[48]

The agreement is contained in the 'Unilateral declarations by the United Kingdom of Great Britain and Northern Ireland and the European Union in the Withdrawal Agreement 8.50

[44] The commitment was of course made in Article 5(3) and (4) of the Protocol by which EU customs legislation was made applicable in Northern Ireland. See European Commission, 'Task Force for Relations with the United Kingdom', *Technical note on the implementation of the Protocol on Ireland/Northern Ireland* (30 April 2020), https://ec.europa.eu/info/sites/info/files/brexit_files/info_site/20200430_note_protocol_ie_ni.pdf.The EU Customs Code is contained in Regulation 952/2013: see Title VIII, Articles 263–277 and in particular Article 271 as to the declarations to made where goods are leaving the EU's customs territory.

[45] In oral evidence to the EU Committee of the House of Lords on 21 October 2019, Minister Stephen Barclay had indicated that 'Exit summary declarations will be required in terms of Northern Ireland to GB'.

[46] Command Paper, p. 3. https://assets.publishing.service.gov.uk/government/uploads/system/uploads/attachment_data/file/950601/Northern_Ireland_Protocol_-_Command_Paper.pdf.

[47] ibid, paragraph 9.

[48] ibid, paragraph 16.

Joint Committee on export declarations' of 17 December 2020.[49] The declarations were in two parts, one by the United Kingdom, the other by the EU. The United Kingdom's unilateral declaration materially states:

In respect of goods moving from Northern Ireland to other parts of the United Kingdom's internal market, the United Kingdom may give effect to Article 263(1) and Article 269(1) of Regulation (EU) No 952/2013 by deeming a pre-departure and/or export declaration to have been made where equivalence regarding the content and timeliness of information provided to the competent customs authorities of the United Kingdom is ensured by other means and by using appropriate electronic data-processing techniques. The United Kingdom will ensure that information relating to the implementation of the preceding sentence will be made available to the Union representatives referred to in the Decision of the Withdrawal Agreement Joint Committee on arrangements under Article 12(2) of the Protocol.

In this regard, the United Kingdom confirms its intention that standard export procedures will apply where goods:

1. are placed under a procedure listed in Article 210 of Regulation (EU) No 952/2013;
2. are in temporary storage in accordance with Article 144 of that Regulation;
3. are subject to provisions of Union law falling within the second sentence of Article 6(1) of the Protocol which prohibit or restrict the exportation of goods;
4. are placed under the export procedure within the Union; or
5. do not exceed EUR 3000 in value and are packed or loaded for export shipment within the Union.

8.51 By virtue of the latter aspect of the declaration, the UK government accepts that export declarations will be needed in a limited number of circumstances. This is acknowledged in the Command Paper on the Northern Ireland Protocol which states that 'for a very small number of international obligations, or where goods are not in free circulation, placed into voluntary special procedures, dispatched from Ireland or where the trader seeks a specific facilitation, export declarations are needed. Specific arrangements are normally applied to 64 areas of trade by the UK and EU: for Northern Ireland to Great Britain movements we have further limited these processes to only 14 areas underpinned by specific international obligations. These concern only very limited categories of trade—such as those involving endangered species—and will have negligible implications for trade as a whole.'[50]

8.52 The EU's unilateral declaration in response simply states: '[t]he European Union takes note of the United Kingdom's declaration setting out the practice it intends to put in place as regards the movement of goods from Northern Ireland to Great Britain'.

8.53 The government considered that removing the need for export declarations would further mean that, in the event that a Free Trade Agreement was reached between the United Kingdom and the EU (which, in the event, occurred later in December 2020 with the parties entering into the Trade and Cooperation Agreement (TCA)), the standalone agreement to remove export declarations would continue to have effect: '[i]t would mean that Northern Ireland businesses using the UK Trader Scheme would not need to complete origin certification; and if goods could not qualify for tariff-free trade under a Free Trade Agreement's Rules

[49] https://assets.publishing.service.gov.uk/government/uploads/system/uploads/attachment_data/file/946660/Unilateral_declarations_by_the_United_Kingdom_of_Great_Britain_and_Northern_Ireland_and_the_European_Union_in_the_Withdrawal_Agreement_Joint_Committee_on_export_declarations.pdf.

[50] Command Paper, paragraph 17.

of Origin requirements, they could still be traded tariff-free under this deal by those businesses within the scheme'.[51]

F. NOTIFICATION OF STATE AID

1. The State Aid Regime in Northern Ireland

As explained in further detail in chapter 9 below, during 2020 it became clear that the UK government was not prepared to accept continued application of EU State aid rules[52] as part of the continuing trade relationship with the EU, but was planning to create its own system of subsidy control.[53] As matters stood before the passage of the Act, the position after the end of the transition period on 31 December 2020 was that the EU State aid rules would no longer apply in the United Kingdom, leaving the devolved administrations (and indeed the United Kingdom Government, in England) free from any constraint on the grant of subsidies that adversely affected other parts of the United Kingdom, subject to whatever regime the UK government decided (or agreed with the EU) to put in place to replace EU State aid rules. 8.54

However, the position in Northern Ireland was different and the Protocol was drafted to ensure that EU state aid law remained, in material part, applicable in Northern Ireland. Article 10 of the Northern Ireland Protocol thus provides: 8.55

1. The provisions of Union law listed in Annex 5 to this Protocol shall apply to the United Kingdom, including with regard to measures supporting the production of and trade in agricultural products in Northern Ireland, in respect of measures which affect that trade between Northern Ireland and the Union which is subject to this Protocol.[54]
2. Notwithstanding paragraph 1, the provisions of Union law referred to in that paragraph shall not apply with respect to measures taken by the United Kingdom authorities to support the production of and trade in agricultural products in Northern Ireland up to a determined maximum overall annual level of support, and provided that a determined minimum percentage of that exempted support complies with the provisions of Annex 2 to the WTO Agreement on Agriculture. The determination of the maximum exempted overall annual

[51] Command Paper, paragraph 22.

[52] As the EU proposed as part of its position on the negotiation of a post-Brexit trading relationship with the EU: see paragraph 94 of the European Council's Directives for the Negotiation of a New Partnership with the United Kingdom of Great Britain and Northern Ireland, https://www.consilium.europa.eu/media/42736/st05870-ad01re03-en20.pdf: 'The envisaged partnership should ensure the application of Union State aid rules to and in the United Kingdom.'

[53] Thus, paragraph 65 of the UK government's negotiating position (The Future Relationship with the EU: The UK's Approach to Negotiations, February 2020, https://assets.publishing.service.gov.uk/government/uploads/system/uploads/attachment_data/file/868874/The_Future_Relationship_with_the_EU.pdf, stated that: '[t]he UK will have its own regime of subsidy control' and that the agreement with the EU should contain only provisions relating to transparency and consultations.

[54] As the Command Paper on the Northern Ireland Protocol of December 2020 put it: 'The Protocol sets out that EU state aid rules will apply in certain cases where this is relevant to trade between Northern Ireland and the EU. However this does not mean that state aid rules will apply to Northern Ireland as they do today: it is limited in scope to the movement of goods and wholesale electricity markets, and concerns only measures that "affect trade" between Northern Ireland and the EU. Northern Ireland will enjoy new freedoms in relation to support for its services and other sectors of the future' ibid, paragraph 49.

level of support and the minimum percentage shall be governed by the procedures set out in Annex 6.[55

3. Where the European Commission examines information regarding a measure by the United Kingdom authorities that may constitute unlawful aid that is subject to paragraph 1, it shall ensure that the United Kingdom is kept fully and regularly informed of the progress and outcome of the examination of that measure.[56]

8.56 Thus, pursuant to Article 10 of the Northern Ireland Protocol, EU State aid rules will apply in relation to trade in goods and electricity between Northern Ireland and the EU.[57] Such EU State aid law will apply in domestic law via section 7A of the European Union (Withdrawal) Act 2018.

8.57 This led to further unilateral declarations being made by the EU and the UK government via the Joint Committee on 17 December 2020.[58] In its unilateral declaration on the approach to Article 10(1) of the Protocol, the EU stated:

> When applying Art. 107 TFEU to situations referred to in Art. 10(1) of the Protocol, the European Commission will have due regard to Northern Ireland's integral place in the United Kingdom's internal market. The European Union underlines that, in any event, an effect on trade between Northern Ireland and the Union which is subject to this Protocol cannot be merely hypothetical, presumed, or without a genuine and direct link to Northern Ireland. It must be established why the measure is liable to have such an effect on trade between Northern Ireland and the Union, based on the real foreseeable effects of the measure.

8.58 This declaration thus addressed the UK government's concern that the Protocol could be interpreted to enable unfair 'reach back' of rules to subsidies given to companies in Great Britain. The UK government's statement of 17 September 2020 rejected any insistence that the EU's State aid provisions should apply in Great Britain where there is no link or only a

[55] The more detailed specifications made for the State aid exemptions in relation to agricultural and fisheries subsidies are contained in the Decision of the Joint Committee on agricultural subsidies of 17 December 2020: https://assets.publishing.service.gov.uk/government/uploads/system/uploads/attachment_data/file/949845/Decision_of_the_Withdrawal_Agreement_Joint_Committee_on_agricultural_subsidies.pdf.The Command Paper on the Northern Ireland Protocol of December 2020 in this regard observed that '[t]hese state aid exemptions enable the Northern Ireland Executive to provide their fisheries and agricultural sectors with the support they need. Northern Ireland will leave the Common Agricultural Policy along with the rest of the UK, with the freedom to design its own subsidy policy to suit local needs and with substantial flexibility with these state aid exemptions' (ibid, paragraph 56).

[56] As paragraph 67 of the Explanatory Notes recalls, other existing statutory powers to provide financial assistance extend to some but not all of the United Kingdom, e.g. section 31 of the Local Government Act 2003 which only extends to England and Wales, or section 126 of the Housing Grants, Construction and Regeneration Act 1996 which does not extend to Northern Ireland.

[57] The Protocol provides the basis for the continued operation of the Single Electricity Market and trade of wholesale electricity across the island of Ireland. See Article 9 which provides: '[t]he provisions of Union law governing wholesale electricity markets listed in Annex 4 to this Protocol shall apply, under the conditions set out in that Annex, to and in the United Kingdom in respect of Northern Ireland'.

[58] https://assets.publishing.service.gov.uk/government/uploads/system/uploads/attachment_data/file/946286/Unilateral_declarations_by_the_European_Union_and_the_United_Kingdom_of_Great_Britain_and_Northern_Ireland_in_the_Withdrawal_Agreement_Joint_Committee_on_Article_10_1__of_the_Protocol.pdf.

trivial link to commercial operations taking place in Northern Ireland. The EU's unilateral declaration of 17 December 2020 thus addresses those concerns.[59]

The Act of course makes provision for the UK Parliament to have the exclusive ability to legislate for a UK subsidy control regime once the United Kingdom ceases to follow EU State aid rules at the end of the transition period. The subsidies regime is considered in detail in chapter 9 below. However, any future subsidies regime that the UK Parliament may bring into being will be subject to Article 10 of the Protocol on Ireland/Northern Ireland in the Withdrawal Agreement whilst it applies to the United Kingdom. **8.59**

Section 48 of the Act is entitled 'Guidance on Article 10 of the Northern Ireland Protocol'. Its purpose is to ensure 'a uniform approach across the UK to the application of EU State aid law under Article 10 of the Northern Ireland Protocol'.[60] Section 48(1) requires the Secretary of State to publish guidance on the practical application of Article 10 of the Northern Ireland Protocol (state aid). Section 48(2)–(5) then provides: **8.60**

> (2) For that purpose Article 10 is to be read in the light of—
> (a) any relevant decision or recommendation of the Joint Committee,[61] and
> (b) any relevant declaration that is made in the Joint Committee by either party, of which the other party takes note.
>
> (3) The guidance must be published before the end of the period of one month beginning with the day on which this section comes into force.
>
> (4) A person with public functions relating to the implementation of Article 10 (including functions involving the provision of financial assistance or other subsidies) must have regard to the guidance when exercising such functions.

Public authorities will be required to have regard to the guidance, helping to ensure a consistent and uniform application of Article 10. **8.61**

Section 48(5) provides that the Secretary of State may (a) revise or replace the guidance; or (b) if satisfied it is no longer necessary, withdraw the guidance. **8.62**

2. Notification of State Aid Under the Northern Ireland Protocol

Section 49 of the Act stipulates that only the Secretary of State may give the European Commission notification or information related to aid where Article 10 applies. EU State aid law requires notification or information relating to aid to be provided to the European Commission. At present, this function is performed by the Secretary of State for Foreign, Commonwealth and Development Affairs via the UK Mission in Brussels. **8.63**

G. THE DEMOCRATIC CONSENT PROCESS

Article 18 of the Protocol on Ireland/Northern Ireland to the Agreement on the withdrawal of the United Kingdom from the EU makes provision for consent to be provided by the **8.64**

[59] The United Kingdom's unilateral declaration in response simply states: '[t]he United Kingdom takes note of the European Union's declaration on its application of Art. 107 TFEU to situations referred to in Art. 10(1) of the Protocol'.

[60] Explanatory Notes, paragraph 7(e).

[61] The Joint Committee again being the committee established by Article 164(1) of the EU Withdrawal Agreement.

Northern Ireland Assembly to the continued application of Articles 5–10 of that Protocol. Article 18(1) thus provides that '[w]ithin 2 months before the end of both the initial period and any subsequent period, the United Kingdom shall provide the opportunity for democratic consent in Northern Ireland to the continued application of Articles 5 to 10'.[62] The initial period and subsequent period are provided for in Article 18(5) as follows:

> For the purposes of this Article, the initial period is the period ending 4 years after the end of the transition period. Where the decision reached in a given period was on the basis of a majority of Members of the Northern Ireland Assembly, present and voting, the subsequent period is the 4 year period following that period, for as long as Articles 5 to 10 continue to apply. Where the decision reached in a given period had cross-community support, the subsequent period is the 8-year period following that period, for as long as Articles 5 to 10 continue to apply.

8.65 Consent must therefore be given every four or eight years depending whether it is given on a simple majority or cross-community basis.[63]

8.66 Section 55 of the Act confirms that when Articles 5–10 of the Northern Ireland Protocol cease to apply (and they will so cease if the requisite consent is not provided for their continuation), section 11 and Part 5 of the Act as well as section 8C(5A) of the European Union (Withdrawal) Act 2018 will also cease to have effect.

8.67 The Protocol on Ireland/ Northern Ireland (Democratic Consent Process) (EU Exit) Regulations 2020[64] make further provision for that democratic consent process. They do so by inserting a new Schedule 6A in the Northern Ireland Act 1998. Part 3 of that Schedule makes provision for the process that will apply in circumstances where there is a functioning Northern Ireland Executive. Part 4 makes provision for the process that will apply in circumstances where there is not a functioning Executive in place. This is consistent with the undertaking made by the UK government in its declaration concerning the operation of the 'Democratic consent in Northern Ireland' provision of the Protocol made on 17 October 2019.

8.68 It has been noted that since any refusal to provide consent to the continued operation of the Protocol would bring back into play the hard border on the island of Ireland that the Protocol is designed to prevent, any such decision seems for the time being improbable.[65]

---

[62] Article 18(2) provides that '[f]or the purposes of paragraph 1, the United Kingdom shall seek democratic consent in Northern Ireland in a manner consistent with the 1998 Agreement. A decision expressing democratic consent shall be reached strictly in accordance with the unilateral declaration concerning the operation of the "Democratic consent in Northern Ireland" provision of the Protocol on Ireland/Northern Ireland made by the United Kingdom on 17 October 2019, including with respect to the roles of the Northern Ireland Executive and Assembly.'

[63] Article 18(6) provides that cross-community support means:

'(a) a majority of those Members of the Legislative Assembly present and voting, including a majority of the unionist and nationalist designations present and voting; or

(b) a weighted majority (60%) of Members of the Legislative Assembly present and voting, including at least 40% of each of the nationalist and unionist designations present and voting'.

[64] SI 2020/1500, which came into force on 10 December 2020.

[65] See Weatherill, 'The Protocol of Ireland/ Northern Ireland', n. 3 above.

H. ADDITIONAL PROVISIONS IN CONNECTION WITH NORTHERN IRELAND

Section 54 of the Act is entitled 'Protection of Act against modification' and inserts references to the United Kingdom Internal Market Act into the Scotland Act 1998, the Government of Wales Act 2006 and the Northern Ireland Act 1998, so that the Act is treated as a protected or entrenched enactment under each. This means that the Scottish Parliament, the National Assembly for Wales, and the Northern Ireland Assembly may not pass legislation that amends the Act or modifies its application. **8.69**

Section 55 also makes clear that nothing in the Act limits the power to make provision under section 8C of the European Union (Withdrawal) Act 2018, or the effect of such regulations, save that section 55(3) inserts a new sub-section 5A into section 8(c) which provides that any such regulations 'may not amend, repeal or otherwise modify the operation of section 47' of the Act, subject to some exceptions. That, evidently, is to reinforce the commitment to ensuring unfettered access of Northern Ireland goods to the UK internal market contained in section 47. **8.70**

I. CONCLUSION

The imperative to avoid a hard border on the Island of Ireland could be achieved in two principal ways. First, the United Kingdom could have agreed to full regulatory alignment with EU law as it applied to goods and related matters such as customs law and indirect tax. That was the approach that Prime Minister May commended to Parliament by way of the Withdrawal Agreement reached in 2018 and which, having been repeatedly rejected in the Commons, cost Mrs May her job. The second, adopted by Mr Johnson, was to accept a customs and regulatory border between Great Britain and Northern Ireland which served to maintain Northern Ireland within the EU and subject to EU legislation applicable to goods. **8.71**

However, having persuaded Parliament to back the latter model, it is misleading to overstate the extent of the UK internal market. Plainly there is now such a market as it concerns England, Wales, and Scotland. But Northern Ireland's regulatory alignment with the EU means that, to a limited extent with regard to the trade in goods moving from West to East, but to a materially greater extent with regard to the trade in goods moving from East to West, there is no single UK internal market. As regulatory divergence between the United Kingdom and the EU grows, so too will the number of instances where, in particular, goods manufactured in or imported into Great Britain will not be capable of being placed on the Northern Irish market. That constraint does not operate in reverse since compliance with EU authorizations and regulatory standards will be treated as entitling Northern Irish exporters to place their goods on the market in Great Britain. It follows that the principle of mutual recognition and the principle of non-discrimination will apply asymmetrically, to the potentially greater detriment of UK producers. That split in the UK internal market was the inevitable consequence of Mr Johnson's preferred solution.[66] **8.72**

[66] The cleavage in the regulatory approach applicable as between Northern Ireland on the one hand and Great Britain on the other, is emphasized in the context of enforcement. EU law will apply to Articles 5 and 7–10 of the Protocol in the same way that EU law applied generally throughout the period of UK membership of the EU, meaning that the Court of Justice of the European Union (CJEU) continues to have jurisdiction to

8.73 By the same token, it is not only the United Kingdom that has accepted a division within its own internal market. As has been pointed out, the EU has, exceptionally, 'agreed that its de facto external frontier will lie within the territory of a third country, the UK, and that the primary responsibility for its policing will belong with the public authorities of that third country, while also accepting that its own de jure external frontier, between Ireland and Northern Ireland, will remain unpoliced. The EU has also conceded the fragmentation of its own internal market *acquis*. Pursuant to the Protocol, Northern Ireland is to be regulated by some but not all the EU rules governing goods, and not at all by EU rules governing workers or service provision. There is, it seems, a core to EU internal market law which must be applied in order for the EU to be prepared to treat the border between Ireland and Northern Ireland as soft in the same way that borders found internally within the EU are soft, and a wider body of internal market law of less pressing significance.' To that extent, the EU has made a concession that has rendered its sacred four, invisible freedoms, divisible.[67]

resolves dispute arising over the application of those provisions and private parties can still seek to rely on the concepts of direct effect and supremacy in private law disputes to which the EU legislation made applicable in Northern Ireland is relevant. Article 13(2) of the Protocol thus provides that 'the provisions of this Protocol referring to Union law or to concepts or provisions thereof shall in their implementation and application be interpreted in conformity with the relevant case law of the Court of Justice of the European Union'.

[67] We are grateful to Professor Stephen Weatherill for this observation, made in his paper, 'The UK Internal Market', a working copy of which he kindly shared with us in the course of writing this guide.

9
FINANCIAL ASSISTANCE AND SUBSIDIES

A. INTRODUCTION

9.01 This chapter examines sections 50–53 of the Act, found in Parts 6 and 7 of the Act, concerning financial assistance and subsidy control.[1] Sections 50 and 51 confer on Ministers of the UK government a wide power to provide financial assistance for a wide range of purposes across the United Kingdom. Sections 52 and 53 deal with the proposed new United Kingdom-wide subsidy regime. Both pairs of provisions gave rise to concern in Parliament and in the devolved administrations as to their implications for the powers of the devolved governments.

B. FINANCIAL ASSISTANCE

9.02 Section 50 provides that a 'Minister of the Crown' (that is to say, a Minister of the UK government[2]) may provide, out of money provided by Parliament, 'financial assistance'[3] to any person for, or in connection with, a list of purposes set out in subsection (1): (a) promoting[4]

---

[1] Each of these provisions commenced at 11 p.m. on 31 December 2020 (defined as 'IP completion day' in Schedule 1 to the Interpretation Act 1978 by reference to section 39 of the European Union (Withdrawal Agreement) Act 2020): see regulation 2 of the United Kingdom Internal Market Act 2020 (Commencement No. 1) Regulations 2020.

[2] See section 58 of the Act, referring to section 8(1) of the Ministers of the Crown Act 1975, which provides that 'Minister of the Crown' means 'the holder of an office in Her Majesty's Government in the United Kingdom, and includes the Treasury, the Board of Trade and the Defence Council'.

[3] Section 51(1) provides that financial assistance may be made by way of grants, loans, indemnities, or in any other form, may be made conditional (including conditional as to repayment), may be provided under a contract, and may be provided to an investment fund for onward investment.

[4] Defined in section 50(2) to include 'taking any measure likely to contribute directly or indirectly to economic development (which might include, for example, measures relating to social inclusion)'.

Blackstone's Guide to the UK Internal Market Act 2020. Alan Bates, Brendan McGurk, George Peretz QC, and Jack Williams, Oxford University Press.

DOI: 10.1093/oso/9780192856203.003.0009

economic development; (b) providing[5] infrastructure;[6] (c) supporting cultural activities; (d) supporting activities relating to sport;[7] (e) supporting international education and training activities and exchanges; and (f) supporting education and training activities and exchanges within the United Kingdom.

9.03 The drafting of the various paragraphs of section 50(1) makes it clear that the purpose for which the financial assistance is granted may relate either to the United Kingdom as a whole or to 'particular areas of', or 'places in', the United Kingdom. There is therefore no requirement that the activity or project concern, or be for the benefit of, the United Kingdom as a whole or of more than one part of the United Kingdom. For example, an activity or project that concerns, or is for the benefit of, only Wales and no other part of the United Kingdom would qualify for financial assistance from the UK government under this section.

9.04 As paragraph 80 of the Explanatory Notes points out,[8] the purposes listed in section 50(1) fall within, or partly within, areas of devolved competence under the various devolution Acts. That paragraph also makes the point that UK Ministers already had some powers in other statutes, in particular the Industrial Development Act 1982, to provide funding in the devolved nations even in areas of devolved competence.[9]

9.05 In parliamentary debates, Ministers argued that this provision would 'ensure that the United Kingdom Government are well positioned following the transition period to deliver investments to replace EU structural funds'[10]—though, as the Scottish government noted, there was no requirement that spending be confined to areas supported by such funds.[11] The point that funding under the new power would replace spending by the 'unelected' EU was also used to reject criticism that the UK government could spend in a way that was not agreed by the relevant devolved government,[12] and to persuade Parliament to reject amendments designed to require the consent of the devolved governments before funding could be provided in their nations. The Minister did, however, state that the government 'intend[ed] to take a much more collaborative approach to delivering replacements to EU programmes than was ever the case with the European Union mandate. This will include engaging heavily with local authorities and the devolved Administrations, as well as with wider organisations.'[13]

[5] Defined in section 50(2) to include 'acquiring, designing, constructing, converting, improving, operating and repairing infrastructure'.

[6] Defined in section 50(2) to include: utilities; transport facilities; health, educational, cultural, and sports facilities; court or prison facilities; and housing.

[7] Defined in section 50(2) to include any physical recreation.

[8] Explanatory Notes to the United Kingdom Internal Market Act 2020 (hereafter, 'Explanatory Notes').

[9] See section 56 of the Scotland Act 1998 and paragraph 1 of Schedule 3A to the Government of Wales Act 2006, both of which provide that UK Ministers jointly exercise powers of funding under the Industrial Development Act 1982 (and various other Acts giving funding powers) with the relevant devolved governments notwithstanding the provision in those Acts for the general transfer of powers within devolved competence from UK Ministers to the devolved governments.

[10] Hansard HC, 16 October 2020, col. 437 (Chloe Smith MP).

[11] Memorandum from the Scottish government on the Internal Market Bill, https://archive2029.parliament.scot/S5_Finance/General%20Documents/SPLCM-S05-47.pdf, paragraph 99.

[12] As the Scottish government pointed out, ibid, the provision 'would allow the UK Government to spend money including in devolved areas without the consent or input of the Scottish Ministers, or the approval of the Scottish Parliament'. It went on (paragraph 106) to express concern that the provision would lead to a 'risk of an uncoordinated and potentially incoherent approach to spending in devolved areas if the UK Government and the Scottish Government have separate spending programmes on, for example, education, culture and infrastructure. Moreover, for the Scottish Government to have to coordinate with the UK Government plans to spend in devolved areas would constrain current devolved decision making.'

[13] Hansard HC, 16 October 2020, col. 437 (Chloe Smith MP).

Ministers also stated that the reason why the UK government was given power to fund projects directly, rather than through the relevant devolved governments, was that it was 'sensible' for the UK government directly to fund projects in the case of 'investment that is strategic, that is at a certain scale, that can be intra-UK and that can provide benefits universally across the UK'[14] and could take place 'across the boundaries of or nations'[15] (though, as noted above, the provision does not restrict funding to projects that have an 'intra-UK' or 'cross-boundary' aspect or are of a 'certain scale'). **9.06**

The UK government has announced a new UK Shared Prosperity Fund, starting in 2022, with investment that will 'at least match EU receipts, on average reaching about £1.5 billion a year': the legal basis for the Fund will be section 50 of the Act. The Fund will include assistance that will 'target places most in need across the UK' and 'will enable joined-up, holistic investment to support local communities and people', and assistance to 'people most in need through bespoke employment and skills programmes that are tailored to local need'. The UK government has stated that 'we intend to work with the Devolved Administrations to ensure that funding is used to best effect and supports citizens across the UK', a commitment that it says that it has demonstrated 'by confirming that the Devolved Administrations will have a place within the governance structures for the [Fund]'.[16] **9.07**

In the period before that Fund is in operation, and while EU structural funds continue to provide investment in the United Kingdom under programmes commenced before Brexit, there will be a UK Community Renewal Fund for 2021/22, providing additional investment of £220 million: this will be used to support local pilot programmes ahead of the UK Shared Prosperity Fund.[17] **9.08**

One issue that has yet to be clarified is how the new UK subsidy control regime[18] will affect, or apply to, the UK Shared Prosperity Fund. **9.09**

C. SUBSIDIES

Section 52 of the Act inserts identical new specific reservations relating to subsidy control into each of the lists of specific reservations in the Scotland Act 1998, the Northern Ireland Act 1998, and the Government of Wales Act 2006. The effect in each case is to remove the area of subsidy control, as defined in the reservations, from devolved competence. That has two effects: first, that the relevant devolved legislature cannot legislate within the area of subsidy control as defined;[19] and, second, that the Sewel convention written into each of those statutes (under which the UK Parliament will not normally legislate for those nations in relation to devolved matters without the consent of the relevant legislatures) will not apply to UK legislation on subsidy control.[20] **9.10**

[14] ibid, col. 438.

[15] ibid, col. 440.

[16] https://www.gov.uk/government/publications/uk-community-renewal-fund-prospectus/uk-community-renewal-fund-prospectus-2021-22, updated 24 March 2021.

[17] ibid.

[18] See the following section.

[19] See e.g. section 29(1) and (2)(b) of the Scotland Act 1998, which provides that legislation by the Scottish Parliament is not law, to the extent that it relates to reserved matters.

[20] See e.g. section 28(8) of the Scotland Act 1998 and, generally, the discussion in *Miller v Secretary of State for Exiting the EU* [2017] UKSC 5, at paragraphs 136–151: the Supreme Court concluded that section 28(8)

9.11 The terms of the reservation are: '[r]egulation of the provision[21] of subsidies[22] which are or may be distortive or harmful[23] by a public authority[24] to persons supplying goods or services in the course of a business'.

9.12 The background to section 52 is that, while the United Kingdom was a member of the EU, it was (and every UK public authority was) subject to the EU State aid rules contained in Articles 107 and 108 of the Treaty on the Functioning of the European Union (TFEU). In particular, Article 108(3) TFEU made it unlawful for any public authority (including the devolved governments and legislatures) to implement any measure that amounted to State aid unless that measure had been notified to, and cleared by, the European Commission under Article 107(2) or (3) TFEU, or fell within specific regulations (so-called 'block exemptions') made by the European Commission.

9.13 Against that background, during the period of UK membership of the EU, devolution legislation did not need to address the question of whether and how the devolved institutions should be restrained from granting subsidies in ways that adversely affected other parts of the United Kingdom or the United Kingdom's trading partners. That possibility—a very real issue in a number of federal or quasi-federal countries where state or provincial governments have wide fiscal and legislative powers[25]—was effectively precluded by EU law, particularly as the threshold condition for a measure being a State aid under the TFEU (that the measure have an actual or potential effect on trade between Member States) is notoriously low,[26] so

of that Act (and parallel provisions in other devolution legislation) was a political convention and not a legal rule justiciable by the courts.

[21] The reservations state that '[a] subsidy is provided "by a public authority" if it is provided by that authority directly or indirectly'.

[22] The reservations define a 'subsidy' as including 'assistance provided to a person directly or indirectly by way of income or price support, grant, loan, guarantee, indemnity, the provision of goods or services and any other kind of assistance, whether financial or otherwise and whether actual or contingent'. It may be noted that that definition (in particular 'any other kind of assistance') would appear to catch tax measures, such as exemptions from tax rules, though the definition does not expressly do so (contrast Article 363(2) of the UK/EU Trade and Cooperation Agreement, which states that the provisions on subsidies do cover tax measures subject to the provisions set out). The Minister stated in debate on the Bill, in response to a suggestion that the provision be amended to make express reference to research and development grants, that: '[f]or the purpose of the reservation of subsidy control, the definition of a subsidy is deliberately broad to ensure that we have sufficient scope to design a future domestic regime that meets the needs of the United Kingdom. To ensure that we cover a broad range of financial interventions, the definition is not currently limited by reference to any specific policy purpose or sector. Subsidies may be given for a variety of purposes, and it would be anomalous to single out just one of them here. The current wording in the clause already encompasses assistance provided to a person directly or indirectly by way of grants and is therefore sufficient to cover research and development grants' (Hansard HL, 9 November 2020, col. 943, Lord Callanan).

[23] The reservations state that a subsidy is 'distortive or harmful' if it 'distorts competition between, or otherwise causes harm or injury to, persons supplying goods or services in the course of a business, whether or not those persons are established in the United Kingdom'. The latter phrase is needed given that one purpose of the proposed new UK subsidy control regime is to implement international agreements that restrain each party from subsidizing in ways that harm industry in the other party.

[24] The reservations define a 'public authority' as meaning 'a person who exercises functions of a public nature'.

[25] See e.g. the 'national beauty contest' between US States competing to be the location of Amazon's second headquarters described in https://www.theatlantic.com/ideas/archive/2018/11/amazons-hq2-spectacle-should-be-illegal/575539/ (which records that 'every year, American cities spend up to $90 billion in tax breaks and cash grants to urge companies to move among states').

[26] See K. Bacon, *EU Law of State Aid* (3rd edn, OUP 2017), paragraphs 2.150–2.153 and Case C-518/13 *Eventech* ECLI:EU:C:2015:9 at paragraphs 65–69.

that it was hard in practice to conceive of a subsidy measure by a devolved government, or the UK government in England, that would have had a significantly adverse effect on another part of the United Kingdom but which would not have been subject to EU State aid rules.

As a result, the devolution statutes contained no provision that limited the ability of the devolved institutions, within their devolved powers, to grant harmful or distortive subsidies. Nor (once all the devolution statutes had moved to the 'reserved powers' model) did they list subsidy control as a reserved competence in relation to which the UK Parliament could legislate without being subject to the Sewel convention, despite the statement by the Minister during passage of the Bill that 'the Government have always been clear in their view that the regulation of state aid ... was a reserved matter'.[27] The closest they came to such a reservation was a paragraph that reserved 'regulation of anti-competitive practices and agreements; abuse of dominant position; monopolies and mergers';[28] but it seemed unlikely that that provision covered subsidies by public authorities as opposed to the regulation of anti-competitive practices and agreements between undertakings that is the subject matter of the Competition Act 1998 (the reference to 'anti-competitive practices' being needed because Chapter I of the Competition Act 1998 applies to 'concerted practices' between undertakings as well as to 'agreements'). 9.14

Further, during 2020 it became clear that the UK government was not prepared to accept continued application of EU State aid rules[29] as part of the continuing trade relationship with the EU, but was planning to create its own system of subsidy control.[30] As matters stood before the passage of the Act, therefore, the position after the end of the transition period on 31 December 2020 was that the EU State aid rules (apart from Article 10 of the Ireland–Northern Ireland Protocol[31]) would no longer apply in the United Kingdom, leaving the devolved administrations (and indeed the UK government, in England) free from any constraint on the grant of subsidies that adversely affected other parts of the United Kingdom, subject to whatever regime the UK government decided (or agreed with the EU) to put in place to replace EU State aid rules. 9.15

On the same date that the UK Internal Market Bill was published (9 September 2020), the UK Department of Business, Energy and Industrial Strategy announced by written statement[32] that the UK government would not produce any proposals for a new regime before 2021, although there would be 'guidance' to public authorities as to ensuring compliance with the United Kingdom's international obligations on subsidies (principally under the World Trade Organization (WTO) Agreement on Subsidies and Countervailing Measures). 9.16

---

[27] Hansard HL, 9 November 2020, col. 942 (Lord Callanan).

[28] See e.g. paragraph C3 of Part II of Schedule 5 to the Scotland Act 1998.

[29] As the EU proposed as part of its position on the negotiation of a post-Brexit trading relationship with the EU: see paragraph 94 of the European Council's Directives for the Negotiation of a New Partnership with the United Kingdom of Great Britain and Northern Ireland, https://www.consilium.europa.eu/media/42736/st05870-ad01re03-en20.pdf: 'The envisaged partnership should ensure the application of Union State aid rules to and in the United Kingdom.'

[30] Thus, paragraph 65 of the UK government's negotiating position (The Future Relationship with the EU: The UK's Approach to Negotiations, February 2020, https://assets.publishing.service.gov.uk/government/uploads/system/uploads/attachment_data/file/868874/The_Future_Relationship_with_the_EU.pdf, stated that: '[t]he UK will have its own regime of subsidy control' and that the agreement with the EU should contain only provisions relating to transparency and consultations.

[31] See chapter 8 above.

[32] https://www.gov.uk/government/news/government-sets-out-plans-for-new-approach-to-subsidy-control.

At some point in 2021, however, there would be a consultation on the shape of the new regime.

9.17 At the time of the Bill's introduction, and throughout the debates on its passage, the position was therefore that it was unclear (a) whether the UK government would accept any obligation to introduce a subsidy control regime as part of the post-Brexit trading relationship with the EU (which was under negotiation until 24 December 2020, after Royal Assent to the Act); and (b) what (if any) subsidy control regime would be proposed after the end of the transition period on 31 December 2020.

9.18 The purpose of section 52 was, therefore, to give the UK government a solid basis for legislating for a system of subsidy control (as and when it chose to propose one) without being subject to the Sewel convention. In the words of the Minister: '[r]eserving will ensure we take a coherent and consistent approach to the way public authorities within the UK subsidise businesses, supporting the smooth functioning of the UK's internal market. A unified approach will reduce uncertainty for UK businesses and prevent additional costs in supply chains and to consumers.'[33]

9.19 In the House of Lords, both the Scottish and Welsh governments supported an amendment put forward by Lord Thomas of Cwmgiedd to the effect that section 52 would take effect only after the United Kingdom and devolved governments had sought to agree a common framework for subsidy control. In response to that, the Minister proposed what became section 53 of the Act, namely a provision that, in the words of the Minister, 'ensures that before publishing any relevant report relating to the outcomes of the UK subsidy control consultation, the Secretary of State will provide a draft of the proposed response to the devolved authorit[ies], inviting [them] to make representations. The Secretary of State will then consider any representations and determine whether to alter the report in the light of that consideration. This proposal makes it clear that the UK Government are committed to involving the devolved Administrations in the forthcoming development of proposals for a UK-wide subsidy control regime.'[34]

9.20 After Royal Assent to the Act, on 24 December 2020 the UK government reached agreement on a new Trade and Cooperation Agreement (TCA) with the EU. Articles 363–375 of the TCA set out requirements for each party to operate a subsidy control regime, with an independent body and provision for domestic courts to review the grant of subsidies for compliance with principles and prohibitions set out in the TCA. Section 29 of the EU (Future Relationship) Act 2020 gives the TCA the force of law in the United Kingdom to the extent that it is required to be implemented:[35] the effect of section 29 is therefore, as from 31

[33] Hansard HL, 9 November 2020, col. 942 (Lord Callanan).

[34] Hansard HL, 25 November 2020, col. 1307 (Lord Callanan).

[35] See e.g. *Lipton v BA City Flyer Ltd* [2021] EWCA Civ 454, at paragraphs 78–82: 'The section 29 mechanism provides that domestic law (as defined) "has effect ... with such modifications as are required for the purposes of implementing in that law the Trade and Cooperation Agreement". The phrase "has effect" is important. Parliament has mandated a test based upon the result or effect. The phrase "has" makes clear that this process of modification is automatic i.e. it occurs without the need for further intervention by Parliament. The concept of modification is interpreted broadly in section 37(1) to "include" (and therefore is not limited to) amendment, repeal or revocation. Section 29 is capable of achieving any one or more of these effects. This does not lay down a principle of purposive interpretation (such as is found in section 3 Human Rights Act) but amounts to a generic mechanism to achieve full implementation. It transposes the TCA into domestic law, implicitly changing domestic law in the process. Applying section 29 to domestic law on a particular issue

December 2020, to control the powers of the United Kingdom and devolved governments to grant subsidies to the extent that that control is required by Articles 363–375 of the TCA. Section 52 of the United Kingdom Internal Market Act had the effect that, to that extent, the Sewel convention did not apply in relation to section 29.

The consultation on a future UK subsidy control regime referred to in section 53(1)(a) of **9.21** the Act was published on 3 February 2021,[36] and the consultation period closed on 31 March 2021. On 29 June 2021 the government published a Subsidy Control Bill: that Bill contained provisions that required all public authorities across the United Kingdom to consider various principles before granting subsidies, and prohibited certain types of subsidy: subsidy decisions were to be subject to judicial review before the Competition Appeal Tribunal. The Bill also applied to legislation passed by the devolved (but not the UK) Parliaments, and provided for the High Court or Court of Session to have power to judicially review such legislation on subsidy control grounds.[37] Certain subsidies would have to be referred (or could be referred by the Secretary of State[38]) to the Competition and Markets Authority to report on their compliance with the subsidy control provisions and prohibitions, though such reports would not bind the granting authority. The Bill contained a specific prohibition on subsidies conditional on relocation from elsewhere in the United Kingdom.[39]

now means what the TCA says it means, regardless of the language used ... Applying section 29 there are three steps to take. The first is to identify the relevant domestic law ... The second step is to determine whether the domestic law is the same as the corresponding provisions of the TCA. If it is then under section 29(1) there is no need to apply the automatic read-across. If there is inconsistency, daylight or a lacuna then the inconsistent or incomplete provision is amended or replaced, and the gap is plugged ... '.

[36] https://assets.publishing.service.gov.uk/government/uploads/system/uploads/attachment_data/file/957958/subsidy-control-consultation-document.pdf.

[37] Schedule 3 to the Bill.

[38] Though not by the devolved governments.

[39] Clause 18.

APPENDIX

United Kingdom Internal Market Act 2020

An Act to make provision in connection with the internal market for goods and services in the United Kingdom (including provision about the recognition of professional and other qualifications); to make provision in connection with provisions of the Northern Ireland Protocol relating to trade and state aid; to authorise the provision of financial assistance by Ministers of the Crown in connection with economic development, infrastructure, culture, sport and educational or training activities and exchanges; to make regulation of the provision of distortive or harmful subsidies a reserved or excepted matter; and for connected purposes. [17th December 2020]

BE IT ENACTED by the Queen's most Excellent Majesty, by and with the advice and consent of the Lords Spiritual and Temporal, and Commons, in this present Parliament assembled, and by the authority of the same, as follows:—

PART 1

UK MARKET ACCESS: GOODS

Introductory

1 Purpose of Part 1

(1) This Part promotes the continued functioning of the internal market for goods in the United Kingdom by establishing the United Kingdom market access principles.

(2) The United Kingdom market access principles are—

(a) the mutual recognition principle for goods (see sections 2 to 4), and

(b) the non-discrimination principle for goods (see sections 5 to 9).

(3) Those principles have no direct legal effect except as provided by this Part.

Mutual recognition: goods

2 The mutual recognition principle for goods

(1) The mutual recognition principle for goods is the principle that goods which—
(a) have been produced in, or imported into, one part of the United Kingdom ("the originating part"), and
(b) can be sold there without contravening any relevant requirements that would apply to their sale,
should be able to be sold in any other part of the United Kingdom, free from any relevant requirements that would otherwise apply to the sale.
(2) Where goods are to be sold in a particular way in the other part of the United Kingdom, the condition in subsection (1)(b) has effect as if the reference to "their sale" were a reference to their sale in that particular way.
So, for example, if goods are to be sold by auction, the condition is met if (and only if) they can be sold by auction in the originating part without contravening any applicable relevant requirements there.
(3) Where the principle applies in relation to a sale of goods in a part of the United Kingdom because the conditions in subsection (1)(a) and (b) are met, any relevant requirements there do not apply in relation to the sale.

3 Relevant requirements for the purposes of section 2

(1) This section defines "relevant requirement" for the purposes of the mutual recognition principle for goods as it applies in relation to a particular sale of goods in a part of the United Kingdom.
(2) A statutory requirement in the part of the United Kingdom concerned which—
(a) prohibits the sale of the goods or, in the case of an obligation or condition, results in their sale being prohibited if it is not complied with, and
(b) is within the scope of the mutual recognition principle,
is a relevant requirement in relation to the sale unless excluded from being a relevant requirement by any provision of this Part.
(3) A statutory requirement is within the scope of the mutual recognition principle if it relates to any one or more of the following—
(a) characteristics of the goods themselves (such as their nature, composition, age, quality or performance);
(b) any matter connected with the presentation of the goods (such as the name or description applied to them or their packaging, labelling, lot- marking or date-stamping);
(c) any matter connected with the production of the goods or anything from which they are made or is involved in their production, including the place at which, or the circumstances in which, production or any step in production took place;
(d) any matter relating to the identification or tracing of an animal (such as marking, tagging or micro-chipping or the keeping of particular records);
(e) the inspection, assessment, registration, certification, approval or, authorisation of the goods or any other similar dealing with them;
(f) documentation or information that must be produced or recorded, kept, accompany the goods or be submitted to an authority;
(g) anything not falling within paragraphs (a) to (f) which must (or must not) be done to, or in relation to, the goods before they are allowed to be sold.

(4) A manner of sale requirement is not within the scope of the mutual recognition principle unless subsection (6) applies.

(5) For this purpose a "manner of sale requirement" is a statutory requirement that governs any aspect of the circumstances or manner in which the goods are sold (such as where, when, by whom, to whom, or the price or other terms on which they may be sold).

(6) A statutory requirement that—

(a) is worded as a manner of sale requirement, but

(b) appears to be designed artificially to avoid the operation of the mutual recognition principle in relation to what would otherwise be a requirement within the scope of that principle,

is to be regarded as a relevant requirement, despite subsection (4).

This subsection would apply, for example, where a manner of sale requirement involves an unusually restrictive condition such that it would be impossible to comply with the condition and have a practical chance of selling the goods.

(7) A statutory requirement which requires the person selling or acquiring the goods to keep or submit, after the sale takes place, any documentation or information required to be produced or recorded beforehand is to be treated as a relevant requirement relating to the sale.

(8) In this Part "statutory requirement" means an obligation, a condition or a prohibition (however described) imposed by legislation (including legislation imposing mandatory terms into contracts for the sale of goods).

4 Exclusion of certain requirements existing before commencement

(1) A statutory requirement in a part of the United Kingdom ("the relevant part") which—

(a) applies in relation to a particular sale of goods in that part of the United Kingdom, and

(b) would otherwise fall within section 3 as a relevant requirement,

is not a relevant requirement (so far as relating to the sale) for the purposes of the mutual recognition principle where the conditions in subsection (2) are met.

(2) The conditions are that, on the relevant day —

(a) the same statutory requirement would have applied in relation to the sale if it had taken place on that day, and

(b) there was no corresponding requirement in force in each of the other three parts of the United Kingdom.

(3) For the purposes of subsection (2) "the relevant day" is the day before the day on which this section comes into force.

(4) The re-enactment (without substantive change) of a statutory requirement does not affect its continuity for the purposes of subsection (2)(a).

(5) For the purposes of subsection (2)(b) "corresponding requirement", in relation to the statutory requirement in the relevant part of the United Kingdom, means a statutory requirement in another part of the United Kingdom that would have had the same effect in relation to the sale (if it had taken place there on the relevant day).

(6) For the purposes of subsections (2) and (5) a statutory requirement is to be regarded as the same as another statutory requirement, or having the same effect, if any differences between them are not substantive.

Non-discrimination: goods

5 The non-discrimination principle for goods

(1) The non-discrimination principle for goods is the principle that the sale of goods in one part of the United Kingdom should not be affected by relevant requirements that directly or indirectly discriminate against goods that have a relevant connection with another part of the United Kingdom.

(2) For the purposes of the application of that principle in any given case—

(a) the part of the United Kingdom where sale should not be affected is referred to as the "destination part";

(b) the goods that have a relevant connection with another part of the United Kingdom are referred to as the "incoming goods";

(c) that other part is referred to as the "originating part".

(3) A relevant requirement (see section 6) is of no effect in the destination part if, and to the extent that, it directly or indirectly discriminates against the incoming goods (see sections 7 and 8).

(4) Goods have a relevant connection with a part of the United Kingdom if they or any of their components—

(a) are produced in that part,

(b) are produced by a business based in that part, or

(c) come from, or pass through, that part before reaching the destination part.

(5) For the purposes of this Part—

(a) "components" includes parts, ingredients and constituent materials;

(b) a business is "based"—

(i) where its registered office is,

(ii) if it does not have a registered office, where its head office is, or

(iii) if it has neither a registered office nor a head office, where its principal place of business is.

6 Relevant requirements for the purposes of the non-discrimination principle

(1) This section defines "relevant requirement" for the purposes of the non- discrimination principle for goods.

(2) A relevant requirement, for the purposes of the principle as it has effect in relation to a part of the United Kingdom, is a statutory provision that—

(a) applies in that part of the United Kingdom to, or in relation to, goods sold in that part, and

(b) is within the scope of the non-discrimination principle.

(3) A statutory provision is within the scope of the non-discrimination principle if it relates to any one or more of the following—

(a) the circumstances or manner in which goods are sold (such as where, when, by whom, to whom, or the price or other terms on which they may be sold);

(b) the transportation, storage, handling or display of goods;

(c) the inspection, assessment, registration, certification, approval or authorisation of the goods or any similar dealing with them;

(d) the conduct or regulation of businesses that engage in the sale of certain goods or types of goods.

(4) A statutory provision is not a relevant requirement—

(a) to the extent that it is a relevant requirement for the purposes of the mutual recognition principle for goods (see section 3), or

(b) if section 9 (exclusion of certain existing provisions) so provides.

(5) The Secretary of State may by regulations amend subsection (3) so as to add, vary or remove a paragraph of that subsection.
(6) Regulations under subsection (5) are subject to affirmative resolution procedure.
(7) Before making regulations under subsection (5) the Secretary of State must seek the consent of the Scottish Ministers, the Welsh Ministers and the Department for the Economy in Northern Ireland.
(8) If consent to the making of the regulations is not given by any of those authorities within the period of one month beginning with the day on which it is sought from that authority, the Secretary of State may make the regulations without that consent.
(9) If regulations are made in reliance on subsection (8), the Secretary of State must publish a statement explaining why the Secretary of State decided to make the regulations without the consent of the authority or authorities concerned.
(10) In this section "statutory provision" means provision contained in legislation.

7 The non-discrimination principle: direct discrimination

(1) A relevant requirement directly discriminates against incoming goods if, for the reason that the goods have the relevant connection with the originating part, the requirement applies to, or in relation to, the incoming goods in a way—
(a) in which it does not or would not apply to local goods, and
(b) that puts the incoming goods at a disadvantage compared to local goods.
(2) Goods are put at a disadvantage if it is made in any way more difficult, or less attractive, to sell or buy the goods or do anything in connection with their sale.
(3) "Local goods", for the purposes of this section, are actual or hypothetical goods that—
(a) lack the relevant connection of the incoming goods with the originating part, but
(b) otherwise are materially the same as, and share the material circumstances of, the incoming goods.
(4) Goods ("the other goods") lack the relevant connection of the incoming goods with the originating part—
(a) where the incoming goods have a relevant connection within section 5(4)(a), if the other goods, or (as the case may be) their components, were produced in the destination part;
(b) where the incoming goods have a relevant connection within section 5(4)(b), if the other goods, or (as the case may be) their components, were produced by a business based in the destination part;
(c) where the incoming goods have a relevant connection within section 5(4)(c), if the other goods, or (as the case may be) their components, came from the destination part and did not pass through anywhere outside that part.

8 The non-discrimination principle: indirect discrimination

(1) A relevant requirement indirectly discriminates against incoming goods if—
(a) it does not directly discriminate against the goods,
(b) it applies to, or in relation to, the incoming goods in a way that puts them at a disadvantage,
(c) it has an adverse market effect, and
(d) it cannot reasonably be considered a necessary means of achieving a legitimate aim.
(2) Goods are put at a disadvantage if it is made in any way more difficult, or less attractive, to sell or buy the goods or do anything in connection with their sale than if the requirement did not apply.

(3) A requirement has an adverse market effect if, because it—

(a) puts at a disadvantage the incoming goods (and any comparable goods that also have a relevant connection with the originating part and are also put at that disadvantage), but

(b) does not put at that disadvantage (at all or to the same extent) some or all comparable goods that have a relevant connection with the destination part and no other part of the United Kingdom,

it causes a significant adverse effect on competition in the market for such goods in the United Kingdom.

(4) "Comparable goods" means like goods or interchangeable goods; and—

(a) "like goods" are goods that are alike the incoming goods in all respects, or otherwise have characteristics closely resembling those of the incoming goods;

(b) "interchangeable goods" are goods that, from the point of view of a purchaser of the goods, could reasonably be said to be interchangeable with the incoming goods.

(5) The application of subsection (3) is to be determined with regard both to the content of the requirement and to the way in which it operates, or is administered, in practice (as a whole or in particular classes of case).

(6) "Legitimate aim" means one, or a combination, of the following aims—

(a) the protection of the life or health of humans, animals or plants;

(b) the protection of public safety or security.

(7) The Secretary of State may by regulations amend subsection (6) so as to add, vary or remove an aim.

(8) Regulations under subsection (7) are subject to affirmative resolution procedure.

(9) Before making regulations under subsection (7), the Secretary of State must seek the consent of the Scottish Ministers, the Welsh Ministers and the Department for the Economy in Northern Ireland.

(10) If consent to the making of the regulations is not given by any of those authorities within the period of one month beginning with the day on which it is sought from that authority, the Secretary of State may make the regulations without that consent.

(11) If regulations are made in reliance on subsection (10), the Secretary of State must publish a statement explaining why the Secretary of State decided to make the regulations without the consent of the authority or authorities concerned.

(12) The application of subsection (1)(d) is to be determined with regard, in particular, to—

(a) the effects of the requirement in all the circumstances, and

(b) the availability of alternative means of achieving the aim in question.

9 Exclusion of certain provision existing before commencement

(1) Statutory provision is not a relevant requirement for the purposes of the non- discrimination principle for goods if the same provision was in force in the part of the United Kingdom concerned on the day before the day on which this section comes into force.

(2) The re-enactment (without substantive change) of statutory provision does not affect its continuity for the purposes of subsection (1).

(3) For the purposes of subsection (1) the same provision is to be regarded as in force on the day concerned if any differences are not substantive.

(4) In this section "statutory provision" has the same meaning as in section 6.

Exclusions from market access principles

10 Further exclusions from market access principles

(1) Schedule 1 contains provision excluding the application of the United Kingdom market access principles in certain cases.

(2) The Secretary of State may by regulations amend that Schedule.

(3) The power under subsection (2) may, for example, be exercised to give effect to an agreement that—

(a) forms part of a common framework agreement, and

(b) provides that certain cases, matters, requirements or provision should be excluded from the application of the market access principles.

(4) A "common framework agreement" is a consensus between a Minister of the Crown and one or more devolved administrations as to how devolved or transferred matters previously governed by EU law are to be regulated after IP completion day.

(5) References in this section to devolved or transferred matters include reference to corresponding matters in England.

(6) When determining whether a matter is a devolved or transferred matter for the purposes of this section, the following provisions are to be ignored—

(a) section 30A of the Scotland Act 1998;

(b) section 109A of the Government of Wales Act 2006;

(c) section 6A of the Northern Ireland Act 1998.

(7) In making regulations under subsection (2), the Secretary of State must have regard to the importance of facilitating the access to the market within Great Britain of qualifying Northern Ireland goods.

(8) Regulations under subsection (2) are subject to affirmative resolution procedure.

(9) Before making regulations under subsection (2), the Secretary of State must seek the consent of the Scottish Ministers, the Welsh Ministers and the Department for the Economy in Northern Ireland.

(10) If consent to the making of the regulations is not given by any of those authorities within the period of one month beginning with the day on which it is sought from that authority, the Secretary of State may make the regulations without that consent.

(11) If regulations are made in reliance on subsection (10), the Secretary of State must publish a statement explaining why the Secretary of State decided to make the regulations without the consent of the authority or authorities concerned.

(12) In this section—

"devolved administrations" means—

(a) the Scottish Ministers,

(b) the Welsh Ministers, and

(c) a Northern Ireland department;

"qualifying Northern Ireland goods" has the same meaning as in section 47.

Supplementary

11 Modifications in connection with the Northern Ireland Protocol

(1) The United Kingdom market access principles for goods apply, in relation to the sale of goods in a part of the United Kingdom other than Northern Ireland, with the following modifications.

(For provision affecting the application of those principles in relation to the sale of goods in Northern Ireland, see, in particular, the Northern Ireland Protocol and sections 7A, 7C and 8C of the European Union (Withdrawal) Act 2018.)

(2) The mutual recognition principle for goods applies in relation to all qualifying Northern Ireland goods as if they were produced in, or imported into, Northern Ireland.

(3) That principle does not apply in relation to goods produced in, or imported into, Northern Ireland that are not qualifying Northern Ireland goods, unless subsection (4) applies.

(4) If goods falling within subsection (3) are moved in a way that would, but for the fact that Northern Ireland is a part of the United Kingdom, amount for the purposes of the mutual recognition principle for goods to the importation of the goods into England, Scotland or Wales, the goods are to be regarded for the purposes of that principle as having been so imported.

(5) Goods that are not qualifying Northern Ireland goods do not have a relevant connection with Northern Ireland for the purposes of the non-discrimination principle for goods (despite section 5(4)).

(6) Subsection (7) applies for the purposes of paragraph 1 of Schedule 1 in a case where Northern Ireland is the "affected part" within the meaning of sub- paragraph (2) of that paragraph.

(7) In determining whether the condition in sub-paragraph (3) of that paragraph is met, a pest or disease is to be taken to be present in Northern Ireland if it is, or may be, present in qualifying Northern Ireland goods (including when the goods are in Great Britain).

(8) In this section "qualifying Northern Ireland goods" has the same meaning as in section 47.

12 Guidance relating to Part 1

(1) The Secretary of State may issue guidance on any matter relating to—
   (a) the practical operation of the United Kingdom market access principles, or
   (b) the effect of any provision of this Part.

(2) Guidance may be directed towards the public generally or towards any description of persons (such as traders, persons with enforcement functions or a class of such traders or persons).

(3) In subsection (2) "enforcement function" means a function relating to the enforcement of anything which is (or is capable of being) a relevant requirement for the purposes of either of the market access principles for goods.

(4) The power of the Secretary of State under subsection (1) includes power to revise or withdraw (in whole or part) any guidance previously issued.

(5) Before issuing, revising or withdrawing guidance under subsection (1), the Secretary of State must consult the Scottish Ministers, the Welsh Ministers and the Department for the Economy in Northern Ireland.

(6) The Secretary of State must arrange for the publication of—
   (a) any guidance that has been issued, as revised from time to time;
   (b) any revisions made under subsection (4);
   (c) notice of the withdrawal of any guidance under subsection (4).

(7) In this section "guidance" means guidance under subsection (1).

13 Duty to review the use of Part 1 amendment powers

(1) In this section "the Part 1 amendment powers" are the powers conferred by sections 6(5), 8(7) and 10(2) (powers to amend certain provisions of Part 1).

(2) The Secretary of State must, during the permitted period—
(a) carry out a review of any use that has been made of the Part 1 amendment powers,
(b) prepare a report of the review, and
(c) lay a copy of the report before Parliament.
(3) In carrying out the review the Secretary of State must—
(a) consult the Scottish Ministers, the Welsh Ministers and the Department for the Economy in Northern Ireland,
(b) consider any relevant reports made, or advice given, by the Competition and Markets Authority under Part 4, and
(c) assess the impact and effectiveness of any changes made under the Part 1 amendment powers.
(4) The permitted period is the period beginning with the third anniversary of the passing of this Act and ending with the fifth anniversary.
(5) If any Part 1 amendment power has not been used by the time the review is carried out, this section has effect—
(a) as if the report required by subsection (2), so far as relating to that power, is a report containing—
(i) a statement to the effect that the power has not been used since it came into force, and
(ii) such other information relating to that statement as the Secretary of State considers it appropriate to give, and
(b) as if the requirements of subsection (3) did not apply in relation to that power.

14 Sale of goods complying with local law

Nothing in this Part prevents goods produced in or imported into a part of the United Kingdom from being sold in another part of the United Kingdom if (apart from this Part) the sale complies with any requirements applicable in that other part of the United Kingdom (or there are no such requirements).

15 Interpretation of references to "sale" in Part 1

(1) This section explains the meaning in this Part of references to the sale of goods (however expressed).
(2) "Sale" does not include a sale which—
(a) is not made in the course of a business, or
(b) is made in the course of a business but only for the purpose of performing a function of a public nature.
(3) Subsection (2)(b) does not exclude a sale which is—
(a) made by a public body or authority for commercial purposes, and
(b) not made for the purpose of performing a function of a public nature (other than a function relating to the carrying on of commercial activities).
(4) "Sale" includes—
(a) agreement to sell,
(b) offering or exposing for sale, or
(c) having in possession or holding for sale.
(5) This Part applies in relation to a supply of goods other than a sale as it applies in relation to a sale (and any reference to "sale", outside this subsection, is to be read accordingly).

(6) For this purpose "supply of goods" means the transfer of possession or property in goods (whether or not under or by virtue of a contract), and includes, for example, supply by way of—
   (a) barter or exchange,
   (b) the leasing or hiring out of goods, hire-purchase, or bailment of goods, or
   (c) gift (or anything else done free of charge).

16 Interpretation of other expressions used in Part 1

(1) This section applies for the purposes of this Part.
(2) "Goods" means any tangible movable, or corporeal moveable, thing (including any packaging or label), but not water or gas that is not offered for sale in a limited volume or set quantity.
(3) Goods are to be regarded as "produced in" a part of the United Kingdom (if not wholly produced there) if the most recent significant production step which is a regulated step has occurred there.
(4) A production step occurring in a part of the United Kingdom is "regulated" for the purposes of subsection (3) if —
   (a) it is the subject of any statutory requirement in that part of the United Kingdom, or
   (b) it is a step that could materially affect a person's ability to sell the goods without contravening—
      (i) any relevant requirement for the purposes of the mutual recognition principle for goods, or
      (ii) any statutory requirement that is excluded from being a relevant requirement by section 4(1),

   that would be applicable to a sale of the goods in that part of the United Kingdom (being a sale of a kind for which the goods are being produced).
(5) A production step is "significant" for the purposes of subsection (3) if it is significant in terms of the character of the goods being produced and the purposes for which they are to be sold or used (but see subsections (6) and (7)).
(6) A production step falling within any of the following descriptions is not significant (whether or not it is regulated)—
   (a) activities carried out specifically to ensure goods do not deteriorate before being sold (such as maintaining them at or below a particular temperature);
   (b) activities carried out solely for purposes relevant to their presentation for sale (such as cleaning or pressing fabrics or sorting different coloured items for packaging together);
   (c) activities involving a communication of any kind with a regulatory or trade body (such as registering the goods or notifying the goods or anything connected with them or their production);
   (d) activities carried out for the purpose of testing or assessing any characteristic of the goods (such as batch testing a pharmaceutical product).
(7) A production step involving the packaging, labelling or marking of goods is not significant (whether or not it is regulated) unless the step is fundamental to the character of the goods and the purposes for which they are to be sold or used.
(8) Goods are "imported into" a part of the United Kingdom only if they are imported into that part from outside the United Kingdom.

   For this purpose the Isle of Man is outside the United Kingdom.

(9) Goods are to be regarded as imported—
(a) for goods brought by sea, when the ship carrying them enters the limits of the port at which they are discharged;
(b) for goods brought by air, when they are unloaded;
(c) for goods brought by land, when they enter the United Kingdom.
In this subsection "port" and "ship" have the same meaning as in the Customs and Excise Management Act 1979 (see section 1 of that Act).

(10) Goods produced in, or imported into, a part of the United Kingdom ("the original part of the United Kingdom") which are—
(a) exported to a place outside the United Kingdom, and
(b) re-imported back into any other part of the United Kingdom, are, despite the re-importation, to continue to be regarded as goods produced in, or imported into, the original part of the United Kingdom.

(11) A reference (however expressed) to the production of anything includes—
(a) cultivation, harvesting and similar activities (in relation to plants or fungi) and
(b) rearing, keeping, handling, killing and similar activities (in relation to livestock or other animals).

(12) A reference (however expressed) to law in a part of the United Kingdom is a reference to—
(a) the law of England and Wales as it applies in (or in relation to) England,
(b) the law of England and Wales as it applies in (or in relation to) Wales,
(c) the law of Scotland, or
(d) the law of Northern Ireland.

(13) "Contravening" includes failing to comply.

(14) "Statutory requirement" has the meaning given by section 3(8).

PART 2

UK MARKET ACCESS: SERVICES

17 Services: overview

(1) This Part governs the regulation of service providers in the United Kingdom.

(2) It makes provision that limits the application and effect of authorisation requirements and regulatory requirements.

(3) An authorisation requirement is a legislative requirement that a service provider must have the permission of a regulator before carrying on a business of providing particular services.

(4) A regulatory requirement is a legislative requirement that would if not satisfied (whether at a particular point or on a continuing basis) prevent a service provider from carrying on a business of providing particular services.

(5) The following are neither authorisation requirements nor regulatory requirements for the purposes of this Part—
(a) relevant requirements as defined for the purposes of the mutual recognition principle for goods (see section 3);
(b) provision of the sort described in section 24(1) or 28(1) (professional qualifications and regulation) to the extent it has the effect described there;

(c) a requirement that—
  (i) is in force, or otherwise has effect, on the day before the day on which this section comes into force and has not been substantively changed after that day, or
  (ii) comes into force, or otherwise takes effect, on or after the day on which this section comes into force if it re-enacts or replicates (without substantive change) a legislative requirement in force or having effect immediately before that day;

(d) a requirement that applies to a service provider, but which also applies to persons who do not provide services (for example, a requirement imposing duties on employers);

(e) a requirement to notify, or register with, a regulator;

(f) a requirement to provide evidence of being authorised to provide services in a part of the United Kingdom other than the part in which the requirement applies.

(6) Subsection (5)(c) does not exclude (and, accordingly, references to authorisation requirements do include) an authorisation requirement that applies in a part of the United Kingdom if, after the relevant day, a corresponding authorisation requirement in another part of the United Kingdom is substantively changed.

(7) For the purposes of subsection (6)—
(a) an authorisation requirement corresponds to another authorisation requirement if it relates to the same, or substantially the same, services;
(b) the "relevant day" is the day before the day on which this section comes into force.

(8) For the purposes of this section, an authorisation requirement is substantively changed if a legislative requirement that would, if not satisfied, prevent a service provider from satisfying the authorisation requirement is substantively changed.

(9) In this Part—
"service provider" means a person—
  (a) that provides, or intends to provide, services in the course of the person's business, and
  (b) that has a permanent establishment in the United Kingdom through which that business is wholly or partly carried on;

"permanent establishment"—
  (a) in relation to a company, is to be read in accordance with Chapter 2 of Part 24 of the Corporation Tax Act 2010, and
  (b) in relation to any other person, is to be read in accordance with that Chapter but as if references in that Chapter to a company were references to that person.

18 Services: exclusions

(1) Schedule 2 contains—
(a) a list of services specified in the first column of the table in Part 1 of that Schedule, to which section 19 (mutual recognition) does not apply;
(b) a list of services specified in the first column of the table in Part 2 of that Schedule, to which sections 20 and 21 (non-discrimination) do not apply;
(c) a list of authorisation requirements in Part 3 of that Schedule, to which section 19 does not apply;
(d) a list of regulatory requirements in Part 4 of that Schedule, to which sections 20 and 21 do not apply.

(2) The Secretary of State must keep Schedule 2 under review, and may by regulations—
(a) remove entries in the tables in Part 1 or Part 2 of that Schedule or entries in the lists in Part 3 or Part 4 of that Schedule;
(b) amend entries in those tables or lists;
(c) add entries to those tables or lists.

(3) The power under subsection (2) may, for example, be exercised to give effect to an agreement that—
   (a) forms part of a common framework agreement, and
   (b) provides that certain cases, matters, requirements or provision should be excluded from the application of this Part.
(4) A "common framework agreement" is a consensus between a Minister of the Crown and one or more devolved administrations as to how devolved or transferred matters previously governed by EU law are to be regulated after IP completion day.
(5) References in this section to devolved or transferred matters include reference to corresponding matters in England.
(6) When determining whether a matter is a devolved or transferred matter for the purposes of this section, the following provisions are to be ignored—
   (a) section 30A of the Scotland Act 1998;
   (b) section 109A of the Government of Wales Act 2006;
   (c) section 6A of the Northern Ireland Act 1998.
(7) Regulations under subsection (2) are subject to affirmative resolution procedure.
(8) Before making regulations under subsection (2), the Secretary of State must seek the consent of the Scottish Ministers, the Welsh Ministers and the Department for the Economy in Northern Ireland.
(9) If consent to the making of the regulations is not given by any of those authorities within the period of one month beginning with the day on which it is sought from that authority, the Secretary of State may make the regulations without that consent.
(10) If regulations are made in reliance on subsection (9), the Secretary of State must publish a statement explaining why the Secretary of State decided to make the regulations without the consent of the authority or authorities concerned.
(11) In this section "devolved administrations" means—
   (a) the Scottish Ministers,
   (b) the Welsh Ministers, and
   (c) a Northern Ireland department.

19 Services: mutual recognition of authorisation requirements

(1) An authorisation requirement in relation to the provision of services in one part of the United Kingdom does not apply to a person who is authorised to provide those services in another part of the United Kingdom.
(2) A person is authorised to provide services in a part of the United Kingdom if they have the permission of a regulator that exercises regulatory functions in relation to the whole of that part to carry on a business of providing those services in that part.
(3) But, for the purposes of this section, a person is not to be treated as authorised to provide services in a part of the United Kingdom where the permission to provide those services only relates to their provision in relation to particular premises or to a particular place or piece of infrastructure.
(4) Subsection (1) does not apply to an authorisation requirement to the extent it can reasonably be justified as a response to a public health emergency.

20 Direct discrimination in the regulation of services

(1) A regulatory requirement that directly discriminates against a service provider is of no effect in relation to that service provider.

(2) A regulatory requirement directly discriminates against a service provider if—
   (a) it has, or would have, the effect of treating the service provider less favourably than other service providers, and
   (b) the reason for that less favourable treatment is the service provider's relevant connection, or lack of relevant connection, to a part of the United Kingdom.

(3) A regulatory requirement is not to be taken to directly discriminate against a service provider to the extent the requirement can reasonably be justified as a response to a public health emergency.

(4) For the purposes of this section, a service provider has a relevant connection to a part of the United Kingdom if the service provider—
   (a) has a registered office, place of business or residence in that part,
   (b) provides services from that part, or
   (c) has members, partners, officers or staff with a registered office, place of business, or residence in that part.

21 Indirect discrimination in the regulation of services

(1) A regulatory requirement that indirectly discriminates against an incoming service provider is of no effect in relation to that incoming service provider.

(2) A regulatory requirement indirectly discriminates against an incoming service provider if—
   (a) it does not directly discriminate against the incoming service provider (within the meaning of section 20),
   (b) it puts the incoming service provider at a relevant disadvantage,
   (c) it has an adverse market effect, and
   (d) it cannot reasonably be considered a necessary means of achieving a legitimate aim.

(3) A regulatory requirement puts an incoming service provider at a relevant disadvantage if—
   (a) it puts the incoming service provider at a disadvantage in relation to the provision of services in the part of the United Kingdom in which the requirement applies, and
   (b) it does not put, or would not put, each local service provider at that disadvantage in relation to the provision of those services in that part (at all or to the same extent).

(4) A regulatory requirement puts a service provider at a disadvantage in relation to the provision of services in a part of the United Kingdom if it makes it in any way more difficult, or less attractive, for the service provider to provide the services in that part.

(5) A regulatory requirement has an adverse market effect if, by putting an incoming service provider (or incoming service providers) at a relevant disadvantage in relation to the provision of services, it has a significant adverse effect on competition in the market for those services in the United Kingdom.

(6) For the purposes of subsections (1) to (5)—
   (a) an "incoming service provider" is a service provider that—
      (i) provides the services in the part of the United Kingdom in which the regulatory requirement applies, but
      (ii) does not have a relevant connection to that part;
   (b) a "local service provider" is a service provider that—
      (i) provides the services in the part of the United Kingdom in which the regulatory requirement applies,
      (ii) has a relevant connection to that part, and
      (iii) does not have a relevant connection to another part of the United Kingdom;

(c) a service provider has a "relevant connection" to a part of the United Kingdom if the service provider—
(i) has a registered office, place of business or residence in that part, or
(ii) provides the services from that part.

(7) In this section "legitimate aim" means one, or a combination of any, of the following aims—
(a) the protection of the life or health of humans, animals or plants;
(b) the protection of public safety or security;
(c) the efficient administration of justice.

(8) The Secretary of State may by regulations amend subsection (7) so as to add, vary or remove a legitimate aim.

(9) Regulations under subsection (8) are subject to affirmative resolution procedure.

(10) Before making regulations under subsection (8), the Secretary of State must seek the consent of the Scottish Ministers, the Welsh Ministers and the Department for the Economy in Northern Ireland.

(11) If consent to the making of the regulations is not given by any of those authorities within the period of one month beginning with the day on which it is sought from that authority, the Secretary of State may make the regulations without that consent.

(12) If regulations are made in reliance on subsection (11), the Secretary of State must publish a statement explaining why the Secretary of State decided to make the regulations without the consent of the authority or authorities concerned.

(13) The application of subsection (2)(d) is to be determined with regard, in particular, to—
(a) the effects of the requirement in all the circumstances, and
(b) the availability of alternative means of achieving the aim in question.

22 Duty to review the use of Part 2 amendment powers

(1) In this section "the Part 2 amendment powers" are the powers conferred by sections 18(2) and 21(8) (powers to amend certain provisions of Part 2).

(2) The Secretary of State must, during the permitted period—
(a) carry out a review of any use that has been made of the Part 2 amendment powers,
(b) prepare a report of the review, and
(c) lay a copy of the report before Parliament.

(3) In carrying out the review the Secretary of State must—
(a) consult the Scottish Ministers, the Welsh Ministers and the Department for the Economy in Northern Ireland,
(b) consider any relevant reports made, or advice given, by the Competition and Markets Authority under Part 4, and
(c) assess the impact and effectiveness of any changes made under the Part 2 amendment powers.

(4) The permitted period is the period beginning with the third anniversary of the passing of this Act and ending with the fifth anniversary.

(5) If either of the Part 2 amendment powers has not been used by the time the review is carried out, this section has effect—
(a) as if the report required by subsection (2), so far as relating to that power, is a report containing—
(i) a statement to the effect that the power has not been used since it came into force, and

(ii) such other information relating to that statement as the Secretary of State considers it appropriate to give, and

(b) as if the requirements of subsection (3) did not apply in relation to that power.

23 Interpretation of Part 2

(1) In this Part—

"authorisation requirement" has the meaning given by section 17(3); "legislative requirement" means a requirement imposed by, or by virtue of, legislation;

"public health emergency" means an event or a situation that is reasonably considered to pose an extraordinary threat to human health; "regulator" means a person exercising regulatory functions, and includes—

(a) a Minister of the Crown,

(b) the Scottish Ministers,

(c) the Welsh Ministers, and

(d) a Northern Ireland department;

"regulatory requirement" has the meaning given by section 17(4).

(2) If a function conferred by legislation may only be exercised in a way that would impose a regulatory requirement in respect of which section 20(1) or 21(1) applies, the function is to be treated as though it were a regulatory requirement for the purposes of those sections (and ignoring section 17(5)).

(3) Subsection (2) does not affect the continuation in force or the continuing effect of a requirement of the sort described in section 17(5)(c) and not preserved by section 17(6) (existing requirements).

(4) Any effect of section 5, 20 or 21 (direct and indirect discrimination for goods and services) is to be disregarded when considering whether a person is authorised to provide services in another part of the United Kingdom for the purposes of section 19 (mutual recognition for services).

PART 3

UK MARKET ACCESS: PROFESSIONAL QUALIFICATIONS AND REGULATION

24 Access to professions on grounds of qualifications or experience

(1) Subsection (2) applies in relation to provision applying in a part of the United Kingdom ("the relevant part") that limits the ability to practise a profession in that part to individuals who have certain qualifications or experience.

(2) A qualified UK resident (see section 25) is to be treated for the purposes of the provision (and any related provision) as if the qualified UK resident had the qualifications or experience required to be able to practise the profession.

(3) Provision does not fall within subsection (1) by making the ability of an individual to continue to practise a particular profession, having started to do so on a fully qualified basis, subject to continuing requirements as to training, learning or other forms of experience.

(4) Subsections (1) and (2) are subject to sections 26 and 27.

25 Meaning of "qualified" UK resident

(1) A UK resident is "qualified" in relation to a profession for the purposes of section 24(2) if, in any part of the United Kingdom other than the relevant part ("the other part"), the resident is qualified (within the meaning of subsections

(3) to (5)) to undertake the full range of corresponding activity.

(2) In this section—

(a) "corresponding activity" means activity that is the same as, or substantially corresponds to, relevant professional activity;

(b) "the full range" of corresponding activity is a range of corresponding activity that substantially corresponds to the full range of relevant professional activity;

(c) "relevant professional activity" means activity that, in the relevant part, ordinarily comprises the practice of the profession in question.

(3) To the extent that—

(a) corresponding activity is ordinarily undertaken by practitioners of a particular profession in the other part, and

(b) provision applying in the other part limits the ability to practise that profession to individuals who have certain qualifications or experience, a UK resident is qualified to undertake the corresponding activity if the resident has the qualifications or experience required to be able to practise the profession in the other part.

(4) To the extent that—

(a) the position is not as described in subsection (3)(a) and (b), and

(b) provision applying in the other part limits the ability to undertake corresponding activity to individuals who have certain qualifications or experience, a UK resident is qualified to undertake the corresponding activity if the resident has the qualifications or experience required to do so in the other part.

(5) To the extent that the position is not as described in subsection (3)(a) and (b) or (4)(b), any UK resident is qualified to undertake corresponding activity in the other part.

(6) For the purposes of subsection (3)—

(a) it does not matter that corresponding activity may also be undertaken by individuals who are not practitioners of a profession;

(b) to the extent that corresponding activity is ordinarily undertaken by practitioners of more than one profession regulated as mentioned in subsection (3)(b), a UK resident is qualified in relation to that activity only if the resident has qualifications or experience required to be able to practise whichever of those professions most closely corresponds to the profession in the relevant part.

(7) For the purposes of subsections (3) and (4)—

(a) qualifications may be relied on only if they were obtained in the United Kingdom, and

(b) experience may be relied on only if it was obtained mainly in the United Kingdom.

26 Exception from section 24 where individual assessment offered

(1) Section 24(2) does not apply in a case where the qualified UK resident—

(a) is able to seek, or has sought, to be able to practise the profession in the relevant part by way of a process that satisfies the requirements of this section, and

(b) has not lawfully practised the profession in the relevant part at any time before being able to seek that ability by way of that process.

(2) The process must have the result that, if the regulatory body so decides on an application by the qualified UK resident, the resident becomes able to practise the profession—

(a) despite the limitation referred to in section 24(1), and

(b) without further assessment of the resident's qualifications, experience, knowledge or skills (except in connection with the sort of provision referred to in section 24(3)).

(3) The process must require the application to be dealt with in accordance with the principles set out in subsection (4).

(4) The principles are that, in connection with the ability to practise a profession in the relevant part—

(a) qualifications or experience obtained in any other part of the United Kingdom should have the same effect as qualifications or experience obtained in the relevant part, to the extent that the former demonstrate the like knowledge and skills to substantially the same standard as the latter;

(b) the applicant should be able to rely on any qualifications or experience obtained in any other part of the United Kingdom in order to demonstrate the necessary knowledge and skills, so far as those qualifications or experience are reasonably capable of demonstrating them;

(c) to the extent that the applicant cannot, on application of the principles set out in paragraphs (a) and (b), demonstrate the necessary knowledge and skills to the satisfaction of the regulatory body, the applicant should (subject to subsection (5)) have an opportunity to do so by way of a test or assessment the demands of which are proportionate to the deficiency;

(d) if the applicant can, on application of the principles set out in paragraphs (a) to (c), demonstrate the necessary knowledge and skills to the satisfaction of the regulatory body, the regulatory body should decide as mentioned in subsection (2).

(5) The process may, without contravening the principle set out in subsection (4)(c), allow the regulatory body in a case to which this subsection applies to decline the application without the applicant first being offered a test or assessment as described in that principle.

(6) Subsection (5) applies if the test or assessment would (having regard to the knowledge and skills demonstrated by the applicant in accordance with the principles set out in subsection (4)(a) and (b)) be similarly demanding to obtaining so much of the usual qualifications or experience as the applicant lacks.

(7) The process must require the regulatory body to inform the applicant of its decision within a reasonable time from the receipt of the application.

(8) Subsection (1) ceases to apply in the case of an applicant if, before the regulatory body informs the applicant of its decision—

(a) the regulatory body accepts in writing, or

(b) a court determines in legal proceedings,

that the regulatory body has failed to satisfy the requirement referred to in subsection (7).

(9) A regulatory body that administers a process to which this section applies must publish information about—

(a) the procedure for making an application within the process, and

(b) the way in which the principles set out in subsection (4) will be given effect in the context of the profession concerned.

But a failure to comply with this duty does not mean that the process does not comply with the requirements of this section.

(10) In this section—

"the usual qualifications or experience" means the qualifications or experience that are, under the provision that falls within section 24(1), required in order to be able to practise the profession concerned in the relevant part;

"the necessary knowledge and skills" means the knowledge and skills that are demonstrated by the usual qualifications or experience;

"regulatory body" means—

(a) the person, if any, responsible for determining whether a person has the qualifications or experience referred to in section 24(1), or

(b) if there is no such person, the responsible administration;

"responsible administration" means—

(a) if the relevant part is Scotland and the provision that falls within section 24(1)—

(i) would be within the legislative competence of the Scottish Parliament if contained in an Act of that Parliament, or

(ii) is provision which could be made in subordinate legislation by the Scottish Ministers, the First Minister or the Lord Advocate acting alone, the Scottish Ministers;

(b) if the relevant part is Wales and the provision that falls within section 24(1)—

(i) would be within the legislative competence of Senedd Cymru if contained in an Act of Senedd Cymru (assuming that any consent by a Minister of the Crown were given), or

(ii) is provision which could be made in subordinate legislation by the Welsh Ministers acting alone, the Welsh Ministers;

(c) if the relevant part is Northern Ireland and the provision that falls within section 24(1)—

(i) would be within the legislative competence of the Northern Ireland Assembly, and would not require the consent of the Secretary of State, if contained in an Act of that Assembly,

(ii) is contained in, or was made under, Northern Ireland legislation, and would be within the legislative competence of the Northern Ireland Assembly, and would require the consent of the Secretary of State, if contained in an Act of that Assembly, or

(iii) is provision which could be made in subordinate legislation by the First Minister and deputy First Minister in Northern Ireland acting jointly, a Northern Ireland Minister or a Northern Ireland department, a Northern Ireland department;

(d) in any other case, the Secretary of State.

27 Other exceptions from section 24

(1) Section 24(2) does not apply to existing provision (subject to subsection (3)).

(2) In subsection (1) "existing provision" means—

(a) provision that is in force on the date that this Act is passed, or

(b) provision that comes into force after that date so far as it is, in substance, a re-enactment or replication of provision within paragraph (a).

(3) Subsection (1) does not apply (and section 24(2) accordingly does apply) if, after the date on which this Act is passed, provision comes into force in a part of the United Kingdom other than the relevant part that changes the circumstances in which individuals are qualified in relation to the profession concerned.

(4) In subsection (3)—

(a) "relevant part" is to be read in accordance with section 24(1);

(b) "qualified" is to be read in accordance with section 25.

(5) Section 24(2) does not apply in relation to provision that limits the ability to practise a legal profession.

(6) In subsection (5) "legal profession" means—
(a) in relation to England or Wales, the profession of barrister, solicitor, notary, chartered legal executive, costs lawyer, licensed conveyancer or licensed CLC practitioner (see section 53 of the Courts and Legal Services Act 1990);
(b) in relation to Scotland, the profession of advocate, solicitor, notary, conveyancing practitioner (see section 17 of the Law Reform (Miscellaneous Provisions) (Scotland) Act 1990), executry practitioner (see section 18 of that Act) or commercial attorney;
(c) in relation to Northern Ireland, the profession of barrister, solicitor or notary;
(d) in relation to any part of the United Kingdom, the profession of patent attorney or trade mark attorney.

(7) Section 24(2) does not apply in relation to provision that limits the ability to practise the profession, or any profession, of school teaching.

28 Professional regulation not within section 24: equal treatment

(1) This section applies in relation to provision that—
(a) is not of the sort described in section 24(1),
(b) makes the ability to practise a particular profession in a part of the United Kingdom ("the relevant part") subject to a requirement or restriction, and
(c) applies differently to individuals according to—
(i) where any qualifications or experience of an individual were obtained, or
(ii) what qualifications or experience an individual has.

(2) "Requirement or restriction" includes, for example, a requirement as to registration, monitoring, insurance or continuing professional development, or a restriction on the undertaking of particular activities in the course of practising the profession.

(3) Subsection (4) applies to the extent that—
(a) the differential application is within subsection (1)(c)(i), and
(b) because of that differential application, the provision has the effect of imposing a more onerous requirement or restriction on an externally qualified UK practitioner than it would have the effect of imposing on a locally qualified practitioner.

(4) The externally qualified UK practitioner is to be treated for the purposes of the provision (and any related provision) as if the practitioner's external UK qualifications or experience had been obtained in the relevant part.

(5) Subsection (6) applies to the extent that—
(a) the differential application is within subsection (1)(c)(ii),
(b) because of that differential application, the provision has the effect of imposing a more onerous requirement or restriction on an externally qualified UK practitioner than it would have the effect of imposing on a locally qualified practitioner, and
(c) the external UK qualifications or experience are of a sort that cannot be obtained in the relevant part.

(6) The externally qualified UK practitioner is to be treated for the purposes of the provision (and any related provision) as if the practitioner's external UK qualifications or experience were the nearest equivalent qualifications or experience that can be obtained in the relevant part.

(7) Subsection (6) does not apply if the more onerous requirement or restriction can reasonably be justified on the grounds of differences between the external UK qualifications or experience and the nearest equivalent qualifications or experience.

(8) In this section—
"locally qualified practitioner" means a UK resident all of whose qualifications and experience were obtained in the relevant part;

"externally qualified UK practitioner" means a UK resident any of whose qualifications or experience was obtained in a part of the United Kingdom other than the relevant part;
"external UK qualifications or experience" means the qualifications or experience by virtue of which a UK resident is an externally qualified UK practitioner.

29 Interpretation of Part 3

(1) References in this Part to the ability to practise a profession include reference to the ability—
   (a) to undertake activities that comprise the practice of a profession,
   (b) to use a particular professional title, or
   (c) to be registered, licensed or similarly authorised, where that is required in order to undertake such activities or use such a title.

(2) Provision that limits the ability referred to in subsection (1)(a) to individuals with certain qualifications or experience falls within section 24(1) only if the activities affected by the provision are, in a significant number of cases, essential to the practice of the profession in question.

(3) Subsection (4) applies if provision applying in a part of the United Kingdom —
   (a) enables individuals to practise a profession—
      (i) on the basis of certain qualifications or experience, or not on the basis of any particular qualifications or experience, only following an individual assessment, and
      (ii) on the basis of certain qualifications or experience, without the need for an individual assessment, or
   (b) generally enables individuals to practise a profession only following an individual assessment, but provides for a less demanding assessment in some cases than in others according to what qualifications or experience an individual has.

(4) References in section 24 to the ability to practise a profession are to be read, in relation to the profession to which the provision relates, as references to the ability to practise the profession—
   (a) if the provision is within subsection (3)(a), without the need for an individual assessment, or
   (b) if the provision is within subsection (3)(b), following an individual assessment of the least demanding sort provided for.

(5) In subsections (3) and (4), "individual assessment" means an assessment of the individual's qualifications, experience, knowledge or skills.

(6) For the purposes of this Part a qualification is "obtained" in the place where the body that issues it is based.
A body is "based"—
   (a) where its registered office is,
   (b) if it does not have a registered office, where its head office is, or
   (c) if it does not have a registered office or a head office, where its principal place of operation is.

(7) References in this Part (however expressed) to the effect of "provision" are to the effect that it would have disregarding this Part.

(8) In this Part—
"profession" includes—
   (a) an occupation or trade, and
   (b) any subdivision of, or distinct specialism within, a profession; "provision" means—

(a) provision contained in legislation, or
(b) provision not of a legislative character but made under, and given effect by, legislation;

"qualification" means any record, issued by a body whose ordinary activities include the issuing of such records, of having attained a particular standard following a course of study or training;

"UK resident" means an individual who is lawfully resident in the United Kingdom; and for this purpose an individual is not lawfully resident in the United Kingdom if the individual requires leave to enter or remain in the United Kingdom but does not have it.

PART 4

INDEPENDENT ADVICE ON AND MONITORING OF UK INTERNAL MARKET

General provision about functions under Part 4

30 Functions of the CMA under Part 4: general provisions

(1) A regulatory provision is within the scope of this Part so far as it meets the conditions in subsections (2) and (4).

(2) The first condition is that the regulatory provision—

(a) imposes a relevant requirement, as defined for the purposes of the mutual recognition principle for goods as that principle applies in relation to a sale of goods in a part of the United Kingdom (see section 3),

(b) imposes a relevant requirement, as defined for the purposes of the non- discrimination principle for goods as that principle has effect in relation to a part of the United Kingdom (see section 6),

(c) imposes an authorisation requirement within the meaning given by subsection (3) of section 17 (services: overview),

(d) imposes a regulatory requirement within the meaning given by subsection (4) of that section, or

(e) comprises provision—

(i) of the sort described in section 24(1) (access to professions on grounds of qualifications or experience), or

(ii) to which section 28 (professional regulation not within section 24: equal treatment) applies.

(3) In its application for the purposes of section 34 (advising etc on proposed regulatory provisions on request) subsection (2) has effect as if—

(a) for each occurrence of "imposes" there were substituted "imposes, varies, or revokes";

(b) in paragraph (e) for "comprises" there were substituted "comprises, varies, repeals or revokes".

(4) The second condition is that the regulatory provision applies to one or more of England, Wales, Scotland and Northern Ireland but does not apply to the whole of the United Kingdom.

(5) In subsection (2)(c) the reference to an authorisation requirement does not include an authorisation requirement to which section 19 does not apply by virtue of section 18(1)(c).

(6) In subsection (2)(d) the reference to a regulatory requirement does not include a regulatory requirement to which sections 20 and 21 do not apply by virtue of section 18(1)(d).

(7) For the purposes of the law relating to defamation, absolute privilege attaches to any advice given, or report made, by the CMA (or a person acting on the CMA's behalf) in the exercise of any functions of the CMA under this Part.

(8) In this Part "regulatory provision" means a provision—
  (a) contained in legislation, or
  (b) not of a legislative character but made under, and given effect by, legislation.

(9) But a provision is not a "regulatory provision" so far as it contains anything that is necessary to give effect to the Northern Ireland Protocol.

(10) In this Part "the CMA" means the Competition and Markets Authority.

31 Objective and general functions

(1) In carrying out its functions under this Part the CMA must have regard to the objective in subsection (2).

(2) The objective is to support, through the application of economic and other technical expertise, the effective operation of the internal market in the United Kingdom (with particular reference to the purposes of Parts 1, 2 and 3).

(3) That objective includes, in particular, supporting the operation of the internal market—
  (a) in the interests of all parts of the United Kingdom, and
  (b) in the interests of consumers of goods and services as well as other classes of person with an interest in its operation.

(4) The CMA must also, in carrying out its functions under this Part, have regard to the need to act even-handedly as respects the relevant national authorities.

(5) The following do not apply in relation to the carrying out of the CMA's functions under this Part—
  (a) section 25(3) of the Enterprise and Regulatory Reform Act 2013 (duty to seek to promote competition), and
  (b) sections 6(1)(b) (function of giving information or advice to the public) and 7 (provision of information and advice to Ministers etc) of the Enterprise Act 2002.

(6) The CMA may give information or advice to the Secretary of State on matters relating to any of its functions under this Part.

32 Office for the Internal Market panel and task groups

(1) The CMA may authorise an Office for the Internal Market task group constituted under Schedule 4 to the Enterprise and Regulatory Reform Act 2013 to do anything required or authorised to be done by the CMA under this Part (and such an authorisation may include authorisation to exercise the power conferred on the CMA by this subsection).

(2) Schedule 3 contains provision about the Office for the Internal Market panel and Office for the Internal Market task groups.

Reporting, advisory and monitoring functions

33 Monitoring and reporting on the operation of the UK internal market

(1) The CMA may from time to time undertake a review of any matter it considers relevant to assessing or promoting the effective operation of—
  (a) the internal market in the United Kingdom;
  (b) provisions of Parts 1 to 3 (for example with regard to particular sectors of the internal market, or trade in different parts of the United Kingdom).

(2) The CMA may receive and consider any proposals that may be made or referred to it for undertaking a review in exercise of its powers under subsection (1).

(3) The CMA may prepare and publish a report on any matter falling within subsection (1).

(4) Any report published by the CMA under subsection (3) is to be published in such manner as it considers appropriate.

(5) The CMA must, no later than 31 March 2023 and at least once in every relevant 12-month period, prepare a report on—
  (a) the operation of the internal market in the United Kingdom, and
  (b) developments as to the effectiveness of the operation of that market.

(6) The CMA must, no later than 31 March 2023 and at least once in every relevant 5-year period, prepare a report on—
  (a) the effectiveness of the operation of provisions of Parts 1 to 3,
  (b) the impact of the operation of those Parts on the operation and development of the internal market in the United Kingdom,
  (c) any interaction between the operation of those Parts and common framework agreements, and
  (d) the impact of common framework agreements on the operation and development of the internal market in the United Kingdom.

(7) The CMA must arrange for a copy of the report prepared under subsection (5) or (6) for any period to be laid before—
  (a) each House of Parliament,
  (b) the Scottish Parliament,
  (c) Senedd Cymru, and
  (d) the Northern Ireland Assembly.

(8) So far as a report under this section is concerned with the effective operation of the internal market in the United Kingdom, the report may consider (among other things)—
  (a) developments in the operation of the internal market, for example as regards—
    (i) competition,
    (ii) access to goods and services,
    (iii) volumes of trade (or of trade in any direction) between participants in different parts of the United Kingdom, and
  (b) the practical implications of differences of approach embodied in regulatory provisions, falling within the scope of this Part, that apply to different parts of the United Kingdom.

(9) In this section—
"common framework agreements" has the meaning given by section 10; "relevant 12-month period" means—
  (a) the period of 12 months beginning with 1 April 2023, and
  (b) each successive period of 12 months;
"relevant 5-year period" means—
  (a) the period of 5 years beginning with 1 April 2023, and
  (b) each successive period of 5 years.

34 Advising etc on proposed regulatory provisions on request

(1) Where the condition in subsection (3) is met, the CMA may at the request of a relevant national authority give advice, or provide a report, to the authority with respect to a qualifying proposal.

(2) In subsection (1) "qualifying proposal" means a proposal of—
  (a) the requesting authority, or
  (b) a person or body on whose behalf the requesting authority makes the request, that a regulatory provision applying to the relevant part of the United Kingdom should be passed or made.

(3) The condition is that it appears to the requesting authority that—
(a) the regulatory provision to which the proposal relates would fall within the scope of this Part and be within relevant competence, and
(b) the proposal should be further considered in the light of the significance of its potential effects on the operation of the internal market in the United Kingdom.
(4) Advice given, or a report provided, under this section may consider among other things the potential economic effects of the proposed regulatory provision on the effective operation of the internal market in the United Kingdom, including—
(a) indirect or cumulative effects;
(b) distortion of competition or trade;
(c) impacts on prices, the quality of goods and services or choice for consumers.
(5) Subsections (1) to (3) apply in relation to two or more relevant national authorities acting jointly as those subsections apply in relation to a single relevant national authority.
(6) A request under subsection (1) must set out the reasons for making it.
(7) If the CMA declines to provide a report requested under subsection (1) it must—
(a) give to the requesting authority (or if more than one, to each of them simultaneously) a notice of its reasons for doing so, and
(b) publish the notice in such manner as it considers appropriate.
(8) Where the CMA gives advice or reasons, or provides a report, under this section to two or more relevant national authorities acting jointly, the CMA must give the advice or reasons, or provide the report, to each of them simultaneously.
(9) Where the CMA has on a particular day ("day 1") given advice, or provided a report, under subsection (1) the CMA must provide a copy of the advice or report to each relevant national authority who did not request the advice or report—
(a) as soon as reasonably practicable after the requesting authority (or each requesting authority) has informed the CMA that it may do so, or
(b) (if sooner), by the end of the 15th day after day 1.
(10) Where the CMA provides a report under this section it must, as soon as reasonably practicable after it has fully complied with subsection (9), publish the report in such manner as it considers appropriate.
(11) In this section "relevant part of the United Kingdom", in relation to a relevant national authority, means—
(a) in the application of this section to the Scottish Ministers as relevant national authority, Scotland;
(b) in the application of this section to the Welsh Ministers as relevant national authority, Wales;
(c) in the application of this section to a Northern Ireland department as relevant national authority, Northern Ireland;
(d) in the application of this section to the Secretary of State as relevant national authority, any part of the United Kingdom.

35 Provision of report on request after regulatory provision is passed or made

(1) The CMA may, at the request of a relevant national authority, provide a report to the authority on the impact on the effective operation of the internal market in the United Kingdom of a regulatory provision specified in the request which—
(a) is passed or made after the day on which this section comes into force,
(b) falls within the scope of this Part, and
(c) applies to the relevant part of the United Kingdom and is within relevant competence.

(2) A relevant national authority may not request a report from the CMA under subsection (1) unless the authority has considered whether any other person or body is qualified to provide an independent report on the matter.
(3) Subsections (1) and (2) apply in relation to two or more relevant national authorities acting jointly as those subsections apply in relation to a single relevant national authority.
(4) A request under subsection (1) must set out the reasons for making it.
(5) If the CMA declines to provide a report requested under subsection (1) it must—
  (a) give the requesting authority a notice of its reasons for doing so, and
  (b) publish the notice in such manner as it considers appropriate.
(6) Where the CMA provides a report under this section—
  (a) if the report was requested by two or more relevant national authorities acting jointly, the CMA must provide the report to each of them simultaneously;
  (b) the CMA must, as soon as reasonably practicable after complying with paragraph (a), publish the report in such manner as it considers appropriate.
(7) In this section "the relevant part of the United Kingdom" means—
  (a) in the application of this section to a relevant national authority who is the Scottish Ministers, Scotland;
  (b) in the application of this section to a relevant national authority who is the Welsh Ministers, Wales;
  (c) in the application of this section to a relevant national authority who is a Northern Ireland department, Northern Ireland;
  (d) in the application of this section to a relevant national authority who is the Secretary of State, any part of the United Kingdom.

36 Report on request on provision considered to have detrimental effects

(1) The CMA may, at the request of a relevant national authority, provide a report to the authority on the economic impact of a regulatory provision passed or made after the day on which this section comes into force, where—
  (a) the regulatory provision falls within the scope of this Part, and
  (b) the requesting authority considers that the operation of the regulatory provision is, or may come to be, detrimental to the effective operation of the internal market in the United Kingdom.
(2) The CMA's function under subsection (1) is exercisable regardless of whether or not a relevant national authority has exercised the power under section 34(1) in relation to the regulatory provision in question.
(3) A relevant national authority may not request a report from the CMA under subsection (1) unless it has considered whether any other person or body is qualified to provide an independent report on the matter.
(4) Subsections (1) to (3) apply in relation to the making of a request by two or more relevant national authorities acting jointly as they apply in relation to the making of a request by a single relevant national authority.
(5) A request under subsection (1) must set out the reasons for making it.
(6) If the CMA declines to provide a report requested under subsection (1) it must—
  (a) give the requesting authority (or each of them simultaneously, if more than one) a notice of its reasons for doing so, and
  (b) publish the notice in such manner as it considers appropriate.

(7) Where the CMA provides a report under subsection (1)—
  (a) it must provide a copy of the report to each relevant national authority who did not request the report, and
  (b) the provision of the report to the requesting authority (or each requesting authority) and each recipient mentioned in paragraph (a) must be simultaneous.

(8) As soon as reasonably practicable after the condition in subsection (9) has been met, but in any case no later than the end of the period of 6 months beginning with the day on which the CMA complies with subsection (7), the CMA must arrange for a copy of the report to be laid before—
  (a) each House of Parliament,
  (b) the Scottish Parliament,
  (c) Senedd Cymru, and
  (d) the Northern Ireland Assembly.

(9) The condition mentioned in subsection (8) is that each relevant national authority has notified the CMA that it does not require any further time for private consideration of the report provided or copied to it under this section.

(10) The CMA must publish the report in such manner as it considers appropriate, but may not do so until it has made the arrangements mentioned in subsection (8) and the report has been laid in accordance with one or more of paragraphs (a) to (d) of that subsection.

37 Statements on reports under section 36

(1) Subsection (2) applies where a report (or copy of it) relating to a regulatory provision has been laid before each House of Parliament, the Scottish Parliament, Senedd Cymru and the Northern Ireland Assembly in accordance with section 36(8).

(2) The following authorities must make a statement on the report to Parliament—
  (a) the responsible authority for each affected part of the United Kingdom;
  (b) the appropriate authority in relation to each relevant national authority which requested the CMA's report.

(3) In subsection (2) "to Parliament" means—
  (a) where the responsible authority or (as the case may be) appropriate authority is the Scottish Ministers, to the Scottish Parliament;
  (b) where the responsible authority or (as the case may be) appropriate authority is the Welsh Ministers, to Senedd Cymru;
  (c) where the responsible authority or (as the case may be) appropriate authority is the First Minister and deputy First Minister acting jointly, to the Northern Ireland Assembly.

(4) A duty of the Secretary of State under subsection (2) to make a statement to Parliament is to be discharged by laying a copy of the statement before each House of Parliament.

(5) In this section—

"affected part of the United Kingdom", in relation to a regulatory provision, means a part of the United Kingdom to which the provision applies;

"appropriate authority", in relation to a relevant national authority who is the Secretary of State, the Scottish Ministers or the Welsh Ministers, means that relevant national authority;

"appropriate authority", in relation to a relevant national authority who is a Northern Ireland department, means the First Minister and deputy First Minister acting jointly.

(6) In this section "responsible authority", in relation to Scotland, means—
 (a) if the regulatory provision is not within Scottish devolved competence, the Secretary of State;
 (b) otherwise, the Scottish Ministers.

(7) In this section "responsible authority", in relation to Wales, means—
 (a) if the regulatory provision is not within Welsh devolved competence, the Secretary of State;
 (b) otherwise, the Welsh Ministers.

(8) In this section "responsible authority", in relation to Northern Ireland, means—
 (a) if the regulatory provision is not within Northern Ireland devolved competence, the Secretary of State;
 (b) otherwise, the First Minister and deputy First Minister acting jointly.

(9) In this section "responsible authority", in relation to England, means the Secretary of State.

38 Reports under Part 4

Where under this Part the CMA publishes (or arranges for the publication of) a report it may exclude from the report—
 (a) any information the disclosure of which the CMA thinks is contrary to the public interest;
 (b) commercial information the disclosure of which the CMA thinks might significantly harm the legitimate business interests of any person;
 (c) information relating to the private affairs of an individual the disclosure of which the CMA thinks might significantly harm the individual's interests.

39 General advice and information with regard to exercise of functions

(1) The CMA must prepare and publish general advice and information about how it expects to approach the exercise of its functions under sections 33 to 36.

(2) Advice (or information) published by virtue of subsection (1) may include advice (or information) about the factors the CMA may take into account in considering whether to exercise a function conferred by any of those sections, including—
 (a) in cases where a person or body has requested the exercise of the function in accordance with the section concerned, and
 (b) in other cases.

(3) The CMA may at any time publish revised, or new, advice or information.

(4) Any advice or information published by the CMA under this section must be published in such manner as it considers appropriate.

40 Laying of annual documents before devolved legislatures

(1) Schedule 4 to the Enterprise and Regulatory Reform Act 2013 (the Competition and Markets Authority) is amended as follows.

(2) In paragraph 12(3) (annual plan to be laid before Parliament), for "Parliament" substitute "—
  (a) Parliament,
  (b) the Scottish Parliament,
  (c) Senedd Cymru, and
  (d) the Northern Ireland Assembly".

(3) In paragraph 13(2) (proposals for annual plan to be laid before Parliament), for "Parliament" substitute "—

(a) Parliament,

(b) the Scottish Parliament,

(c) Senedd Cymru, and

(d) the Northern Ireland Assembly".

(4) In paragraph 14(3)(a) (performance report to be laid before Parliament), for "Parliament" substitute "—

(i) Parliament,

(ii) the Scottish Parliament,

(iii) Senedd Cymru, and

(iv) the Northern Ireland Assembly".

Information-gathering powers

41 Information-gathering powers

(1) The powers under this section may be exercised for the purpose of assisting the CMA in carrying out any of its functions under—

(a) section 33, 34, 35 or 36; or

(b) section 5 of the Enterprise Act 2002 (acquisition of information etc) in connection with a matter in relation to which the CMA proposes to undertake a review, prepare a report, or give advice under any of the sections mentioned in paragraph (a).

(2) The CMA may by notice in writing require a person to produce any document which—

(a) is specified or otherwise identified in the notice; and

(b) is in that person's custody or under that person's control.

(3) The CMA may by notice in writing require any person who carries on a business to provide such estimates, forecasts, returns or other information as may be specified or otherwise described in the notice.

(4) A notice under subsection (2) or (3) may specify—

(a) the time and place at which,

(b) the form and manner in which, and

(c) the person to whom, a document or information is to be produced or provided.

(5) A notice under subsection (2) or (3) may require the provision of a legible and intelligible copy of information which is recorded otherwise than in legible form.

(6) A notice under subsection (2) or (3) must—

(a) state the purpose for which the notice is given, including which of the functions mentioned in subsection (1) is relevant; and

(b) include information about the potential consequences of not complying with the notice.

(7) The person to whom any document is produced in accordance with a notice under subsection (2) or (3) may copy the document.

(8) A notice under subsection (2) or (3) may not require a person—

(a) to produce or provide any document or information which the person could not be compelled to produce, or give in evidence, in civil proceedings before the court; or

(b) to go more than 10 miles from the person's place of residence, unless the person's necessary travelling expenses are paid or offered to them.

(9) In this section "the court" means—
(a) in relation to England and Wales or Northern Ireland, the High Court; and
(b) in relation to Scotland, the Court of Session.

(10) In Schedule 14 to the Enterprise Act 2002 (disclosure of information: specified functions) at the appropriate place insert—
"Part 4 of the United Kingdom Internal Market Act 2020.".

42 Enforcement

(1) Where the CMA considers that a person has, without reasonable excuse, failed to comply with any requirement of a notice under section 41, it may impose a penalty in accordance with section 43.

(2) Where the CMA considers that a person has intentionally obstructed or delayed any person in the exercise of the power under section 41(7), it may impose a penalty in accordance with section 43.

(3) In deciding whether and, if so, how to proceed under subsection (1) or (2), the CMA must have regard to the statement of policy which was most recently published under subsection (6) or (8) at the time the failure or (as the case may be) the obstruction or delay concerned occurred.

(4) Subject to subsection (5), no penalty may be imposed by virtue of subsection (1) or (2) after the end of the period of 4 weeks beginning with—
(a) where the penalty is imposed in connection with the exercise of the CMA's functions under section 33—
(i) if that exercise involves the publication of a report in accordance with subsection (3) of that section, the day on which the report is published,
(ii) if that exercise involves arranging for a copy of a report to be laid in accordance with subsection (7) of that section, the day on which the laying mentioned in paragraphs (a) to (d) of that subsection is fully accomplished, or
(iii) in the case of a review under subsection (1) of that section which does not involve the publication or laying of a report as mentioned in sub-paragraph (i) or (ii), the day on which the review is concluded,
(b) where the penalty is imposed in connection with the exercise of the CMA's functions under section 34, the day on which the advice or report is given or provided in accordance with subsection (1) of that section,
(c) where the penalty is imposed in connection with the exercise of the CMA's functions under section 35, the day on which the report is provided in accordance with subsection (1) of that section,
(d) where the penalty is imposed in connection with the exercise of the CMA's functions under section 36, the day on which the report is provided in accordance with subsection (1) of that section, or
(e) where the penalty is imposed in connection with the exercise of the CMA's functions under section 5 of the Enterprise Act 2002 in the circumstances mentioned in section 41(1)(b), the day on which the CMA finally concludes the carrying out of those functions.

(5) Subsection (4) does not apply in relation to any variation or substitution of the penalty which is permitted by virtue of section 43(11).

(6) The CMA must prepare and publish a statement of policy in relation to the enforcement of notices given under section 41.

(7) The statement must include a statement about the considerations relevant to the determination of the nature and amount of any penalty imposed under subsection (1) or (2).

(8) The CMA may revise its statement of policy under subsection (6) and, where it does so, it must publish the revised statement.

(9) The CMA must consult—

(a) each relevant national authority, and

(b) such other persons as it considers appropriate,

when preparing or revising its statement of policy under subsection (6) or (8).

(10) Any statement or revised statement published by the CMA under this section is to be published in such manner as the CMA considers appropriate.

43 Penalties

(1) A penalty imposed under section 42(1) or (2) may be of such amount as the CMA considers appropriate.

(2) The amount of a penalty imposed under section 42(1) may be—

(a) a fixed amount,

(b) an amount calculated by reference to a daily rate, or

(c) a combination of a fixed amount and an amount calculated by reference to a daily rate.

(3) The amount of a penalty imposed under section 42(2) must be a fixed amount.

(4) A penalty imposed under section 42(1) may not exceed—

(a) in the case of a fixed amount, such amount as the Secretary of State may specify in regulations,

(b) in the case of an amount calculated by reference to a daily rate, such amount per day as the Secretary of State may so specify, and

(c) in the case of a fixed amount and an amount calculated by reference to a daily rate, such fixed amount and such amount per day as the Secretary of State may so specify.

(5) A penalty imposed under section 42(2) may not exceed such amount as the Secretary of State may specify in regulations.

(6) Regulations under subsection (4) or (5) may not specify—

(a) in the case of a fixed amount, an amount exceeding £30,000,

(b) in the case of an amount calculated by reference to a daily rate, an amount per day exceeding £15,000, and

(c) in the case of a fixed amount and an amount calculated by reference to a daily rate, a fixed amount exceeding £30,000 and an amount per day exceeding £15,000.

(7) Regulations under subsection (4) or (5) are subject to negative resolution procedure.

(8) Before making regulations under subsection (4) or (5) the Secretary of State must consult—

(a) the CMA,

(b) each other relevant national authority, and

(c) such other persons as the Secretary of State considers appropriate.

(9) In imposing a penalty by reference to a daily rate—

(a) no account is to be taken of any days before the service on the person concerned of notice of the penalty under section 112 of the Enterprise Act 2002 (as applied by subsection (11)), and

(b) unless the CMA determines an earlier date (whether before or after the penalty is imposed), the amount payable ceases to accumulate at the beginning of the earliest of the days mentioned in subsection (10).

(10) The days mentioned in subsection (9) are—

(a) the day on which the requirement of the notice concerned under section 41 is satisfied;

(b) the day referred to in paragraph (a)(i), (a)(ii), or (a)(iii), (b), (c), (d) or (e) (as the case may be) of section 42(4).

(11) Sections 112 to 115 of the Enterprise Act 2002 (procedural requirements, appeals etc in relation to penalties) apply in relation to a penalty imposed under section 42(1) or (2) as they apply in relation to a penalty imposed under section 110(1) of that Act.

Review

44 Duty to review arrangements for carrying out Part 4 functions

(1) The Secretary of State must, within the permitted period—
   (a) carry out a review of the appropriateness, for the purpose of securing the most effective and efficient performance of the Part 4 functions, of—
      (i) the provision made by section 32(1) and the amendments made by Schedule 3, and
      (ii) any arrangements made under or in connection with that provision and those amendments;
   (b) prepare a report of the review (see subsection (4) for specific requirements relating to the report), and
   (c) lay a copy of the report before Parliament, the Scottish Parliament, Senedd Cymru and the Northern Ireland Assembly.

(2) The review must, among other things, assess—
   (a) the way in which Part 4 functions have been carried out by the CMA through Office for the Internal Market task groups authorised under section 32(1), and
   (b) any advantages or disadvantages of continuing with—
      (i) the provision made by section 32 and the amendments made by Schedule 3, and
      (ii) the arrangements made under or in connection with that provision or those amendments, as compared with other possible ways of providing for the Part 4 functions to be carried out (including possible arrangements not involving the CMA).

(3) In carrying out the review the Secretary of State must consult the other relevant national authorities.

(4) Before finalising the report required by subsection (1)(b) the Secretary of State must—
   (a) send a draft of the proposed report to each of the other relevant national authorities, inviting the authority to make representations as to the content of the proposed report within a period specified by the Secretary of State, and
   (b) consider any representations duly made in response to that invitation and determine whether to alter the report in the light of that consideration.

(5) The Secretary of State need not consult the devolved authorities further if the draft is altered as mentioned in subsection (4)(b) (but is free to do so if the Secretary of State thinks fit).

(6) The permitted period for the review is the period beginning with the third anniversary of the day on which section 32 comes into force (or first comes into force to any extent) and ending with the fifth anniversary.

(7) In this section "Part 4 functions" means functions of the CMA under this Part.

Interpretation

45 Interpretation of Part 4

(1) This section applies for the purposes of this Part.

(2) "The CMA" has the meaning given by section 30(10).

(3) References to the "operation of the internal market in the United Kingdom" are to be read as including a reference to aspects of its operation, for example its operation in relation to a particular description of goods or services or in a particular area or region of the United Kingdom.

(4) "Regulatory provision" has the meaning given by section 30(8).

(5) "Relevant competence" means—

(a) in relation to the Scottish Ministers, Scottish devolved competence;

(b) in relation to the Welsh Ministers, Welsh devolved competence;

(c) in relation to a Northern Ireland department, Northern Ireland devolved competence;

(d) in relation to the Secretary of State, reserved competence.

(6) "Relevant national authority" means any of the following—

(a) the Secretary of State;

(b) the Scottish Ministers;

(c) the Welsh Ministers;

(d) a Northern Ireland department.

(7) "Scottish devolved competence", "Welsh devolved competence", "Northern Ireland devolved competence" and "reserved competence" are to be interpreted in accordance with subsections (8) to (11).

(8) A regulatory provision, so far as applying to Scotland—

(a) is within Scottish devolved competence if it—

(i) would be within the legislative competence of the Scottish Parliament if contained in an Act of that Parliament, or

(ii) is provision which could be made in subordinate legislation by the Scottish Ministers, the First Minister or the Lord Advocate acting alone;

(b) otherwise, is within reserved competence.

(9) A regulatory provision, so far as applying to Wales—

(a) is within Welsh devolved competence if it—

(i) would be within the legislative competence of Senedd Cymru if contained in an Act of Senedd Cymru (assuming that any consent by a Minister of the Crown were given), or

(ii) is provision which could be made in subordinate legislation by the Welsh Ministers acting alone;

(b) otherwise, is within reserved competence.

(10) A regulatory provision, so far as applying to Northern Ireland—

(a) is within Northern Ireland devolved competence if it—

(i) would be within the legislative competence of the Northern Ireland Assembly, and would not require the consent of the Secretary of State, if contained in an Act of that Assembly,

(ii) is contained in, or was made under, Northern Ireland legislation, and would be within the legislative competence of the Northern Ireland Assembly, and would require the consent of the Secretary of State, if contained in an Act of that Assembly, or

(iii) is provision which could be made in subordinate legislation by the First Minister and deputy First Minister in Northern Ireland acting jointly, a Northern Ireland Minister or a Northern Ireland department;

(b) otherwise, is within reserved competence.

(11) A regulatory provision, so far as applying to England, is within reserved competence.

PART 5

NORTHERN IRELAND PROTOCOL

Northern Ireland's place in the UK internal market and customs territory

46 Northern Ireland's place in the UK internal market and customs territory

(1) An appropriate authority must have special regard to the following matters when exercising any function for a relevant purpose—

(a) the need to maintain Northern Ireland's integral place in the United Kingdom's internal market;

(b) the need to respect Northern Ireland's place as part of the customs territory of the United Kingdom; and

(c) the need to facilitate the free flow of goods between Great Britain and Northern Ireland with the aim of—

(i) streamlining trade between Great Britain and Northern Ireland, and

(ii) maintaining and strengthening the integrity and smooth operation of the internal market in the United Kingdom.

(2) A function is exercised for "a relevant purpose" if it is exercised for—

(a) the purpose of—

(i) implementing, or

(ii) otherwise dealing with matters arising out of, or related to, the Northern Ireland Protocol,

(b) the purpose of enabling or facilitating a purpose described in paragraph (a) to be achieved, or

(c) a purpose relating to movement of goods within the United Kingdom (including movement that involves movement in a country or territory outside the United Kingdom).

(3) In this section "appropriate authority" means—

(a) a Minister of the Crown;

(b) the Scottish Ministers;

(c) the Welsh Ministers;

(d) the First Minister and deputy First Minister in Northern Ireland acting jointly, a Northern Ireland Minister or a Northern Ireland department;

(e) any other person who exercises functions of a public nature.

Unfettered access

47 Unfettered access to UK internal market for Northern Ireland goods

(1) On or after IP completion day, an appropriate authority must not exercise any function in a way that would—

Part 5 — Northern Ireland Protocol

(a) result in an existing kind of NI-GB check, control or administrative process being used—
   (i) for the first time, or
   (ii) for a new purpose or to a new extent; or
(b) result in a new kind of NI-GB check, control or administrative process—
   (i) being introduced, or
   (ii) being used.

(2) This section does not prevent the exercise of a function if the exercise—
(a) is necessary for the administration of arrangements which have the purpose of facilitating access for qualifying Northern Ireland goods to the internal market in the United Kingdom,
(b) is necessary to secure compliance with, or to give effect to, any international obligation or arrangement to which the United Kingdom is a party (whenever the United Kingdom becomes a party to it),
(c) is necessary where goods have been declared for a voluntary customs procedure,
(d) is necessary for the purposes of VAT or excise duty in consequence of the Northern Ireland Protocol,
(e) is necessary for the purpose of dealing with a threat to biosecurity in Great Britain, or
(f) is necessary for the purpose of dealing with a threat to food or feed safety in Great Britain.

(3) Subsection (2)(b) authorises (in particular) the exercise of a function in relation to a check, control or administrative process if the exercise is necessary to secure compliance with, or to give effect to, Article 6(1) of the Northern Ireland Protocol.

(4) For the purposes of this section the exercise of a function "is necessary for the purposes of VAT or excise duty in consequence of the Northern Ireland Protocol" if—
(a) the appropriate authority exercising the functions is the Treasury, the Commissioners for Her Majesty's Revenue and Customs, or the Director of Border Revenue,
(b) the function is exercised for the purposes of VAT or excise duty (including for the purposes of preventing double taxation, partial or complete non-taxation, or evasion), and
(c) the appropriate authority exercising the function considers that the exercise is necessary in consequence of the Northern Ireland Protocol.

(5) For the purposes of this section the exercise of a function "is necessary for the purpose of dealing with a threat to biosecurity in Great Britain" if the exercise of the function consists of—
(a) the making, or operation, of legislation which satisfies the conditions set out in paragraph 1 of Schedule 1, or
(b) any other activity which satisfies the conditions set out in paragraph 1(2), (3), (4) and (6) of Schedule 1 (reading any reference in those conditions to "legislation" as a reference to the activity in question).

(6) In determining for the purposes of subsection (5)(b) whether the condition in paragraph 1(3) of Schedule 1 is met, a pest or disease is to be taken to be present in Northern Ireland if it is, or may be, present in qualifying Northern Ireland goods (including when the goods are in Great Britain).

(7) For the purposes of this section the exercise of a function "is necessary for the purpose of dealing with a threat to food or feed safety in Great Britain" if the exercise of the function consists of—

(a) the making, or operation, of legislation which satisfies the conditions set out in paragraph 2 of Schedule 1, or

(b) any other activity which satisfies the conditions set out in paragraph 2(2), (3), (4) and (6) of Schedule 1 (reading any reference in those conditions to "legislation" as a reference to the activity in question).

(8) For the purposes of this section—

(a) an "NI-GB" check, control or administrative process is one applicable to the direct movement of qualifying Northern Ireland goods from Northern Ireland to Great Britain;

(b) an "existing kind" of NI-GB check, control or administrative process is one that—

(i) was in use or available for use immediately before IP completion day, or

(ii) is the same as, or substantially similar to, one that was in use or available for use immediately before IP completion day (the "predecessor");

(c) a "new kind of" NI-GB check, control or administrative process is one that is not of an existing kind;

(d) where an NI-GB check, control or administrative process is of an existing kind because of paragraph (b)(ii), that check, control or administrative process and the predecessor are to be treated as a single function for the purpose of determining whether subsection (1)(a) prevents its exercise;

(e) the purpose for which, or extent to which, a function would be used is "new" if the function has not been used for that purpose, or to that extent, before IP completion day.

(9) A Minister of the Crown may by regulations amend this section so that it applies to a type of movement instead of, or in addition to, a type of movement to which it already applies (whether that type of movement is direct movement or another type of movement provided for by regulations under this subsection).

(10) Regulations under subsection (9) are subject to affirmative resolution procedure.

(11) In this section—

"appropriate authority" means—

(a) a Minister of the Crown;

(b) the Scottish Ministers;

(c) the Welsh Ministers;

(d) the First Minister and deputy First Minister in Northern Ireland acting jointly, a Northern Ireland Minister or a Northern Ireland department;

(e) any other person who exercises functions of a public nature;

"declared for a voluntary customs procedure" means declared, in accordance with the Taxation (Cross-border Trade) Act 2018, for a special Customs procedure or temporary storage;

"direct movement" means movement that does not involve movement by land in a country or territory other than the United Kingdom;

"excise duty" means any excise duty under—

(a) the Alcoholic Liquor Duties Act 1979,

(b) the Hydrocarbon Oil Duties Act 1979, or

(c) the Tobacco Products Duty Act 1979;

"qualifying Northern Ireland goods"—

(a) has the same meaning that it has in the European Union (Withdrawal) Act 2018, including any meaning defined for the purposes of that Act from time to time by regulations made under the power conferred by section 8C(6) of that Act (and, if those regulations provide for different meanings to be defined for different purposes of that Act, regulations under section 8C(6) may make provision about the meaning or meanings that are to apply for the purposes of this section);

(b) is to be taken to have had, immediately before IP completion day, the same meaning that it has (under paragraph (a)) at the time when this section comes into force.

State aid

48 Guidance on Article 10 of the Northern Ireland Protocol

(1) The Secretary of State must publish guidance on the practical application of Article 10 of the Northern Ireland Protocol (state aid).

(2) For that purpose Article 10 is to be read in the light of—

(a) any relevant decision or recommendation of the Joint Committee, and

(b) any relevant declaration that is made in the Joint Committee by either party, of which the other party takes note.

(3) The guidance must be published before the end of the period of one month beginning with the day on which this section comes into force.

(4) A person with public functions relating to the implementation of Article 10 (including functions involving the provision of financial assistance or other subsidies) must have regard to the guidance when exercising such functions.

(5) The Secretary of State may—

(a) revise or replace the guidance;

(b) if satisfied it is no longer necessary, withdraw the guidance.

(6) In this section "Joint Committee" means the committee established by Article 164(1) of the EU withdrawal agreement.

49 Notification of state aid for the purposes of the Northern Ireland Protocol

(1) No public authority apart from the Secretary of State may comply with a requirement of a provision of EU law applied to the United Kingdom by Article 10 of the Northern Ireland Protocol (state aid) to give the European Commission a notification or information relating to aid.

(2) In subsection (1), "public authority" means a person who exercises functions of a public nature.

PART 6

FINANCIAL ASSISTANCE

50 Power to provide financial assistance for economic development etc

(1) A Minister of the Crown may, out of money provided by Parliament, provide financial assistance to any person for, or in connection with, any of the following purposes—

(a) promoting economic development in the United Kingdom or any area of the United Kingdom;
(b) providing infrastructure at places in the United Kingdom (including infrastructure in connection with any of the other purposes mentioned in this section);
(c) supporting cultural activities, projects and events that the Minister considers directly or indirectly benefit the United Kingdom or particular areas of the United Kingdom;
(d) supporting activities, projects and events relating to sport that the Minister considers directly or indirectly benefit the United Kingdom or particular areas of the United Kingdom;
(e) supporting international educational and training activities and exchanges;
(f) supporting educational and training activities and exchanges within the United Kingdom.

(2) In this section—

"infrastructure" includes—
(a) water, electricity, gas, telecommunications, sewerage or other services (for example, the provision of heat),
(b) railway facilities (including rolling stock), roads or other transport facilities,
(c) health, educational, cultural or sports facilities,
(d) court or prison facilities, and
(e) housing;

"promoting", in relation to economic development, includes taking any measure likely to contribute directly or indirectly to economic development (which might include, for example, measures relating to social inclusion);

"providing", in relation to infrastructure, includes acquiring, designing, constructing, converting, improving, operating and repairing infrastructure;

"sport" includes any physical recreation.

51 Financial assistance: supplementary

(1) Financial assistance under section 50—
(a) may be provided by way of grants, loans, guarantees or indemnities or in any other form;
(b) may be provided subject to conditions (which may include conditions about repayment with or without interest or other return);
(c) may be provided under a contract;
(d) may be provided to an investment fund for onward investment or administrative costs relating to onward investment.

(2) The power to provide financial assistance under section 50 is in addition to (and does not limit or replace) any other power of a Minister of the Crown to provide financial assistance.

PART 7

SUBSIDY CONTROL

52 Regulation of distortive or harmful subsidies

(1) In Part 2 of Schedule 5 to the Scotland Act 1998 (specific reservations), under Head C (trade and industry), at the end insert—

"C16. Distortive or harmful subsidies

Regulation of the provision of subsidies which are or may be distortive or harmful by a public authority to persons supplying goods or services in the course of a business.

Interpretation

"Public authority" means a person who exercises functions of a public nature.

"Subsidy" includes assistance provided to a person directly or indirectly by way of income or price support, grant, loan, guarantee, indemnity, the provision of goods or services and any other kind of assistance, whether financial or otherwise and whether actual or contingent.

A subsidy is provided "by a public authority" if it is provided by that authority directly or indirectly.

A subsidy is "distortive or harmful" if it distorts competition between, or otherwise causes harm or injury to, persons supplying goods or services in the course of a business, whether or not those persons are established in the United Kingdom."

(2) In Schedule 2 to the Northern Ireland Act 1998 (excepted matters), after paragraph 16 insert—

"16A Regulation of the provision of subsidies which are or may be distortive or harmful by a public authority to persons supplying goods or services in the course of a business.

In this paragraph—

"Public authority" means a person who exercises functions of a public nature.

"Subsidy" includes assistance provided to a person directly or indirectly by way of income or price support, grant, loan, guarantee, indemnity, the provision of goods or services and any other kind of assistance, whether financial or otherwise and whether actual or contingent.

A subsidy is provided "by a public authority" if it is provided by that authority directly or indirectly.

A subsidy is "distortive or harmful" if it distorts competition between, or otherwise causes harm or injury to, persons supplying goods or services in the course of a business, whether or not those persons are established in the United Kingdom."

(3) In Part 2 of Schedule 7A to the Government of Wales Act 2006 (specific reservations), under Head C (trade and industry), at the end insert—

"C18. Distortive or harmful subsidies

Regulation of the provision of subsidies which are or may be distortive or harmful by a public authority to persons supplying goods or services in the course of a business.

Interpretation

"Public authority" means a person who exercises functions of a public nature.

"Subsidy" includes assistance provided to a person directly or indirectly by way of income or price support, grant, loan, guarantee, indemnity, the provision of goods or services and any other kind of assistance, whether financial or otherwise and whether actual or contingent.

A subsidy is provided "by a public authority" if it is provided by that authority directly or indirectly.

A subsidy is "distortive or harmful" if it distorts competition between, or otherwise causes harm or injury to, persons supplying goods or services in the course of a business, whether or not those persons are established in the United Kingdom."

53 UK subsidy control consultation: engagement with the devolved authorities on the Government response

(1) For the purposes of this section—

(a) "the UK subsidy control consultation" is the consultation announced by the Secretary of State for Business, Energy and Industrial Strategy in a written Ministerial statement made in the House of Commons on 9 September 2020 (consultation on whether the United Kingdom should go further than its existing international commitments in relation to subsidy control, including whether legislation is necessary);

(b) a "relevant report" is a report containing the whole or part of the Government's response to that consultation (and for this purpose "response" includes any conclusions and proposals, resulting from that consultation, as to arrangements in the United Kingdom for controlling the provision by public authorities of subsidies which are or may be distortive or harmful);

(c) subsidies are "distortive or harmful" if they distort competition between, or otherwise cause harm or injury to, persons supplying goods or services in the course of a business, whether or not established in the United Kingdom;

(d) the "devolved authorities" are the Scottish Ministers, the Welsh Ministers and the Department for the Economy in Northern Ireland.

(2) The Secretary of State must, before publishing any relevant report relating to the UK subsidy control consultation—

(a) provide a draft of the proposed Government response to each devolved authority, inviting it to make representations about the proposed response within a period specified by the Secretary of State, and

(b) consider any representations duly made by any of the devolved authorities in response to that invitation and determine whether to alter the report in the light of that consideration.

(3) The Secretary of State need not consult the devolved authorities further if the draft is altered as mentioned in subsection (2)(b) (but is free to do so if the Secretary of State thinks fit).

(4) The consultation required by subsection (2) is in addition to any engagement with the devolved authorities in the course of the UK subsidy control consultation.

PART 8

FINAL PROVISIONS

54 Protection of Act against modification

(1) In Schedule 4 to the Scotland Act 1998 (enactments etc. protected from modification), after paragraph 1(2)(g) insert ", and

(h) the United Kingdom Internal Market Act 2020."

(2) In paragraph 5(1) of Schedule 7B to the Government of Wales Act 2006 (protected enactments), in the table after the entry for the European Union (Withdrawal) Act 2018 insert—

"The United Kingdom Internal Market Act 2020 The whole Act."

(3) In section 7(1) of the Northern Ireland Act 1998 (entrenched enactments)—

(a) omit the "and" at the end of paragraph (d), and

(b) after paragraph (e) insert "; and

(f) the United Kingdom Internal Market Act 2020."

(4) No power to make subordinate legislation contained in primary legislation passed or made before this section comes into force may be exercised so as to amend, repeal or otherwise modify the operation of this Act.

55 Further provision in connection with the Northern Ireland Protocol

(1) The following provisions cease to have effect when Articles 5 to 10 of the Northern Ireland Protocol cease to apply—

(a) section 11 and Part 5, and

(b) section 8C(5A) of the European Union (Withdrawal) Act 2018 (as inserted by subsection (3)).

(2) Nothing in this Act except the amendment made by subsection (3) (including, in particular, section 54(4)) limits—

(a) the power to make provision under section 8C of the European Union (Withdrawal) Act 2018 (regulations in connection with the Protocol) (including as that power may be used to modify this Act), or

(b) the effect of any regulations under that section.

(3) In section 8C of the European Union (Withdrawal) Act 2018, after subsection (5) insert—

"(5A) Regulations under subsection (1) may not amend, repeal or otherwise modify the operation of section 47 of the United Kingdom Internal Market Act 2020 ("the 2020 Act"), except by making—

(a) provision of the sort that is contemplated by section 47(2) of the 2020 Act (permitted checks);

(b) provision under subsection (6);

(c) provision of the sort described in paragraph 21(b) of Schedule 7 (supplementary and transitional provision etc) in connection with—

(i) provision within either of the preceding paragraphs;

(ii) Articles 5 to 10 of the Northern Ireland Protocol ceasing to apply (and the resulting operation of section 55(1) of the 2020 Act)."

56 Regulations: general

(1) Any power to make regulations under this Act is exercisable by statutory instrument.

(2) Any power to make regulations under this Act includes power—

(a) to amend, repeal or otherwise modify legislation;

(b) to make different provision for different purposes;

(c) to make supplementary, incidental, consequential, transitional, transitory or saving provision (including provision made in reliance on paragraph (a)).

(3) This section does not apply to regulations under section 59(3).

57 Regulations: references to parliamentary procedures

(1) Where regulations under this Act are subject to affirmative resolution procedure, the regulations may not be made unless a draft of the statutory instrument containing them has been laid before and approved by a resolution of each House of Parliament.

(2) Where regulations under this Act are subject to made affirmative procedure—

(a) the statutory instrument containing them must be laid before Parliament as soon as reasonably practicable after being made; and

(b) the regulations cease to have effect at the end of the period of 40 days beginning with the day on which they are made unless, during that period, the instrument is approved by a resolution of each House of Parliament.

(3) In calculating the period of 40 days, no account is to be taken of any time during which—

(a) Parliament is dissolved or prorogued, or

(b) both Houses of Parliament are adjourned for more than 4 days.

(4) Where regulations cease to have effect as a result of subsection (3) that does not—

(a) affect anything previously done under or by virtue of the regulations, or

(b) prevent the making of new regulations.

(5) Subsections (2) to (4) do not apply to regulations if a draft of the statutory instrument containing them has been laid before, and approved by a resolution of, each House of Parliament.

(6) Where regulations under this Act are subject to negative resolution procedure the statutory instrument containing them is subject to annulment in pursuance of a resolution of either House of Parliament.

(7) Any provision that may be made by regulations under this Act subject to negative resolution procedure may be made in regulations subject to affirmative resolution procedure or made affirmative procedure.

58 Interpretation: general

In this Act—

"affirmative resolution procedure" is to be construed in accordance with section 57(1);

"legislation" means primary legislation, subordinate legislation and retained direct EU legislation;

"made affirmative resolution procedure" is to be construed in accordance with section 57(2);

"Minister of the Crown" has the same meaning as the Ministers of the Crown Act 1975 (see section 8(1) of that Act);

"negative resolution procedure" is to be construed in accordance with section 57(6);

"Northern Ireland Protocol" means the Protocol on Ireland/Northern Ireland in the EU withdrawal agreement;

"part of the United Kingdom" means England, Wales, Scotland or Northern Ireland;

"primary legislation" means—

(a) an Act of Parliament;

(b) an Act of the Scottish Parliament;

(c) an Act or Measure of Senedd Cymru; or

(d) Northern Ireland legislation;

"subordinate legislation" means an instrument made under primary legislation or retained direct EU legislation.

59 Extent, commencement and short title

(1) This Act extends to England and Wales, Scotland and Northern Ireland.

(2) This section comes into force on the day on which this Act is passed.

(3) The other provisions of this Act come into force on such day as the Secretary of State may by regulations made by statutory instrument appoint.

(4) Regulations under subsection (3) may—

(a) appoint different days for different purposes;

(b) make transitional or saving provision in connection with the coming into force of any provision of this Act.

(5) This Act may be cited as the United Kingdom Internal Market Act 2020.

SCHEDULES

SCHEDULE 1

SECTION 10

EXCLUSIONS FROM MARKET ACCESS PRINCIPLES

Threats to human, animal or plant health

1 (1) The United Kingdom market access principles do not apply to (and sections 2(3) and 5(3) do not affect the operation of) legislation so far as it satisfies the conditions set out in this paragraph.

(2) The first condition is that the aim of the legislation is to prevent or reduce the movement of a pest or disease into the part of the United Kingdom in which the legislation applies ("the restricting part") from another part of the United Kingdom ("the affected part").

(3) The second condition is that it is reasonable to believe that the pest or disease—

(a) is present in the affected part, and

(b) is not present, or is significantly less prevalent, in the restricting part.

(4) The third condition is that the potential movement of that pest or disease into the restricting part from the affected part poses (or would in the absence of the legislation pose) a serious threat to the health of humans, animals or plants in the restricting part.

(5) The fourth condition is that the responsible administration has provided to the other administrations an assessment of the available evidence in relation to—

(a) the threat referred to in sub-paragraph (4), and

(b) the likely effectiveness of the legislation in addressing that threat.

(6) The fifth condition is that the legislation can reasonably be justified as necessary in order to address the threat referred to in sub-paragraph (4).

(7) In determining whether the fifth condition is met the following consideration is to be taken into account: whether the legislation, taken together with any similar legislation applying in the restricting part, imposes measures of similar severity arising from the potential movement of the pest or disease into, or within, the restricting part (wherever those threats originate).

(8) In this paragraph "pest or disease" includes any organism or agent that is liable to cause a disease or other harm to the health of humans, animals or plants.

2 (1) The mutual recognition principle for goods does not apply to (and section 2(3) does not affect the operation of) legislation so far as it satisfies the conditions set out in this paragraph.

(2) The first condition is that the aim of the legislation is to prevent or reduce the movement of unsafe food or feed into the part of the United Kingdom in which the legislation applies ("the restricting part") from another part of the United Kingdom ("the affected part").

(3) The second condition is that it is reasonable to believe that the food or feed affected by the legislation is, is likely to be, or is at particular risk of being unsafe in a particular respect.

(4) The third condition is the potential movement of food or feed that is unsafe in that respect into the restricting part from the affected part poses (or would in the absence of the legislation pose) a serious threat to the health of humans or animals in the restricting part.

(5) The fourth condition is that the responsible administration has provided to the other administrations an assessment of the available evidence in relation to—

(a) the threat referred to in sub-paragraph (4), and

(b) the likely effectiveness of the legislation in addressing that threat.

(6) The fifth condition is that the legislation can reasonably be justified as necessary in order to address the threat referred to in sub-paragraph (4).

(7) In this paragraph—

"food" and "feed" have the same meaning as in Regulation (EC) No 178/2002 (see Articles 2 and 3);

"unsafe"—

(a) in relation to food, has the same meaning as in Article 14 of Regulation (EC) No 178/2002;

(b) in relation to feed, means "unsafe for its intended use" within the meaning given by Article 15(2) of Regulation (EC) No 178/2002;

"Regulation (EC) No 178/2002" means Regulation (EC) No 178/2002 of the European Parliament and of the Council of 28 January 2002 laying down the general principles and requirements of food law (etc), as it forms part of retained EU law on IP completion day.

3 Where a decision is taken to exercise powers conferred by legislation in a particular way for the purpose referred to in paragraph 1(2) or 2(2), references to "legislation" in paragraph 1 or 2 (except in paragraph 1(1) or 2(1)) are to be read as references to the use of the legislation in that way.

4 (1) In paragraphs 1 and 2, "responsible administration" is to be interpreted in accordance with sub-paragraphs (2) to (5).

(2) The responsible administration is the Scottish Ministers if—

(a) the restricting part is Scotland, and

(b) the provision contained in the legislation in question, so far as it applies in Scotland—

(i) would be within the legislative competence of the Scottish Parliament if contained in an Act of that Parliament, or

(ii) is provision which could be made in subordinate legislation by the Scottish Ministers, the First Minister or the Lord Advocate acting alone.

(3) The responsible administration is the Welsh Ministers if—

(a) the restricting part is Wales, and

(b) the provision contained in the legislation in question, so far as it applies in Wales—

(i) would be within the legislative competence of Senedd Cymru if contained in an Act of Senedd Cymru (assuming that any consent by a Minister of the Crown were given), or

(ii) is provision which could be made in subordinate legislation by the Welsh Ministers acting alone.

(4) The responsible administration is a Northern Ireland department if—

(a) the restricting part is Northern Ireland, and

(b) the provision contained in the legislation in question, so far as it applies in Northern Ireland—

(i) would be within the legislative competence of the Northern Ireland Assembly, and would not require the consent of the Secretary of State, if contained in an Act of that Assembly,

(ii) is contained in, or was made under, Northern Ireland legislation, and would be within the legislative competence of the Northern Ireland Assembly, and would require the consent of the Secretary of State, if contained in an Act of that Assembly,

(iii) is provision which could be made in subordinate legislation by the First Minister and deputy First Minister in Northern Ireland acting jointly, a Northern Ireland Minister or a Northern Ireland department.

(5) In any other case the responsible administration is the Secretary of State.

(6) In paragraphs 1 and 2, "the other administrations" means each of the Scottish Ministers, the Welsh Ministers, a Northern Ireland department and the Secretary of State, other than the responsible administration.

5 (1) A relevant requirement is not to be taken to directly discriminate against incoming goods for the purposes of section 7 to the extent that it can reasonably be justified as a response to a public health emergency.

(2) In this paragraph—

"public health emergency" means an event or a situation that is reasonably considered to pose an extraordinary threat to human health in the destination part;

"relevant requirement", "incoming goods" and "destination part" have the meanings they have in relation to the non-discrimination principle for goods (see sections 5 and 6).

Chemicals

6 An authorisation under Chapter 2 of Title 7 of the REACH Regulation is to be disregarded in determining (for the purposes of the mutual recognition principle for goods) whether goods can be sold as mentioned in section 2(1)(b).

7 The mutual recognition principle for goods does not apply to (and section 2(3) does not affect the operation of)—

(a) Article 67 of the REACH Regulation, or

(b) a restriction imposed in accordance with Article 129 of that Regulation.

8 In paragraphs 6 and 7, "the REACH Regulation" means Regulation (EC) No 1907/2006 of the European Parliament and of the Council of 18 December 2006 concerning the Registration, Evaluation, Authorisation and Restriction of Chemicals (etc), as it forms part of retained EU law.

Fertilisers and pesticides

9 The mutual recognition principle for goods does not apply to (and section 2(3) does not affect the operation of) any of the following—

(a) a prohibition or condition imposed in accordance with Article 15(1) of Regulation (EC) No 2003/2003 of the European Parliament and of the Council of 13 October 2003 relating to fertilisers, as it forms part of retained EU law;

(b) regulations under section 74A(1) of the Agriculture Act 1970, to the extent that such regulations can reasonably be justified as a response to a risk to—

(i) the health or safety of humans, animals or plants, or

(ii) the environment.

10 The mutual recognition principle for goods does not apply to (and section 2(3) does not affect the operation of) any of the following—

(a) Regulation (EC) No 1107/2009 of the European Parliament and of the Council of 21 October 2009 concerning the placing of plant protection products on the market (etc), as it forms part of retained EU law;

(b) the Plant Protection Products Regulations 2011 (S.I. 2011/2131);

(c) the Plant Protection Products Regulations (Northern Ireland) 2011 (S.R. (N.I.) 2011 No. 295).

Taxation

11 The United Kingdom market access principles do not apply to (and sections 2(3) and 5(3) do not affect the operation of) any legislation so far as it imposes, or relates to the imposition of, any tax, rate, duty or similar charge.

Provision having effect in more than one part of the United Kingdom

12 (1) A relevant requirement is not to be taken indirectly to discriminate against goods for the purposes of section 8 if—

(a) it is statutory provision contained in, or in subordinate legislation made under, an Act of Parliament,

(b) the same, or substantially the same, statutory provision applies in the originating part,

(c) the statutory provision that applies in the originating part is also contained in, or in subordinate legislation made under, an Act of Parliament, and

(d) no substantive change to the statutory provision has come into force—

(i) in the destination part but not the originating part, or

(ii) in the originating part but not the destination part.

(2) In sub-paragraph (1), "relevant requirement", "statutory provision", "originating part" and "destination part" have the meanings they have in relation to the non-discrimination principle for goods (see sections 5 and 6).

SCHEDULE 2

SECTION 18

SERVICES EXCLUSIONS

PART 1

SERVICES TO WHICH SECTION 19 (MUTUAL RECOGNITION) DOES NOT APPLY

Services	*(examples of those services)*
Audiovisual services	terrestrial, cable or satellite television, video on demand, film services, radio services, video sharing services, video recording services, video games services
Debt collection services	services of bailiffs, messengers-at-arms and sheriff officers
Electronic communications services and networks, and associated facilities and services	
Financial services	banking, credit, insurance and re-insurance, occupational or personal pensions, securities, investment funds, payment and investment advice
Gambling services	accepting bets, operating a lottery or providing facilities for gambling
Healthcare services	healthcare services provided in hospitals, other healthcare facilities or at other places, xenotransplantation, human genetics, human fertilisation, embryology, services in connection with surrogacy
Legal services	provision of legal advice, litigation services
Notarial services	
Private security services	
Services of temporary work agencies	services of employment businesses within the meaning given by section 13(3) of the Employment Agencies Act 1973

Services	*(examples of those services)*
Services provided by a person exercising functions of a public nature or by a person acting on behalf of such a person in connection with the exercise of functions of a public nature	
Social services relating to social housing, childcare, adult social care and support of families and persons permanently or temporarily in need	
Transport services	railways, operation of ports, air transport, air traffic services, road transport of goods and passengers, ancillary services

PART 2

SERVICES TO WHICH SECTIONS 20 AND 21 (NON-DISCRIMINATION) DO NOT APPLY

Services	*(examples of those services)*
Audiovisual services	terrestrial, cable or satellite television, video on demand, film services, radio services, video sharing services, video recording services, video games services
Debt collection services	services of bailiffs, messengers-at-arms and sheriff officers
Electronic communications services and networks, and associated facilities and services	
Financial services	banking, credit, insurance and re-insurance, occupational or personal pensions, securities, investment funds, payment and investment advice
Gambling services	accepting bets, operating a lottery or providing facilities for gambling
Healthcare services	healthcare services provided in hospitals, other healthcare facilities or at other places, xenotransplantation, human genetics, human fertilisation, embryology, services in connection with surrogacy
Notarial services	

Services	*(examples of those services)*
Postal services	delivery of letters and parcels by post, sorting and collection of letters and parcels for delivery by post
Private security services	
Services connected with the supply of natural gas through pipelines or production or storage of natural gas	transportation of gas, retail supply, operation of a gas interconnector
Services connected with the supply or production of electricity	distribution or transmission of electricity, retail supply, operation of an electricity interconnector
Services of a statutory auditor within the meaning of Part 42 of the Companies Act 2006	
Services of temporary work agencies	services of employment businesses within the meaning given by section 13(3) of the Employment Agencies Act 1973
Services provided by a person exercising functions of a public nature or by a person acting on behalf of such a person in connection with the exercise of functions of a public nature	
Social Services relating to social housing, childcare, adult social care and support of families and persons permanently or temporarily in need	
Transport services	railways, operation of ports, air transport, air traffic services, road transport of goods and passengers, ancillary services
Waste services	disposal of waste, importation or exportation of waste, waste processing
Water supply and sewerage services	

PART 3

AUTHORISATION REQUIREMENTS TO WHICH SECTION 19 (MUTUAL RECOGNITION) DOES NOT APPLY

Any authorisation requirement in connection with taxation

PART 4

REGULATORY REQUIREMENTS TO WHICH SECTIONS 20 AND 21 (NON-DISCRIMINATION) DO NOT APPLY

Any regulatory requirement in connection with taxation

SCHEDULE 3

SECTION 32

CONSTITUTION ETC OF OFFICE FOR THE INTERNAL MARKET PANEL AND TASK GROUPS

1 Schedule 4 to the Enterprise and Regulatory Reform Act 2013 (the Competition and Markets Authority) is amended as follows.

2 (1) Paragraph 1 is amended as follows.

(2) In sub-paragraph (1)(b)—

(a) in the words before paragraph (i), for "to membership of" substitute "as follows";

(b) in paragraph (i), at the beginning insert "persons appointed to membership of";

(c) in paragraph (ii), at the beginning insert "persons appointed to membership of";

(d) in paragraph (iii), at the beginning insert "persons appointed to membership of";

(e) after paragraph (iii) insert—

"(iv) a person (the "OIM panel chair") appointed to chair the Office for the Internal Market panel and to membership of the CMA Board;

(v) other persons appointed to membership of the Office for the Internal Market panel ("the OIM panel") (see Part 3A)."

(3) After sub-paragraph (2) insert—

"(2A) In making appointments under paragraphs (iv) and (v) of sub- paragraph (1)(b), the Secretary of State must have regard to the desirability of securing that—

(a) a variety of skills, knowledge and experience is available among the members of the OIM panel, and

(b) there is an appropriate balance among the members of that panel of persons who have skills, knowledge or experience relating to the operation of the United Kingdom internal market in different parts of the United Kingdom.

(2B) Before making an appointment under paragraph (iv) or (v) of sub- paragraph (1)(b), the Secretary of State must seek the consent of—
(a) the Scottish Ministers,
(b) the Welsh Ministers, and
(c) the Department for the Economy in Northern Ireland. (2C) Sub-paragraph (2D) applies if consent to an appointment is not given by any of those authorities within the period of one month beginning with the day on which it is sought from that authority.

(2D) In that event the Secretary of State—
(a) may make the appointment without the consent of the authority or authorities concerned, and
(b) must, if the appointment is made, inform each authority which did not give consent of the reasons for the decision to proceed with the appointment."

3 (1) Paragraph 3 is amended as follows.
(2) After sub-paragraph (2), insert—
"(2A) Appointment to membership of the OIM panel under paragraph 1(1)(b) is to be for a term of not more than eight years."
(3) At the end insert—
"(4) Where at the beginning of a person's term of appointment to membership of the CMA panel the person has already begun (and continues) to hold office as a member of the OIM panel, the term of the person's appointment to membership of the CMA panel is to be treated for the purposes of sub-paragraph (2) as beginning when the person's term of appointment to membership of the OIM panel began.
(5) Where at the beginning of a person's term of appointment to membership of the OIM panel the person has already begun (and continues) to hold office as a member of the CMA panel, the term of the person's appointment to membership of the OIM panel is to be treated for the purposes of sub-paragraph (2A) as beginning when the person's term of appointment to membership of the CMA panel began."

4 (1) Paragraph 4 is amended as follows.
(2) After sub-paragraph (1), insert—
"(1A) A person who has been appointed to membership of the OIM panel may be re-appointed to membership of the OIM panel only for the purpose of continuing to act as a member of a group constituted under paragraph 58B before the expiry of the person's term of office."
(3) In sub-paragraph (2), for "sub-paragraph (1)" substitute "sub-paragraphs (1) and (1A)".

5 (1) Paragraph 6 is amended as follows.
(2) In sub-paragraph (2), for "of either the CMA Board or the CMA panel (but not of both)" substitute "of one, but not more than one, of the CMA Board, the CMA panel and the OIM panel,".
(3) In sub-paragraph (3)—
(a) in the words before paragraph (a), after "panel" insert "or both the CMA panel and the OIM panel";
(b) for paragraph (a) substitute—
"(a) resign from one of those memberships (without resigning from the other), or".
(4) After sub-paragraph (3) insert—
"(4) The OIM panel chair may at any time resign from membership of the CMA by giving written notice to this effect to the Secretary of State (and may not resign from the OIM panel, or any other office to which the person is appointed by virtue of paragraph 1(1)(b)(iv), except in accordance with this sub-paragraph)."

6 In paragraph 9(2)—
(a) omit "or" at the end of paragraph (a);
(b) after paragraph (b) insert ", or
(c) a member of the OIM panel."
7 In paragraph 10(2)(b), at the end insert "or the OIM panel".
8 After Part 3 insert—

"PART 3A
THE OIM PANEL

The OIM panel

58A (1) The OIM panel is a panel of persons available for selection as members of a group constituted in accordance with this Part of this Schedule.
(2) The OIM panel is to consist of—
(a) the OIM panel chair appointed under paragraph 1(1)(b)(iv), and
(b) the other members of the panel appointed under paragraph 1(1)(b)(v).

Constitution of OIM task groups

58B (1) The OIM panel chair may at any time constitute a group in accordance with this Part of this Schedule for the purpose of carrying out on the CMA's behalf functions of the CMA under Part 4 of the United Kingdom Internal Market Act 2020.
(2) A group constituted as mentioned in sub-paragraph (1) is to be known as an Office for the Internal Market task group (or "OIM task group").

Membership of OIM task groups

58C (1) The members of an OIM task group are to be selected by the OIM panel chair.
(2) Each OIM task group is to consist of at least three members of the OIM panel.
(3) The OIM panel chair must appoint one of the members of an OIM task group to chair the group ("the task group chair").
58D The validity of anything done by an OIM task group is not affected by—
(a) a vacancy;
(b) a defective appointment.

Termination of person's membership of an OIM task group

58E A member of the OIM panel may at any time resign from an OIM task group by giving written notice to this effect to the OIM panel chair.
58F (1) Sub-paragraph (2) applies if the OIM panel chair considers that—
(a) a member of an OIM task group will be unable, for a substantial period, to perform their duties as a member of the group, or
(b) because of a particular interest of a member of an OIM task group, it is inappropriate for that person to remain a member of the group.

(2) The OIM panel chair may remove the person in question from membership of the task group.

58G A person ceases to be a member of an OIM task group on ceasing to be a member of the OIM panel.

Replacement of a member of an OIM task group

58H (1) Sub-paragraph (2) applies if a person ceases to be a member of an OIM task group, whether by being removed under paragraph 58F, or otherwise.

(2) The OIM panel chair may select a replacement member of the group from the OIM panel.

Continuity on removal or replacement

58I (1) A person's ceasing to be a member of an OIM task group, whether by being removed under paragraph 58F, or otherwise, does not prevent—

(a) the group from continuing with anything begun before the person ceased to be a member of it;

(b) any decision made or direction given by the person while a member of the group from having effect after they have ceased to be a member of the group.

(2) Sub-paragraph (1) applies whether or not a replacement member of the group is selected under paragraph 58H.

Powers of chair pending group's constitution and first meeting

58J (1) While an OIM task group is being constituted, the OIM panel chair may take such steps as the OIM panel chair considers appropriate to facilitate the work of the group once it has been constituted.

(2) The steps taken must be steps that it would be within the power of the group to take, had it already been constituted.

Independence of OIM task groups

58K (1) In exercising functions which they are authorised to exercise by virtue of any enactment, OIM task groups must act independently of the CMA Board.

(2) Nothing in sub-paragraph (1) prevents—

(a) the CMA Board giving information in its possession to an OIM task group, or

(b) an OIM task group giving information in its possession to the CMA Board.

Casting votes

58L If an OIM task group's vote on any decision is tied, the task group chair is to have a casting vote.

Procedure of OIM task groups

58M (1) An OIM task group may determine its own procedure (including determining its quorum).

(2) In determining its procedure under sub-paragraph (1), an OIM task group must have regard to any guidance issued by the CMA Board."

Index